DOLL COSTUMING

How to Costume French & German Bisque Dolls

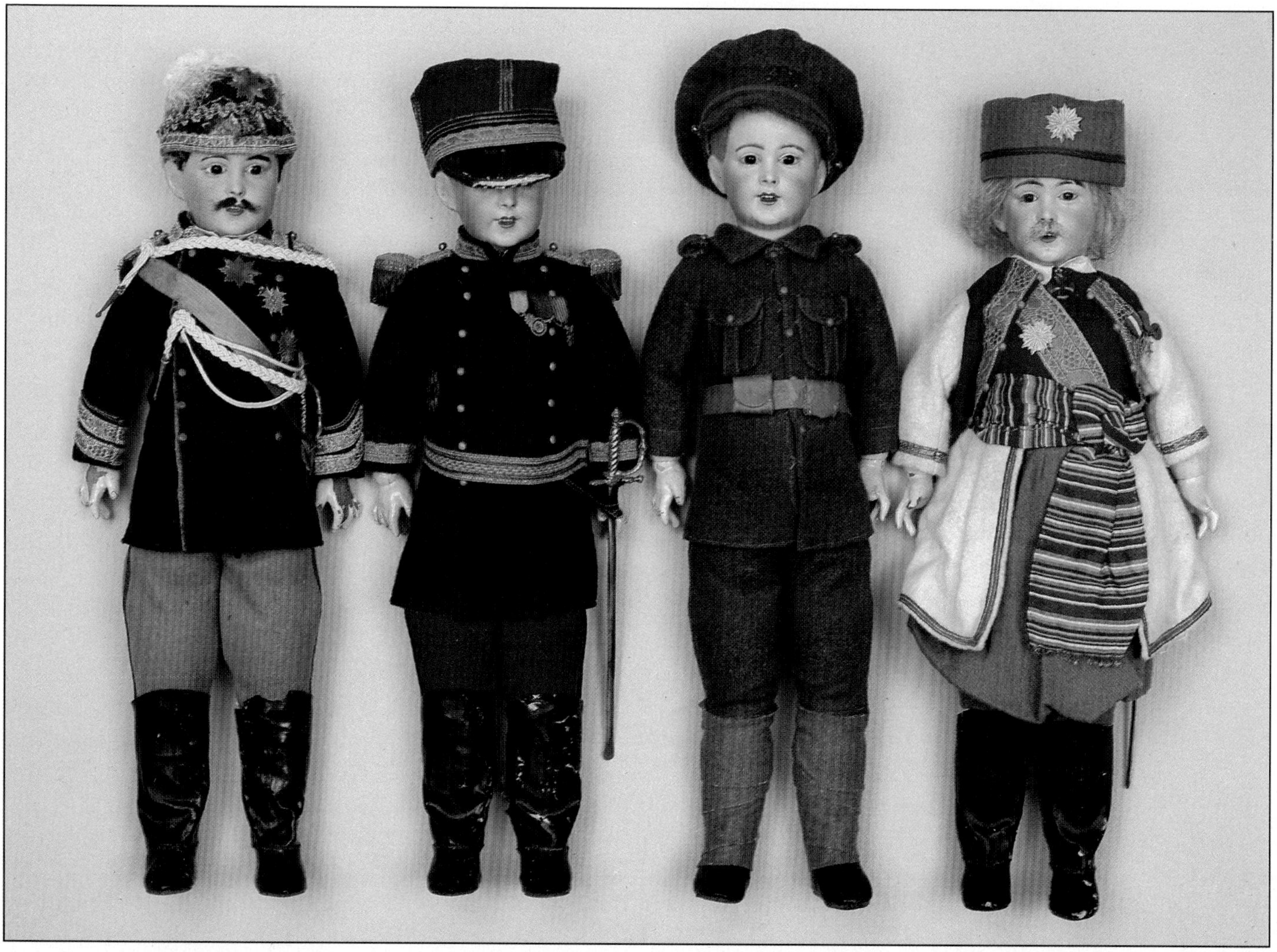

Four SFBJ boy dolls marked *235,* dressed in original costumes. These beautiful dolls were sold at a Robert W. Skinner Auction in 1983. Auctions are a good source to find dolls with original costumes. Picture courtesy of Robert W. Skinner Auctions Inc., Bolton, Massachusetts.

By Mildred & Colleen Seeley

Mildred Seeley shown with four dolls, from left to right: AT7, wire-eyed Steiner, Bru Jne. 3 and AT2.

ABOUT THE AUTHORS

Mildred Seeley is well-known in the doll world. She is a doll maker and collector, and has been involved with dolls all her life.

An active member of the United Federation of Doll Clubs, Mildred has worked hard to get people all over the world interested in collecting dolls. She founded the Doll Artisan Guild, an organization for reproduction-doll makers.

Mildred is affectionately called the "First Lady of Dolls," a title bestowed on her by the International Ceramic Association and Expo Enterprises. She was given this recognition in 1982 at the California Doll Convention.

Always interested in telling the public about dolls, Mildred founded and edited for a number of years *The Dollmaker* magazine. She was also the founder and special editor of the *Doll Artisan* magazine, published by the Doll Artisan Guild.

Mildred's appreciation of dolls is heightened by her appreciation of art. She holds a bachelor's degree in art, and a master's in art education, and has studied sculpture and painting.

Colleen Seeley is Mildred's daughter. She has been collecting dolls since she was old enough to walk. During her childhood, Colleen received a handmade doll from her mother on every birthday. She soon became interested in making dolls herself.

At the age of 11, Colleen started making and selling folk dolls. For almost 12 years, she made and sold her handcrafted wood dolls to museums and gift shops.

Colleen's professional background is in communication arts. During high school, she edited an international magazine for youth. After college, she set up a freelance communications business, writing and editing publications for non-profit organizations. She holds a bachelor's and master's degree.

Although she lives away from her family, Colleen still enjoys her dolls and keeps up with what's happening in the doll world. Writing this book with her mother was another project of love and sharing fond memories.

Mildred and Colleen are also co-authors of HPBooks' *Doll Collecting for Fun & Profit*, a comprehensive guide for doll collectors.

Publisher: Rick Bailey
Executive Editor: Randy Summerlin; Editor: Judith Schuler
Art Director: Don Burton; Managing Editor: Cindy Coatsworth
Book Assembly: Paul Fitzgerald, Leslie Sinclair; Typography: Michelle Carter
Director of Manufacturing: Anthony B. Narducci
Cover Photography: Ray Manley Studios, Tucson, Arizona
Photography: Ray Manley Studios and Mildred Seeley; Illustrations: Arlene Seeley

Published by HPBooks, a division of HPBooks, Inc.
P.O. Box 5367, Tucson, Arizona 85703 (602) 888-2150
ISBN: 0-89586-299-9 Library of Congress Catalog Card Number: 84-80056
© 1984 HPBooks, Inc.
Printed by Dong-A Printing Co., Ltd., Seoul, Korea
Represented by Codra Enterprises, Torrance, California
3rd Printing

Cover: Sitting on left, open-mouth AT3; sitting on trunk, Bébé Jumeau; standing, AT7 Snow Angel; sitting on right, Simon and Halbig doll.

All rights reserved. No part of this work may be reproduced or transmitted in any form by any means, electronic or mechanical, including photocopying and recording, or by any information storage or retrieval system, without written permission from the publisher, except in the case of brief quotations embodied in critical articles or reviews.

NOTICE: The information in this book is true and complete to the best of our knowledge. All recommendations are made without guarantees on the part of the authors or HPBooks. The authors and publisher disclaim all liability in connection with the use of this information.

TABLE OF CONTENTS

Costuming Dolls 5
Preserving Doll Heritage 25
French Doll Costumes 43
German Doll Costumes 63
Getting the Doll Ready to Costume 81
Patterns and Color 93
Doll Wigs and Styles 103
Hats and Bonnets 111
Shoes, Stockings and Underwear 121
Completing the Costume 137
Crochet Baby Doll Pattern 147
Glossary 154
Books and Pamphlets 157
Resources 158
Index 159

Back view of Schmitt dress shows elaborate appliqué work and bustle substitute, made of folds and pleats of jacket fabric.

Costuming Dolls

Doll collecting is one of the world's most popular hobbies. Information on costuming and preservation of these art pieces is important for all doll collectors and doll makers. A *costume* is a doll's complete outfit, including underclothing, dress, shoes, hat and accessories.

Dolls are an important part of our heritage. They represent people as they were at the particular time when the dolls were made. Doll costumes are replicas of adult and child fashions of the time. To reflect its true history, a doll and its costume must be preserved or accurately reproduced.

Fashion dolls were popular tools for 18th-century dress designers. They were used as models for fashion, and popular fashions were displayed on them. Dolls were dressed and sent all over the world as mannequins displaying current fashions of the times. This is why we see many beautifully dressed dolls from France. Paris was one of the centers of fashion, and dolls were made and dressed there to be sent to other countries.

Today, many bisque dolls made a hundred years ago are still in beautiful condition. But we see costumes in all stages of deterioration. Collectors must find ways to preserve, restore and re-create this important part of the doll.

There are few authentic sources of information on antique doll costumes. Our best source of information is dolls that have been preserved in museums or private collections. Not everyone can go to a museum. When we visit museums, we may not be allowed to take pictures and must rely on sketches and notes to record ideas.

Another source of information is catalogs that sold dolls. Many catalogs have been reproduced and are available today, and information they contain is authentic. The problem with catalogs is dolls often were not identified, and only the front of a costume was shown in a black-and-white line drawing. Even though information is limited, we recommend catalogs as a resource because they are authoritative.

You may be able to find old magazines, such as the *Ladies' Home Journal* or *Peterson's* magazine, with doll patterns. Costumes shown are correct for their time.

In this book, we describe dolls in original costumes. We show reproduction costumes that have been copied in detail from original ones that are deteriorating. We provide details about the front and back of original costumes. It is beneficial to see costumes in color, with a description of fabric, construction and trim. We have done this so doll makers and collectors can use this book as a resource in many different ways.

Left: Original silver-and-white-satin jacket on marked 31-inch Schmitt doll. Hand-sewn appliqué work was used in various patterns on silver-satin background. Box-pleated ruffles at neck and sleeves are edged in white satin. Elaborately designed dorset thread buttons are used on front, sleeves and back. Full skirt is cotton, with three layers of ruffles. Underneath are two petticoats and a chemise. Hat is layered and decorated with silver plume and flowers. Handbag is deteriorating. Umbrella has cotton fabric that matches skirt and is in good condition. Doll wears original shoes.

Left: Doll is dressed in light moss-green. Bodice is gathered silk with lace-trimmed bretelles going over the shoulder. Cummerbund is folded silk. Dress has lace overskirt, and lace covers sleeves.

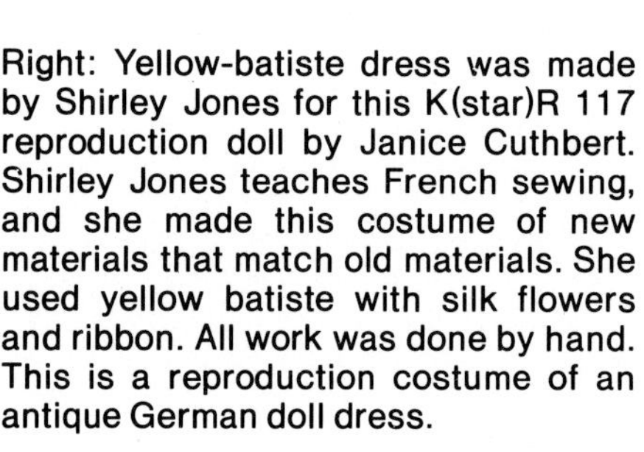

Right: Yellow-batiste dress was made by Shirley Jones for this K(star)R 117 reproduction doll by Janice Cuthbert. Shirley Jones teaches French sewing, and she made this costume of new materials that match old materials. She used yellow batiste with silk flowers and ribbon. All work was done by hand. This is a reproduction costume of an antique German doll dress.

You will learn to distinguish old costumes from new ones. This will give you more confidence to determine which are old costumes and which are reproduction costumes when you see them.

The number of original costumes is so small, many collectors do not have even one in a collection. Dolls were toys to be played with, and they were dressed and undressed. The finer the costume fabric was, the faster it disintegrated.

In the 1960s and 1970s, doll collectors did not realize the importance of a costume. They discarded old costumes and dressed a doll as they wished. They paid little attention to the authenticity of new clothing. Unfortunately, many original costumes were lost this way.

By providing you with photographs of antique costumes, you will be able to reproduce authentic designs for your dolls. There are a few talented doll dressmakers and designers in the United States. They are important to doll collectors, yet many collectors know little about them.

This book also helps reproduction-doll artists because it can be used as a reference book for costuming ideas. Each artist must costume her dolls. With the help of this book, he or she can find what the doll wore or should have worn. Many reproduction-doll artists forget how important a costume is.

Many costumers must make their own patterns because dolls vary in size and shape. This book shows styles of different costumes and authentic variations and trims. We share over 50 of our dolls in original costumes to give you ideas. Feel free to copy them.

CLASSIFYING DOLLS

We discuss three types of dolls and costumes—the antique doll in original costume, the antique doll with a reproduction costume of old fabric and the reproduction doll with reproduction costume of new material. We do not deal with antique dolls dressed in new materials because this should be avoided if possible. When there is no other solution, choose fabrics that are the same as the old, such as silk, satin and cotton.

Dolls in original costumes are very expensive. Sometimes one dressed in original clothing brings a third more at auction.

We do not present patterns, except for some shoe patterns, stocking patterns, bonnet patterns and a crochet pattern for a doll outfit. We do not give you directions for making particular garments. We pre-

Right: Paris Bébé in original burnt-orange, cotton-satin outfit, which is still in good condition. Hat, socks, underclothing and shoes are original. Shoes are marked *Paris Bébé*. Doll was made to celebrate completion of Eiffel Tower.

sent ideas and tell you how a costume can and should be made. Doll collectors have needed this information for a long time. If they had had access to this information, many doll costumes might have been saved.

We have used the word *she* for a collector and doll maker—this is a matter of convenience. Men, women and children collect, costume and make dolls. Often, men's collections are superior, and dolls made by men equal those made by women. Each year the *Millie Award* is given to the best doll makers. In 1983, a man won the award.

Doll Dressmakers—Names of original dressmakers who made the first costume a doll wore have often been forgotten or lost because a garment was not labeled. We discovered names of several Parisian dressers but do not know what dolls they costumed. Some of the names we have found are Mme. Lavallie-Peronne, Mlle. Deschamois and J. Carail. These people were listed in a Paris directory of doll costumers. You can always hope to find a costume with one of their labels.

Some old Bru costumes have *Judith Barrier, Paris* labels. These costumes were low-neck or off-the-shoulder dresses with puffed, short sleeves. Most dresses were made of silk and fell just below the knee. In 1923, Mme. Corene designed clothes for Regal Dolls, which were produced in Europe.

Katherine A. Rauser was an American designer of doll clothes who lived and worked in Chicago. She designed clothes for Horsman and Schoenhut from 1915 to 1925. Do not be surprised if your German doll wears American clothing.

Mrs. Arnoldt designed Blue Bird Doll Clothes, which were used by many companies in the United States around 1914. These costumes were labeled. The American Doll's Outfit Co. manufactured doll clothes in the United States around 1905.

There were other dressmakers for dolls, but no glory was ever given to them. It may be the same with today's doll costumers if they do not label the costumes they make.

Preserved Costumes—It is a miracle a doll 75 to 100 years old has any clothing left. The doll almost has to have been forgotten, kept away from dust, dirt, moths, dampness and vermin. This is where great-grandmother's trunk did a great service to doll lovers and history. Usually, a doll Grandma wrapped in a clean piece of white sheet and put in a trunk is preserved in the best condition.

Other dolls in good condition have been found in small doll museums. Often museums were closed after the original owner died or retired. We have a few museum dolls in our collection.

Sometimes we find dolls preserved under a glass dome for many years. Although costumes are in better shape, they are usually extremely faded.

OUR GOAL FOR DOLL COLLECTORS

Sometimes dolls dressed from old fabric are so skillfully and correctly done even an expert cannot tell if a costume is original. Our ultimate aim is to help costumers achieve perfection in their work. It will become a reality when you can select the proper pattern and correct fabric and finish a costume with the proper decorations.

A reproduction costume is an *exact* copy of an original costume. Often the tiniest details betray the modern doll dressmaker. The dress may be perfect, but modern ribbon, buttons, flowers or nylon lace ruin the effect.

You must first know where to begin, such as selecting the proper antique fabric. Colors must enhance the appearance of the doll. Patterns must be correct for the doll and the period when it was made. Stitching must be delicate and done with the correct thread. Machine-stitching may be used on *inside* seams, but finishing and hemming must be done by hand. Pleating must be uniform. Outside trim must be old ribbon, buttons or a facsimile.

Determine When Doll was Made—Before you select patterns and fabrics for reproduction costumes, you must know when a doll was made. Many dolls from the same mold were made over a period of years. A good example is a small, open-mouth German doll that was produced over a 25-year period.

Some dolls were made for a specific purpose and were made only for a short time. Paris Bébé was made to commemorate the completion of the Eiffel Tower, so there are only a few dress styles Paris Bébé can wear. Other bisque dolls can wear many different styles.

Today, many large dolls wear dresses made originally for young children. It is not always possible to tell if a dress was made for a child or a large doll. In

Right: Unmarked Belton with blue eyes that match her blue dress. Unique, hand-sewn costume represents many hours of work. Fabric is frail and shredding in places. Skirt and bodice are three shades of blue silk. Skirt is triple pleated, with lighter stripes folded inward. Bodice has five rows of gathering at bottom and three at top. Stripe of dark blue is puffed at neckline. Sleeves are tight at forearm, and puffed and gathered above. Vest is separate, but tacked on, and back bodice is plain. Pleats go around skirt.

Jullien doll wears original commercial frock. Dress is in original condition, except where we have repaired it.

this book, we include several examples of large dolls wearing children's dresses. See page 15. If you have a large doll, you may be able to find a child's dress in an antique shop. It will cost about the same to buy as a doll costumer would charge to make a dress. About 90% of children's dresses are white. Many were made from 1900 to 1920 and are appropriate for large dolls of the same period.

Children's dresses can be cut up and good parts used to make a smaller doll's dress. Baby dresses can be cut up to dress baby dolls. These make authentic dresses and are acceptable to use.

HOW TO DETERMINE IF COSTUMES ARE ORIGINAL

In the world of dolls, *original costume* is the clothing made for a particular doll at the time the doll was made. This could be a handmade costume made by a French seamstress or a commercially made frock or chemise. The costume could have been designed and made for one doll or a group of dolls all dressed alike and made at the same time. This costume can be a homemade costume if the doll was purchased undressed.

Contemporary costume is the term used for clothing made about the same time as, but not necessarily for, the doll. This could mean a costume changed from one doll to another, but made within 10 years of the origin of the doll. An example of this would be two sisters who received matching dolls for Christmas and interchanged clothes between the dolls.

Dolls wear *old* or *antique* costumes. These are attic finds with no regard for whom they were made. The dresses and bonnets mother and grandmother made fall into this group. These clothes were played with and changed from one doll to another. Often doll clothes were passed from one generation to the next.

Finding a doll in an original costume is difficult. If you find one, the doll was probably packed away. Few dolls that children played with remain in original clothing unless they came with a trunk of clothing and some outfits were not used.

You must be a detective to determine if the costume with a doll is original. Even experts cannot always be sure.

Know What to Look for—There are some things to look for to help you decide if a doll and its costume are original. Study the doll. Look at the way hair is arranged. Does it look as it was when she was new? Hair can be uncurled but should not have been combed much or played with.

Look at the doll's hands and knees. Are they soiled? Is paint worn or chipped off? Look at the feet. Has the doll been played with without shoes? Do feet show dirt or chipped paint? Look at the body. Is it bruised? Wear and dirt usually indicate a doll was played with, and her costume is probably gone or was washed until it fell apart.

Dolls with original costumes were often forgotten. They were left in the attic or a trunk. Usually if a costume is original, shoes and socks are also original. Carefully remove shoes and socks. Often there is a ring around the leg where leg paint has darkened with age. Sometimes, shoes and socks stick to the doll, so do this slowly and gently.

If the dress is original, underclothing may be original. Underclothing was usually all made of the same fabric, with matching lace.

If the doll has a matching bonnet, it is usually a good indication a costume is original.

If everything about the doll says *original*, chances are it is. Study the costume. Does it fit the doll? Is it

Right: Oliver, an original doll designed by Nicholas Bramble, is dressed in Kate Greenaway style. Doll was reproduced and costumed by Janice Cuthbert.

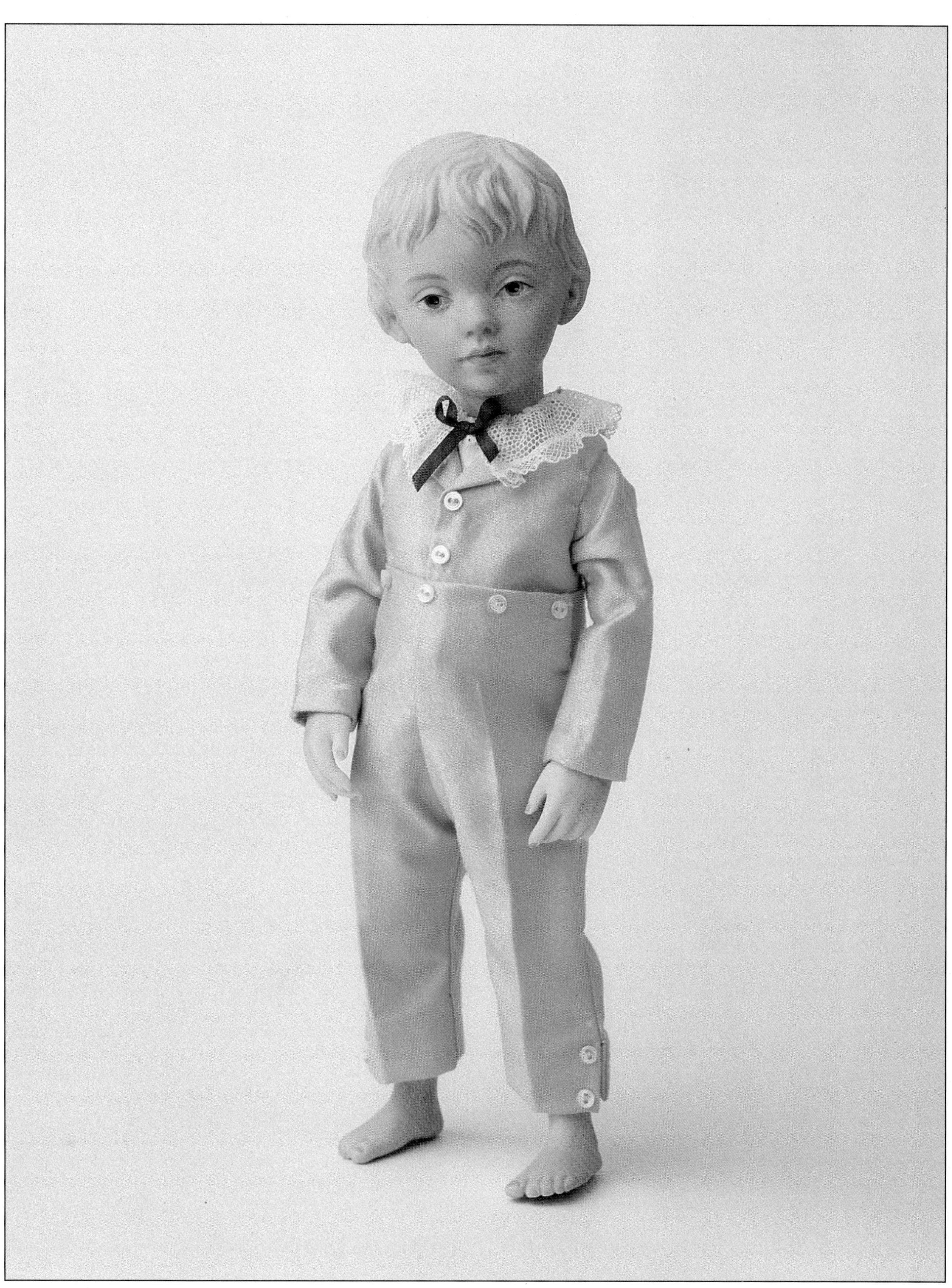

Parisienne Costumes by Dee Robinson, who is a modern-day costumer. This is the label Dee proudly attaches to her fine work.

Original label found inside clothing of Albert Marque dolls. Margaine Lacroix was a Parisienne couturier for dolls.

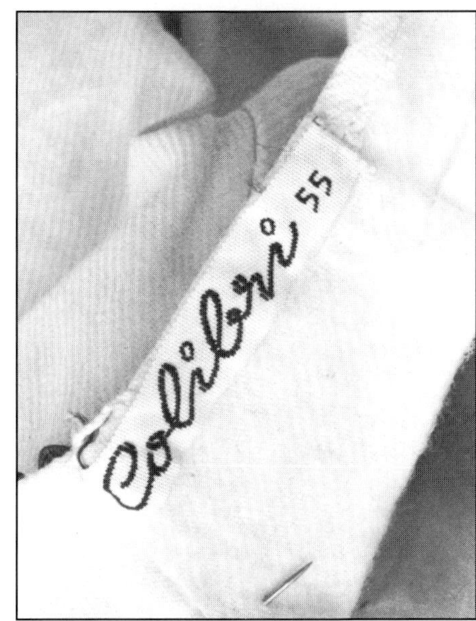

Original label from nightie worn by the boy Heubach, page 72. Vivian Iob purchased the nightie and got a doll too!

too long? Incorrect length is one sign a dress was moved from doll to doll. Check the length of the petticoat to see if it is too long.

Study stitching on the costume. Is it done with new thread? You can tell by looking closely—does it look the same as new thread or is it soiled? Is the fabric old? If it is an old French costume, expect a closure of brass hooks. The closure is always hidden in the front or back. French costumes were always lined, usually with a stiff, loosely woven cotton. Everything was carefully finished and workmanship was perfect.

Expect colors to be faded. Fading is usually more evident on the front than back. Look under edges of hems and jackets, and check inside to see if a costume is faded. To be original, it almost *has* to be faded.

Determine if fabric is one that was used when the doll was made. Check ribbons on the costume. Silk ribbon often deteriorated before the rest of the costume. Almost all ribbon on old costumes was silk.

Checking these things usually gives you a strong feeling about the originality of a costume. Study photographs of original costumes and dolls in museums to help you learn to judge whether a costume is original.

Exceptions—There are exceptions to all the rules. A doll with a trunk of clothes or large wardrobe could have been played with, paint scrubbed up and underclothing gone, yet still have a dress that was used little. This is often the case with lady dolls and other dolls that had large wardrobes.

Treasure old costumes passed from doll to doll. You can change a costume from one doll to another if dolls are about the same size and age. But a costume usually looks better and fits better on the doll it was made for. A doll is more valuable with her original costume.

It is wonderful to have a doll in original clothing, but those found in old or contemporary clothing are wonderful. Each item of old clothing is valuable. Preserve everything, even if the doll is broken and gone. Many antique dolls have no original clothing, so it is better to have some other clothing than none at all.

Labels—Another way to determine if a costume is original is to check labels. Jumeau and Bru labeled shoes and dresses. Jumeau labels were often on the *outside* of the doll's costume, across the front or as arm bands. See page 55. Most labels were removed from play dolls, but labels on underskirts may have survived. Labels at the back of the neck or on a petticoat may have been left on.

Marque dolls were costumed by Margaine Lacroix in Paris. The label on our boy Marque is sewn upside down in the jacket. When you turn up the back edge of the jacket, the label reads correctly.

Labels in bonnets are not common, but you may find some. If the color and fabric of the dress matches the hat, and shoe markings match head markings or a body stamp, the costume is usually original.

Shoes are a good indication of original clothing. Many had labels or letters impressed on the soles. Most had numbers that indicated size, and this number matched the size number on the doll's head. Sometimes these same numbers were stamped on the bottom of the doll's foot. Shoes were often transferred from one doll to another, so check fit.

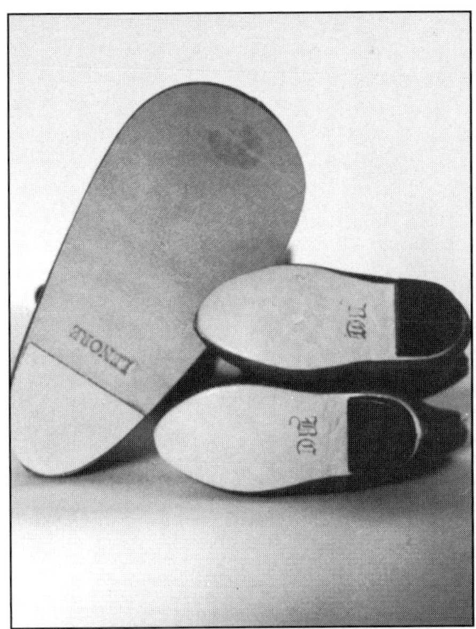

Modern shoes marked by their maker.

Bessie Green, a doll costumer, has a commercial label that indicates she made this reproduction Bru costume.

German dolls in original costumes, which are soiled. Originality of costumes is easily proven by matching these dolls with dolls shown in Butler Brothers' 1911 Christmas catalog.

Match the Costume—Another way to determine if a costume is original is to look at reprints of old catalogs. You might find the exact costume if many similar ones were made at the same time.

You may be able to match a costume to one in a museum. Sometimes you can use photos in books. In John Nobel's book, *Beautiful Dolls*, we found a photo of a Jumeau doll with labeled clothing similar to our Lyric Jumeau.

If there is a question about originality on a fancy French outfit, check for fine hand-sewing. This does not apply to a cotton chemise or a frock that was machine-sewn and put on the doll until she could be better dressed.

Finding Original Costumes—Expensive or large dolls are more apt to be found in original costumes. If a high price was paid for it, the doll was protected. A child may have played with it only on holidays or special occasions. The doll may have sat in a chair for decoration. Large dolls were not usually carried around because they were so cumbersome.

We have never found a label in a German costume, yet we know some costumes are original. Most German dolls came in heavily sized gauze underclothing or simple dresses.

We purchased a toddler JDK from a lady in her late 70s. The doll was in a shoe box. The grandmother had purchased it as an Easter gift when the woman was a 6-year-old girl. She was so excited to receive the gift, she ran across the yard to show a neighbor child and fell and broke a piece out of the neck. This released the head button, and the doll came apart. Grandmother put the doll in a box in the attic and replaced it with another doll.

When we received it, the unstrung doll was attic grimy, and its white outfit was gray. It wore a simple white Easter bonnet of sized, fine cotton. The white dress was of the same fabric, and shoes and socks matched. White gloves had stuck to her hands. When put together, with clothing cleaned up, she was a fine example of a German doll in original clothing.

Dolls 28 inches and larger are more often found in original clothing. In studying old catalogs, we find these large dressed dolls were sold to merchants for display. The size of large dolls made it almost impossible to play with them. They are heavy and awkward—even we have trouble moving and dressing them. For this reason, large dolls may be in better condition and are more apt to wear original clothing. See the 31-inch Schmitt doll in original costume, page 4.

REPRODUCTION COSTUMES

You may buy an undressed antique or reproduction doll. You need to determine the kind of outfit it should wear. You need to know where to locate the type of fabric it needs. You may need to know where you can get a costume made.

First, try to get the approximate date when the doll was made. Most were made over a period of years. After a company paid for a doll to be designed and molds were made, the company usually reproduced the doll until molds wore out. Dolls were often made over a long period of time, perhaps as long as 20 years.

Auction people often do research and can tell you the approximate date of a doll. Sometimes they date a doll too early to create a better sale. Go through books and locate a doll that is similar or perhaps the same as the one you are researching. See what costume is shown on the doll. Check the description, and see if the costume is listed as original or contemporary.

Some books contain reprints of pages from old catalogs. Find your doll or another doll of the same type and date. If you are near a museum, study dolls and try to make a match. Look at doll shows. If you purchase a reproduction doll without clothing, follow the same process.

Materials for Costumes—You must search for materials to make a costume. If the doll is old, dress it in old fabric, if possible. Some companies sell old fabrics. Some antique shops salvage good parts of garments and sell those for costuming. You can purchase an old garment to cut up yourself.

If you are unable to find old fabric, purchase new fabric that is identical or similar to old fabrics, such as cotton or silk. In dressing reproduction dolls, use new fabric as similar to old fabric as possible. The *Resource* section, page 158, lists places carrying different types of fabric.

Getting Ready—When you are ready to costume a reproduction or antique doll, you must decide who will do it. Today many amateurs and professionals costume dolls. Prices vary with the skill and expertise of the dresser. You may have the skill and be able to do it yourself.

Next, search for a pattern. There are good patterns, bad patterns, authentic patterns and patterns that are concoctions of ideas, with no historical background. Many patterns for doll dresses on the market today are a mixture of ruffles, lace and fabric, with no regard for how a costume was originally made.

Selection of a pattern or style must be done carefully. You must know what is correct. Some doll-costume patterns are copied from old magazines, such as the *Delineator.* These patterns are excellent because they are detailed and authentic. Patterns made from a dress still worn by a doll are even better. Original costumes cannot be questioned as to authenticity.

Many doll costumers can make their own patterns by looking at a picture of an old costume. This is a true talent. You may find this is your hidden talent if you try. If you are a beginner, the section on making a pattern to fit, page 94, is helpful.

USING BABY AND CHILD CLOTHING

There is a place for a child's antique dress on large dolls, and these are considered authentic clothes.

This 36-inch Jumeau doll wears a child's hand-embroidered dress. Her shoes belonged to a child.

Millie Baby, an artist's doll made in the likeness of Mildred Seeley, wears Colleen Seeley's baptismal dress and bonnet. Family dresses are nice on dolls.

Unmarked German doll in a child's dress and child's shoes.

Left: Maureen Beattie, from Australia, made this reproduction Jumeau doll and dressed her in a beautiful reproduction costume copied from an old photograph. Costume was made from satin and polished cotton. This is a prize-winning doll.

Unmarked French doll wears plum-colored silk dress with white polka dots. Dress originally had a lace guimpe, but it has completely deteriorated.

You may find old baby dresses for baby dolls in antique shops, at yard sales and auctions. Babies grew out of their dresses before they could wear them out.

White, embroidered or lace-trimmed dresses were used, especially for German dolls. This clothing was popular from 1890 to 1920.

Baby dresses are ideal for making doll costumes. There is enough fabric to make a costume for a small or medium doll. Sometimes a baby dress can be used as it is on large dolls.

If you find a baby or child's dress that seems suitable for cutting up, inspect it carefully to be sure fabric is strong enough to make your time and effort worthwhile. Wash the dress, and use a little bleach if necessary, then iron, using some spray starch. This makes cutting and sewing easier. For more information on washing cotton fabric, see page 25.

Before you begin to cut, make sure the pattern is appropriate and fits your doll. Study the garment before you cut to see where you can lay pieces to take advantage of existing decorations.

Consider each dress separately because decorations are different. Cut the front bodice from the center front of the dress with decorations. Cut sleeves from the bottom of the sleeve to use gathers and sleeve decorations. Determine the length of the skirt you want on the finished dress, then measure it from the *bottom* of the dress.

Use the center front and back of the dress so decorations are centered. When you finish, your new dress is trimmed and hemmed. Carefully remove lace from old garments to add to the new dress around the neck.

You can do the same with an old petticoat for underclothes. Use the lace or eyelet-trimmed bottom of an old petticoat for a doll's petticoat. Cut drawers so legs are the trimmed bottom of the petticoat. This gives you matched underwear.

USING PAPER DOLLS

Paper dolls were printed as long ago as the Victorian era—beginning about 1867. Costumes for paper dolls from the Edwardian period, 1898 to 1920, are fine examples of clothing of the time. They can serve as authentic ideas for costuming because detail is well-illustrated in these drawings.

Paper dolls that can help you design a costume from a particular date are listed below. They are available from Doll and Craft World and Hobby House Press, listed in the *Resource* section, page 158.

- **Antique Paper Dolls.** Arnold has 20 1915-to-1920 full-color costumes.
- **The Edwardian Era.** Epinal has 32 costumes and shows back and front of each costume.
- **Erte Fashion Paper Dolls of the Twenties.** Book has 43 full-color costumes.
- **Victorian Fashion Paper Dolls.** From *Harper's Bazaar.* This book shows 28 Victorian fashions in full color, covering period from 1867 to 1898.
- **Fashion Paper Dolls.** Godey's *Lady's Book* covers 50 fashion costumes from 1840 to 1850. All are in color.
- **Kate Greenaway Paper Dolls.** By Kathy Albert, this book has 28 costumes from the Victorian era.
- **Lettie Lane Paper Dolls.** By Sheila Young, book contains color pictures of paper dolls from 1908.
- **Betty Bonnet Paper Dolls.** By Sheila Young, taken from the *Ladies' Home Journal,* 1915 to 1917. This book shows many costumes for that period, especially child dolls.

There are several Dolly Dingle paper-doll books. They are good for dressing child dolls from 1915 to 1924.

COSTUMING DOLLHOUSE DOLLS

From records and pictures, we learn dollhouse dolls were sold without clothing. These dolls were shoulder heads, with cloth bodies and bisque arms and legs. Dollhouse dolls were made in the proportion of real people—children and adults.

Right: Hazel Samuelson specializes in costuming dollhouse dolls. Here is a spectacular group of her 4- to 5-inch reproduction dolls.

Few dollhouse dolls came dressed. They were sold rolled in a cloth similar to a container for silverwear, with a pocket for each doll. This doll was dressed about 40 years ago. Beige silk has green-velvet stripe. Lace is extremely fine.

Pair of dollhouse dolls in early costumes. Lady doll's dress is olive-green taffeta, which is cracking and falling apart. Man's gold pants are made of sturdy, ribbed fabric.

Prize-winning reproduction miniature-doll costume by Mary K. Stevens shows beautiful work of modern doll artists. Doll is only 4 inches high. Mary has won more Millie awards than any other reproduction-doll artist.

Kämmer and Reinhardt produced a series of dressed dollhouse dolls in the 1920s. From advertisements, they appeared to be dressed as men for different occupations, such as a mailman, policeman, fireman, horseman, sailor, blacksmith, storekeeper and other occupations we cannot distinguish.

OUTDOOR CLOTHING FOR DOLLS

Some dolls made in the 1880s came with trunks, such as French fashion dolls or bébés. Dolls had a complete set of clothes, from extra outdoor boots to coats, capes, bonnets and gloves. Sometimes they had summer and winter coats of cashmere or velvet.

Our Bru Breveté, next page, is a fine example of a doll with a trunk and outdoor clothing. She has a gray cashmere coat with a cape and gray gloves to match. Her maroon hat matches her extra dress. She has high boots—her other shoes were lost.

We have a doll in a reproduction costume that is dressed for winter. The Snow Angel A7T, pages 30, 31 and 32, was dressed by Jim Fernando. She wears a quilted coat, edged in eiderdown, and a fur-trimmed hood and quilted leggings.

The only other dolls we have in outdoor clothing are a Circle and Dot Bru doll in a pink-cashmere coat with cape, and an F.G. doll in a walking or automobile coat.

We had some SFBJ dolls dressed in wool sailor suits with berets. Clothes are similar to winter clothes but are not necessarily outdoor clothes.

Occasionally we find a wool or velvet coat in boxes of old doll clothes. Many outdoor clothing items were probably made of wool, and wool has a problem with moths. This may be the reason we find few wool items today—they were moth-eaten and discarded. See page 26.

We have a peddler doll in our collection that came to us with the remains of a red-wool cape. There was not much left of the cape. It was so full of moths we were afraid it would contaminate our other dolls' clothes, so we threw it out. Other outdoor wool clothing may have gone the same route to protect a collection.

Some wool sweaters and pants have survived. Many knit garments are found on boy dolls or baby dolls. Most of these are found on dolls from the 1920s or a few years earlier.

Right: Special dolls came with trunks—our Bru came from England. Trunk is covered on the outside with embossed fabric in yellow-cocoa and is decorated with stripes of black zinc. Lid is curved, and trunk measures 14x9x8". Tray is still in the trunk and has two compartments. Inside is papered with striped, two-tone beige fabric with fine purple stripe. This doll lived in the trunk after she was put away. Bright-pink, handmade wool dress is moth-eaten, but not faded. Her gray-cashmere coat and gloves indicate she originally wore fancy clothes. When dolls are found with trunks, preserve doll *and* trunk. Contents and trunk are a bit of history.

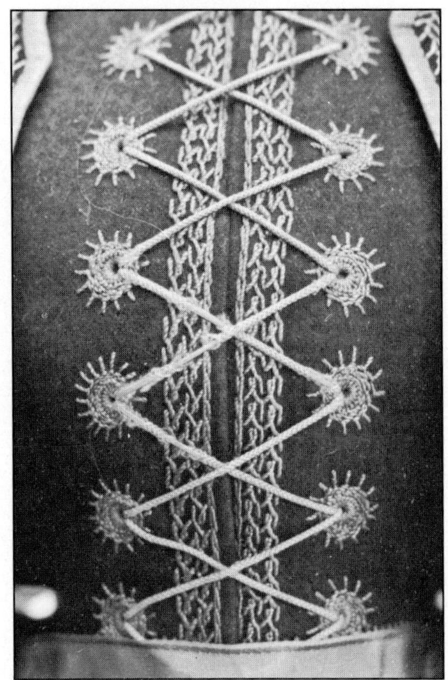

Fancy stitchery was often used on doll clothing. This close up of lady doll on the next page shows front lacing and many stitches.

At one auction, we saw a *Just Me* doll dressed in a yellow button-down wool cloak with matching leggings and yellow-wool hat. This doll was made in the 1920s.

In a reproduction Marshall Field's catalog, originally published in 1897, we found listed, but not shown, dolls dressed in winter suits and summer suits. No maker was listed, but we assume clothes were factory made.

In several old doll catalogs, individual items such as wigs, clothing and accessories were sold. Knit sweaters and caps, fur neck pieces and muffs were shown.

When we visited the Margaret Strong Museum in Rochester, New York, we looked at the French dolls. They have twin Jumeaus in blue-wool, princess-style coats with cape collars. Collars are trimmed with two rows of frilled pink-silk edging. Sleeves are edged in the same decoration. Pink-silk edging decorates the underdresses that show in the coat opening. Bonnets are gathered velvet edged in the front with the same pink-silk edging and topped with a small, deep-pink feather and bow of coat fabric. Each doll has a gathered pink-velvet muff.

We have found only a few other dolls dressed in outdoor clothing. Some were dressed in wool or cashmere dresses and suits. If you prefer to dress your doll in outdoor clothing, it is correct. You will find patterns in the *Ladies' Home Journal, Dolly's Dressmaker* and other pattern books for coats and capes. Hobby House Press carries copies of old patterns and pattern books. See *Resource* section, page 158.

CHILDREN-DRESSED DOLLS

In 1888, *Youth's Companion*, a periodical for children, had a campaign to sell subscriptions. When a certain number of subscriptions were sold, the seller received a doll. The doll came with patterns so the child could learn to sew. The doll was advertised as a Jumeau, but fine print in the advertisement states, "Made after the celebrated Jumeau model."

Another promotion with dolls was the "giving away" of *Daisy*. Actually she was sold for $4.50. The *Ladies' Home Journal* ran a paper-doll series created by Sheila Young, and the doll was named Lettie Lane. In the paper dolls, Lettie introduced her doll Daisy. If a child sold three subscriptions to the magazine and sent in $4.50, she would receive a Daisy doll. Along with the doll were patterns of the same fashion as the paper doll's many outfits. A total of 31,000 Daisy dolls were sent to children.

The child was to dress Daisy, but probably mothers and grandmothers used these patterns to dress many dolls. We do not have a Daisy doll, but many collectors may have her.

In 1898, the *Delineator* gave directions for crocheting suits for dolls. The December 1912 edition of *Ladies' Home Journal* had patterns for the Playmates. Playmates were used to advertise the K(star)R 100 character series. Two packages of patterns, one for a boy and one for a girl, were offered. The advertisement stated clothes were easy and quick to make. The girl's clothes were cut from a basic kimono shape, eliminating the need to make sleeves. Each garment had few seams and could be cut from a small piece of fabric.

Patterns came in four sizes, ranging from 14 to 26 inches. The girl's patterns consisted of a coat, cap, overblouse, dress, jumper, peasant dress, kimono, playsuit, nightgown, petticoat, combination suit of underwear, sandals and stockings.

The boy's patterns included a coat, cap, two blouse suits, rompers, pajamas, bathrobe, union suit, sandals and stockings. It was suggested on the pattern that sandals be made of old gloves or shoe tops.

These patterns are proof that K(star)R dolls were dressed in simple play clothes.

Clothing Decoration—Many doll clothes had embroidery or fancy stitches on them. Stitches were used down the front of dresses, on collars and cuffs. Often there was a line or two of stitches around the bottom of the skirt.

Plain underclothing was decorated with stitches. A flannel petticoat almost always had feather-stitching around it. Drawers were often decorated with tucks, and sometimes tucks had a row of feather-stitching.

Right: Pair of 26-inch adult dolls in ornate regional costumes. They came with a label reading *Brittany Wedding 1869*. Note beautiful color scheme.

Stitches were taught to children at a young age. This is a sample one girl did. The child was given pieces and helped to copy grandma's work. A second piece was barely started.

Embroidery and hand-sewing were taught to young girls. We find books, pamphlets and old magazines with patterns for children to use for their dolls.

Another useful resource we found was *The Sewing Book of Round-About Dolls,* by Betty Campbell. This hard-cover folder included two girl dolls of heavy cardboard with stands. With the dolls came paper clothing for the front and back of each doll.

Directions instructed the child to paint the dresses, then embroider with wool yarn along dots. On an opposite page, an *Embroidery Lesson* showed six different stitches. Stitches are not labeled by name, such as cross-stitch, but are given a number. On the dresses, it instructs the child to use stitch 1 or 2 or whatever, and shows how to tie a bow and a rosette.

In the book we purchased, clothing for dolls is in many stages of completion, from uncut to were finished. Some clothes were crayoned and stitches were finished. This was probably a good learning tool to help a child learn embroidery.

An interesting pamphlet for children, published in 1896, was *Dolly's Dressmaker,* by the Publishers to the Queen, Raphetuck & Sons, LTD, London, Paris, New York. The beginning paragraph of the book states, "This book will show you how to make new dresses for your dear Dolly, so you will have something to do on a rainy day, and Dolly will always look lovely."

The cover shows a child holding a finished doll dress. By the child is an undressed doll, sewing box, scissors and thread. Tacked on the wall are patterns and illustrations.

The 14-page booklet has six pages of pattern directions and three pages of color paper dolls wearing the fashions. The booklet is an excellent source of information for a doll costumer. It shows accessories, such as hats, caps and gloves. The booklet is reprinted by Barbara Jendrick and is available from doll suppliers. Addresses are listed in the *Resource* section, page 158.

PRESERVING THE PAST

Dolls must be preserved for posterity, and their clothing is part of their historic value. We have written this book to help inspire doll keepers and collectors to preserve old costumes, to do as little as necessary in repairing a doll and to use costume examples from this book to make authentic reproduction costumes of the correct period.

We hope this book gives you enjoyment and appreciation of a doll and its costume. We want to prevent doll collectors from stripping dolls and dressing them in new, modern fabrics. When dressing dolls, we want to help you select fabrics, prepare the doll and wig, and understand how to costume different dolls.

The name of the maker and date when a costume was made should appear somewhere on the costume. It will add to the doll's history. We recommend the history of each doll be kept with the doll.

Right: Costume in daring colors of red satin and peach satin. Dress is lined with stiff, loose-weave cotton. Pattern is unusual, with split upper sleeves exposing puckered peach satin. Front inset is same gathered peach, with tiny pointed collar. Vestlike front is finished in two points and decorated with three braid buttons. Two strips on peach come down front edge of jacket and are anchored at points with red-braid buttons. This is repeated on back of dress. Twelve box pleats go around peach skirt. Dress was sold to us as original, but does not pass our test. Our intuition said, "No, it isn't," so we had to find facts to support our decision. Hand-sewing is beautiful, but machine-sewn stitches of *white* thread on peach fabric were found. Fabric is old, but there are signs it was ripped from another garment—there are many seam lines and needle marks in fabric. But dress is still an unusual, well-made costume.

Photo of back of costume shows how silk has completely deteriorated, leaving only lining.

Preserving Doll Heritage

Sometimes people become so involved in current practices or the promise of the future they lose sight of their heritage. In the 1950s and 1960s, we dreamed of the Great Society. Our focus was on newer, bigger horizons. Many people threw out things that represented their heritage.

With the Bicentennial, we realized how important our past was. We rediscovered the value of many things. We have continued our interest in preserving and saving our collectables and surrounding ourselves with them. This interest has included toys because they are a reminder of our past. Our sense of pride in our heritage has helped us preserve dolls and their costumes.

NEW COSTUME OR OLD?

When possible, leave a costume as it is. It may not be possible to do this and still have something beautiful. You must start by making decisions about what must be done to a costume and how it will be done.

If a costume is in shreds, take a picture or make a sketch of it. Do both as a way to record how the costume is made. Have a new costume made in the same style of the same kind of fabric. Or make one as close as possible to the original, with the same colors and decorations. Stitch a note on underclothing indicating the change and stating who made the costume and the year it was made.

If you are not happy with an old costume and how it looked on a doll, check to see what other styles were popular at the time the doll was made. Check fabrics used at that time. If the doll is dressed correctly, its value will be retained.

DRY-CLEANING AND WASHING

Some doll dresses can be dry-cleaned. We took a fashion-lady's wool costume to the dry-cleaners, and the owner volunteered to do it by hand. It came out beautifully and did not shrink. We had another doll's wool-challis skirt dry-cleaned, and it was perfect.

Silk dresses can be dry-cleaned if they are strong enough to stand the stress. Many dresses were made of cotton-backed satin or sateen. You may be able to wash these in cold-water wash. When we use the term *washing*, we mean soaking and rinsing, not wringing or twisting. Cotton fabrics are washable.

Dresses made of cotton lace can be washed in cold-water wash, such as Woolite. Add bleach to the first *rinse water.* Do not let garments soak in bleach water because it weakens old fabric. Rinse garments thoroughly several times. They can be further bleached by drying them in the sun. Add body to old lace dresses by using spray starch when you iron.

Left: Belton doll wears hand-stitched dress of sapphire-blue silk, reinforced with white cotton. This two-piece French design has carefully fitted, four-piece skirt. Jacket is tacked with slight bustle in back. Shell-design ecru lace is used at neck and tight-fitting sleeves. Lace outlines two added, decorative pieces down front opening. Opening has six tiny black buttons. This costume shows what can happen to an outfit if a doll's back is exposed to strong sunlight or if she lies on her face in the attic. Back is completely disintegrated. See photo at top of page. This unmarked doll looks more French than German, but could be either. If this is a German doll, her costume looks similar to those made by fine French seamstresses.

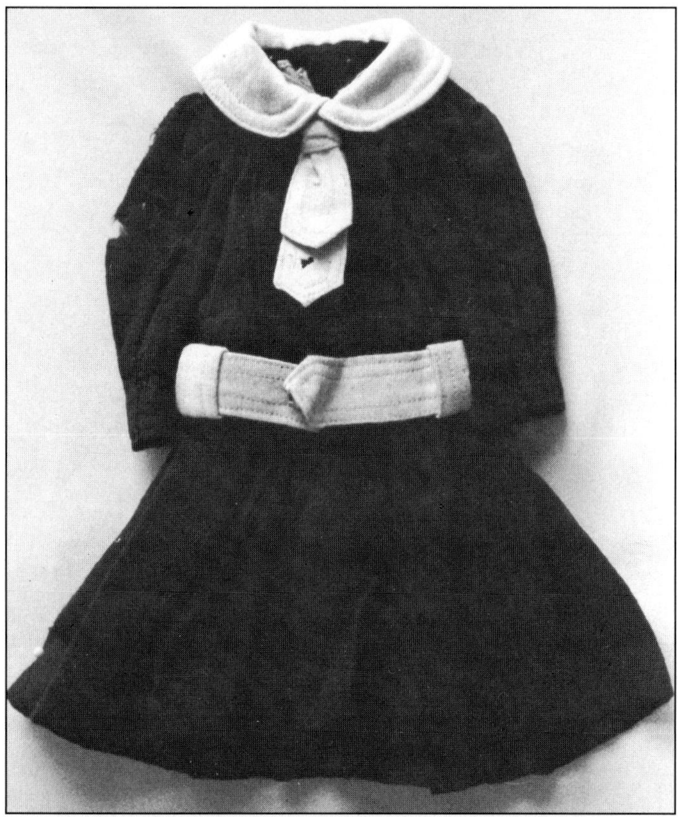

Sometimes clothing gets moth-eaten, as shown by this original wool Jumeau dress. Doll was re-dressed, and outfit was saved as a record.

Most underclothing was made of cotton, which is easily washed and bleached. Use a little more bleach than you would for a lace dress. Lightly spray undergarments with starch as you iron, and they will stay neat. Sometimes just pressing a costume that cannot be washed will give it new life and take out attic odors.

With colored cotton dresses, add 1 teaspoon of vinegar to each quart of water for the final rinse. This brightens colors.

Remove flowers and ribbons before washing because colors might run. Press trim, and sew it back on after dress is finished.

If you need a pressing cloth, use cotton organdy. When pressing old fabric, be sure the setting on the iron is correct. Test the iron first in an inconspicuous spot on the garment.

INSECTS

Two types of insects attack doll clothing—the *clothes moth* and the *museum beetle*. Most of us are familiar with the clothes moth. The museum beetle is tiny and black or gray. You will see them on the inside of your glass doll case after they have done their damage. Get rid of insects with moth crystals or pieces of pest strips.

If a dress is wool and has moths or any indication of insects, put the garment in a brown paper bag with moth crystals. Close the bag tightly. Move the garment and crystals around once each day for three days without opening the bag. After three days, remove the garment from the bag and press it. You can use the same method for a doll with moths in her hair.

SOCKS AND STOCKINGS

Often, after socks and stockings are washed, they dry with a yellow streak down the front and back if they are folded while drying. Extra washing and rinsing helps, but putting a piece of dry paper towel inside to hold them open will prevent a line from forming. Put socks or stockings outside or in a current of air to dry. Cotton can be bleached.

Old stockings on dolls with kid bodies were often held up with pins stuck into the doll. Underclothing was often pinned closed in the same manner. One pin hole is not much, but some dolls have been pinned and unpinned until leather is worn. Instead of using pins, run a double thread around the stocking top and tie it. Elastic thread works well. You can use rubber bands, but these deteriorate.

For more information on socks and stockings, see the *Stocking* section, beginning on page 130.

DOLLS IN SATIN

Many dolls were dressed in a type of satin that deteriorates with up and down splits. If shredding has gone too far, it is almost impossible to repair. Repair small splits with a fusible adhesive. The adhesive melts with a warm iron and seals the splits. Sometimes lining a garment with non-adhesive netting extends its life.

DECORATIONS

Small decorations or cords that are falling off a dress can sometimes be put back with glue or liquid thread, which can be purchased at a fabric store.

Do not replace buttons with new ones of modern materials. Look in antique shops that carry old ones. Some shops carry buttons from France similar to original buttons. If you have two rows of buttons and no old ones to use as replacements, remove a button at the top or bottom to even up the two rows.

Remove hair ribbons and rinse them in cold-water wash. Press them with a warm iron or lay flat on a countertop and let dry. Add extra body with spray starch. If a ribbon must be replaced, replace it with another *old* ribbon, if possible. Do not get bleach on ribbons because it changes their color.

For more information on decorations, see the *Completing the Costume* section, beginning on page 136.

Right: Even the Margaret Strong Museum, in Rochester, New York, with the world's largest collection of dolls, must have some doll costumes made. This reproduction costume is by Hazel Ulseth.

SHOES

Many shoes are missing a sole. To correct this problem, trace the other shoe sole upside down on material, such as cardboard or leather, that is similar to the other shoe. Put rubber cement on the shoe and new sole, let dry a few minutes and press together.

Repair tears in shoes by putting a piece of old glove leather inside to cover the tear. Put rubber cement on shoe and patch, and press together. Buttonholes that are torn out can be repaired by putting a piece of leather or fabric *under* the hole. Stitch or glue in place, then sew on the button.

If shoelaces are gone, use narrow ribbon the same color as shoes. Tie small, neat bows, and cut off ribbon ends. Dip each end in clear nail polish, then roll.

Do not glue shoes and socks on dolls. Some were glued on to keep the doll from losing them when it was played with by a child. On leather-body dolls, we sometimes find pins stuck in the heel to hold shoes on. Too many pin holes make a weak spot in the leather, and stuffing can come out.

Old shoes may be the most difficult piece of clothing to find if they are lost. Always keep shoes on a doll, even in storage. Many people have shoes from extra clothes and doll trunks. Some people buy old shoes at auctions. For information on making shoes, see the *Shoe* section, beginning on page 121.

Storing Shoes—Match shoes, then tie or button them together in pairs. Stuff shoes with tissue paper to keep their shape. Soften leather shoes with shoe polish. Do not leave excess polish on a shoe—it could rub off on a costume. For storing, put shoes in a box so they do not get squashed. New ribbon bows and buckles can be added to old shoes.

STORING DOLLS

When storing dolls, be careful with the costume. Insert white tissue paper under the skirt to keep it from crushing. If sleeves are full, add tissue there. Wrap the entire doll in tissue, then wrap it in a piece of white sheet or a white towel.

Old garments last longer wrapped this way than when wrapped in paper diapers or plastic bags. Many old dolls were preserved in white sheets in grandmother's trunk. Preserve old garments and old fabric the same way.

Stuff a bonnet with tissue, then wrap it in a piece of white sheet. Put the wrapped bonnet in a box to preserve its shape.

Tightly fitting glass-door cabinets are ideal for doll storage. Space dolls so garments hang loose and air can circulate around them. Take dolls out occasionally and fluff up dresses so creases are not always in the same spot. If a doll is sitting, stand her for a while.

Do not have your dolls or doll cabinet facing bright window light. Protect dolls as much as possible from fading.

Dolls in glass domes are well protected from everything but fading. Keep domes out of direct sunlight.

MOVING DOLLS

If you take your dolls in the car, leave them on their stands. Put wadded white tissue paper under costumes to keep them from wrinkling. Place dolls in boxes with clean tissue around them. Save boxes and tissue to carry them home.

If you are flying, do not put dolls in your luggage. It is better to carry them, and put them under the seat or in the overhead compartment. Stuff the costume with tissue paper, then wrap the doll with small-bubble plastic paper. Put the wrapped doll in a box about the same size. Tape the box shut, and carry it with you. Save the box and wrapping for the return trip.

If you are going by bus, wrap the doll as though you are shipping it by registered mail. Make sure the doll stand is anchored so it cannot bounce around and hit the doll. We prefer to tape the bottom part of the stand to the inside of the box.

For more information, HPBooks' *Doll Collecting for Fun & Profit,* by Mildred and Colleen Seeley, contains step-by-step instructions on packing and shipping dolls.

MUSEUM METHODS OF PRESERVING COSTUMES

There are many museum methods of cleaning and preserving costumes. Museum people have a code to which they strictly adhere—*they will not change anything that cannot be changed back.* In repairing or cleaning a doll costume, curators use no irreversible processes. If you have dolls, keep this in mind.

Curators consider light to be one of the hardest things on cloth and fibers. It is one of the most difficult things to control. Other things work against doll clothing, such as molds, insects, humidity, air pollution and dirt.

Most vacuum doll clothing and hair, instead of washing it. With many dolls, gentle vacuuming is the only way to preserve the original hairstyle and clothing. This is where you should begin.

Right: H-1 doll costumed in delicate pastels. A-line dress is green, iridescent silk taffeta, trimmed with salmon-pink silk. The front panel has three box pleats, with knife pleat on each side. Pleats are held together with bowlike arrangements of pink. Puffy appliqué is added at bottom right. Back has two side panels and center closing. Bottom of dress is row of tiny box pleats. Top of each box pleat, above the seam, is drawn into a pattern and tacked, making interesting detail. Dress was created by Sandy Rankow and her label is inside.

Jumper of Snow Angel is beautiful antique sateen. Puffed sleeves are silk organza. See complete costume on opposite page.

If clothing is cotton or linen and has been washed before, museum personnel wash it using their own method. Washing garments helps keep them from deteriorating by removing dirt and acid that accumulates in fabrics. Any trim that is not cotton or linen is removed.

Museum personnel use distilled water or softened water and a neutral soap, which can be purchased at a pharmacy or drugstore. Water temperatures are about 85F (30C) for washing and rinsing.

Washing is done by placing the fragile garment on a fiberglass screen. A screen holds the garment so it is not moved until it is dry. The screen is lowered into the water, and the garment soaks for an hour. The garment is then washed in soapy water by lifting it up and down. It is rinsed several times using the same method. The garment is shaped and pressed with the fingers. Lay garment on terry towel. Terry towels are used to soak up excess moisture.

Curators do not recommend bleaches, scrubbing, wringing or other washing methods. They do not pull or stretch fabrics or use clothes dryers, hair dyers or sunshine.

Most doll costumers use spray sizing and spray starches. Curators do not recommend it. They do not even recommend ironing clothing!

Museum personnel do not recommend storing dolls in cardboard boxes without something between the box and doll. Cardboard contains an acid material that speeds the deterioration of fabric. Curators do not recommend storing dolls in plastic bags or covering dolls sitting in chairs with plastic covers. They do recommend using washed, unbleached muslin around or over the doll.

DOLL COUTURIERS

If a costume is beyond repair or cleaning, you will need to find someone to replace it. Doll costuming as a profession is not new, but interest in it has recently been renewed.

A *doll couturier* or *costumer* is a skilled, artistic costume designer and seamstress. A *doll dressmaker* is anyone who makes doll dresses using existing patterns. A *doll dresser* is anyone who sews any part of a costume or puts together existing pieces of a costume.

In the early 1900s, Katherine A. Rauser lived and worked in Chicago. She set the clothing styles for dolls and was one of the leading maker of doll costumes in the United States. Her costumes rivaled those made at the same time in Europe. She dressed some boy dolls in dresses and some in rompers or jumpers. Dolls she dressed for Marshall Field's are pictured in their 1914 Christmas catalog. Rauser dressed dolls with underclothing, dresses, hoods, hats, bonnets, aprons, coats and accessories. She dressed baby dolls, lady dolls and character dolls, including boy dolls.

Today, many people dress dolls. At shows, booths display doll dresses in different styles, colors, materials and quality of design and workmanship. You might find the perfect dress for your old doll there, but it is more likely you will find something suitable for a reproduction doll. It is not economically feasible for dressmakers to use old fabrics to produce many dresses.

In this book, we show costumes by leading couturiers in the United States. Many people do beautiful costuming, but you must search for them.

Right: Snow Angel is a masterpiece by Jim Fernando, a present-day doll couturier. Doll is an A7T and wears old, lace-trimmed underclothing. Blouse is ivory organza with long, full sleeves and collar with smocking design. Ivory jumper with box pleats goes over this. Shoes and leggings are antique ivory satin and finely quilted. Coat is soft antique aqua satin, quilted and trimmed in eiderdown. Cap is aqua and trimmed with box-pleated rows of lace around the face. The surprise comes when the doll is turned around. She has wings! Wings are made of white feathers and eiderdown. Children and adults from cold areas are familiar with snow angels. They are made when a child lies down in new-fallen snow and moves arms up and down to make wings. This is an example of how ideas for costuming come into being. This doll is shown on the cover.

Back of Snow Angel shows her incredible wings!

This Simon and Halbig doll wears gold-silk costume from Spain. It is machine-sewn and poorly made. Note the long bloomers.

Close-up photo of front of dress shown on opposite page.

Costumers in Great Britain make dresses from antique fabric for antique dolls. We purchased costumes so you can compare styles, colors and workmanship. These are shown on pages 35 and 41. We purchased a reproduction costume from Spain, shown above.

Every year we judge reproduction dolls and select the *Millie Award* winners. Millie awards are trophies given for the best reproduction dolls made each year. We have found costumers from Australia and New Zealand the most superior. They do exquisite handwork, and their designs are extraordinary. They do not care how long it takes to complete a costume. When they produce a costume, they are only interested in the end result. See the Australian reproduction dolls and their beautiful costumes on pages 15 and 36.

HOW TO SELECT A DOLL COUTURIER

A couturier must be someone you enjoy working with. She must understand the value of dolls and know how to handle and protect them from damage.

Doll costuming is expensive. Carefully select the costumer or you will waste your money and may have to do the job over again.

Several costumers dress dolls by mail order. Some require the doll be sent to them; others make the costume from your measurements.

There are advantages to both ways. A costume fits better if the couturier has the doll. She will have a better chance of selecting colors to go with the doll's hair, eyes and bisque if she has the doll.

If you do the measuring, the dress might be too snug or too loose. This will not happen if the costumer has the doll.

We do not like to mail an expensive doll to have it dressed but will, if there is no other way to have it dressed. Even with insurance, if a doll breaks, it cannot be replaced. The doll will be gone for weeks. You do not know if it will come back with color rubbed off the nose or rub marks on the cheeks. A finger might even be broken.

Usually costumers are reliable, and they protect your dolls as though they were their own. Despite what could occur, we have not had any bad experiences leaving our dolls or mailing them.

POINTS FOR EVALUATION

Costumes must be creative and look different from other doll dresses. A costumer should dress the

Right: Doll's auburn hair suggested ivory for this elaborate costume, which flatters and frames the face. Main part of dress is moire silk designed with a polonaise. Fluted silk is used at wrists and as dust ruffle under skirt. Inverted box-pleated walking skirt is finished at bottom with arrow-shape scallops. Filmy georgette over fluted silk circles shoulders and decorates skirt. Jacket is pulled together over vest with corded knots and buttons. Silk lace edges jacket and vest. All materials are antique. This masterpiece is by Dee Robinson.

doll according to your standards, in your favorite colors that look beautiful on the doll.

Check workmanship to see if hemming and parts that show are done by hand. Machine-stitching can be used on inside seams. Check to see if pleats are even.

A costume should be completed and the doll returned at the time originally agreed upon.

MAKING ARRANGEMENTS

Make arrangements by letter or phone *before* mailing a doll to be dressed. Arrange the time with the costumer so she is ready to work on your doll when it arrives. Pack the doll carefully, and ship it by registered mail. Be sure you insure the doll for its full value. There are different types of insurance policies for dolls, but ours does not cover a doll when she is in someone else's home being costumed.

MAIL-ORDER COSTUMES

We only ship small or medium dolls to be dressed, not large ones. We measure large dolls and send their measurements. Below is a sample questionnaire one costumer sent to us. We filled it in, added a deposit of $10 and mailed it instead of mailing our doll. This sheet can be used by new dressmakers setting up their own business.

REPRODUCTION COSTUMES

A costume made of old materials from an old design, similar to an antique costume, is a *reproduction costume*. It is a copy of a costume made at an earlier date. It is impossible to match color, fabric, stitching and every detail exactly, so you must be lenient. Most collectors are satisfied with this solution to what could be an unsolvable problem in costuming.

Making reproduction costumes and costuming antique dolls is as intriguing and satisfying as any fine art or craft. To be a fine doll costumer, a person must be a fine seamstress. Hand-sewing must rival that of French dress designers of the past. Detailing must be lovely, with gentle shaping, perfect tucking and a lavish flurry of pleating. A costumer must be able to reproduce elegant finishing touches and styling.

Right: The English make reproduction dresses for dolls. This one was made of antique materials for Countess Maree Tarnowska. There is no label in the dress.

MAIL-ORDER COSTUMES

Elsie's Doll Costumes
409 Doll Arena
Somewhere, Your State

All materials used in dressing dolls will be from the period of the doll. All ribbons, flowers and other decorations will be old. Stitching will be done in the manner of fine French hand-sewing. Costume will bear my label.

Manufacturer of doll ______
Head circumference over hair ______
Height ______
Doll's date, if known ______
Hair color ______ Hair length ______
Eye color ______
Is the doll: boy, girl, lady, baby ______
Is body: jointed, composition, leather, other ______
Waist—measure over undies ______
Neck ______ Length of arm to wrist ______
Length of skirt—waist to below knee joint ______
Color preferences (more than one) ______
Style desired—long-waisted, high-waisted, natural-waist, child, rompers, other ______

Circle fabrics you prefer: satin, silk, cotton, wool, polyester.
Other ______
Circle items of clothing you want made: petticoat, drawers, dress, bonnet, coat, shoes, stockings.
Your Name ______
Address ______
Date ______
Telephone number ______
After I receive this, I will call you collect with an estimate.

Please allow at least three weeks for each costume. Fill in the following questions. Measure accurately.

Prize-winning reproduction doll and dress. Doll is *Portrait of Jeanne,* by Jill Gray of Upwey, Victoria, Australia. Doll wears delicate antique lace over yellow batiste. Hat, umbrella and shoes are yellow tones. The only other colors used are light and dark moss-green for ribbon and flower foliage.

Back view of reproduction dress shows Gray's skill as designer and seamstress.

Left: Front of dress shown on opposite page has interesting detail. Edging jacket with net softens lines. Colors blend together.

Right: Blond Jumeau wears a dark-cranberry faille-and-velvet suit with matching bonnet. Skirt is separate, but jacket and vest are one piece, opening down the front with antique gold-and-enamel buttons. Skirt has one large inverted box pleat in front and two on sides. Bottom is fly-fringe, with gold cord and black net under the edge. Jacket sleeves are velvet, decorated with fringe and gold cord. More fringe and gold cord decorate vest and collar. This combination of textured materials and color is by Dee Robinson.

To costume dolls, a person must be able to select and use delicate colors, soft hues or a flash of bright color. She must be able to envision an antique costume on a nude doll. For all of this, you will pay a high price.

Old fabrics are often used for dressing valuable antique dolls. Old fabric is expensive and difficult to find, so parts of old dresses women wore are often used. These dresses are usually found in antique shops and at estate sales. Unused old fabrics can be found at flea markets, swap meets, auctions, antique shops and from doll shops that save fabric for doll seamstresses.

Old thread, especially spools of silk thread, may be found in old sewing kits. Sometimes it is sold by the spool in antique shops, flea markets or swap meets.

Check old fabric before buying. Do not buy it if it has started to deteriorate. If the costume will not last 10 years or more, it is not worth the effort, expense and time to make it.

Fine, beautiful old laces can be found in certain areas of New England. Laces from France, Belgium or Spain are beautiful and still in good condition. You may be able to find these at garage sales, estate sales or by word of mouth. We once found some in an old country store.

Undergarments of dolls are the easiest items to reproduce. Fine white fabric in good condition can still be found. Some new fabrics that are available almost match old fabrics. Tatting for decorative edging is the same today, and old lace is available.

The shoe or boot situation is difficult. You can hope to find a pair of old shoes or boots to fit. Often, only one shoe is missing, so you know what to look for or reproduce. If one shoe is gone, it is better to replace both shoes because a reproduction shoe never matches exactly. If the doll has one old shoe, use it to make a pattern. See page 124 for information on making a shoe pattern.

CHOOSING OLD FABRICS FOR DOLL CLOTHES

When we use old or antique fabrics, we are trying to achieve authenticity. We do not believe a piece of nainsook made in 1912 is any better to dress a doll in than one made in 1925. But do not use fabrics that were not produced at the time of the doll's manufacture.

Using fabric that was used for costuming when the doll was made would be the ideal way to choose fabric for a doll. Nylon, rayon and man-made fabrics are not suitable for dolls made before these fabrics were developed. On old dolls, it is better to use cotton, wool or silk. These fabrics are available today.

Most people cannot tell the age of a fabric by looking at it. Elderly women who sewed can often tell the approximate age of a fabric. They remember fab-

Large Bru wears a dress with separate, full-bustle jacket. Pink-silk jacket has piping around armholes and edges and is decorated with beige lace. Knife-pleated skirt matches jacket. Inset of tissue silk is light pink. Front panel is gathered in three places and ends in three rows of ruffles. Dress was made by Helen Kramer.

rics that were popular. But this does not help most of us. Determining the age of fabrics is usually guesswork.

A friend of ours, Florence Lennox, is now in her 80s. She recently gave us a box of fabric left from her mother's sewing. We feel confident fabric in this box is old enough for any doll we have.

Once we located a store that was selling lace and trim. Trims were on original wood spools, and many were marked *France*. The owner said they had been in the store since before 1920, and they looked it! We are still using some of this lace.

When buying old fabric, inspect it carefully. Many cottons age perfectly and seem as strong today as when made. Some fabrics do not hold up as well. Some silks, especially heavier ones, were weighted with metallic salts. These weaken the fabric and cause it to split. Some silks deteriorate in 25 years. Wool is often weakened by moths. Do not make costumes from weakened fabric. It is not worth the effort, money or time.

When you find old fabric, buy it and worry about when you will use it later. Make quick assessments by the age of boxes and age signs of lace. Learn to depend on your own judgment. Usually the price for old fabric and trim is low, unless you buy from an antique dealer.

Occasionally at doll shows, a dealer will offer old fabric for sale. These fabrics are expensive. Try to find your own fabric at small estate sales, auctions and from friends, neighbors or family.

CLASSIFYING ANTIQUES

One hundred years is given as a general rule for the age of antiques. With dolls, it is different. The United Federation of Doll Clubs (UFDC) is the largest doll club in the United States, and it sets the rules. The UFDC considers a doll less than 35 years old to be *modern*. A doll that is over 75 years is *antique*. Any doll falling between the two is considered *collectable* or an *old* doll.

In this book, we consider any material or costume over 75 years as *antique*. We use the term *old* for materials that were made between 35 and 75 years ago. Some fabrics were produced over a 20- to 25-year period, and it is difficult to pin an exact date on them. We do not consider it necessary to be that exact.

WEIGHT OF FABRICS

We often speak of fabrics in weight, such as lightweight fabric or heavyweight fabric. Some patterns only specify fabric by weight. In the next column is a list of fabrics divided into four categories. Many fabrics can be moved up or down to the next classification with no sewing problem.

WEIGHT OF FABRICS

Heavyweight:

- **Velveteen**
- **Corduroy**
- **Worsteds**
- **Heavy-texture linens**
- **Velvet**
- **Wool**
- **Denim**

Mediumweight:

- **Calico**
- **Satin**
- **Gingham**
- **Flannel**
- **Cambric**
- **Cashmere**
- **Broadcloth**
- **Sateen**
- **Muslin**
- **Silk brocade**
- **Cotton eyelet**

Medium-lightweight:

- **Chambray**
- **Percale**
- **Pongee**
- **Silk**

Lightweight:

- **Lawn**
- **China silk**
- **Silk taffeta**
- **Some lace fabric**
- **Nainsook**
- **Dotted Swiss**
- **Voile**
- **Silk organza**

Size of Doll—When choosing fabric for a doll's outfit, consider the size of the doll. Often an amateur chooses velveteen to dress a 12-inch doll. Velveteen is a *heavy* fabric and can only be used on large dolls or in small areas on medium dolls. Heavy fabric smothers a small doll. In dressing tiny dolls, lightweight fabric must be used.

ARTIST SIGNS HER WORK

Doll couturiers are special people—they are artists and hard workers. They are anxious to dress dolls to please the owner and keep a design within the time frame of the manufacture of the doll.

They study complexions, coloring, hair shades and eye colors of dolls. A couturier camouflages any faults a doll has. Only a costumer can cover ugly, unshapely, mismatched body pieces.

A costumer is the collector's right arm. Often a doll collector does not give credit where it is due. Old dolls, with sawdust falling out, hair half gone and paint cracked off the bodies, do not look good until a costumer finishes her work.

If a couturier is good, when she finishes you will not be able to tell if the dress came on the doll or was made later of old materials. Couturiers do such a wonderful job they can, and do, fool experts.

For many years, we have worked with reproduction-doll artists. These artists are proud of their work and mark each head with their name, initials or symbol. They do not try to make anyone think a doll is an antique. This applies to dressmakers and costumers. *Costumers should label their work!* They should be proud of the fine job they do. Reproduction costumes should never be passed off as old or original costumes.

A doll costumer can mark a costume by putting labels and her name where they can be found on each costume and hat. Labels should include the year the costume was produced. This is how reputations are established. Soon, doll-dress designers will be as well known as artists who make reproduction dolls. Some collectors say, "Ask me anything but the name of my doll costumer." These people forget costumers should receive credit for their creations.

Labeling Clothing—Clothing can be labeled in several ways. Commercial labels can be made with the artist's name. Include the date the garment was made. A side seam is a good place to attach a label. Double the label, and sew both ends into the seam. In a bonnet, put the label against the back of the neck. Collectors should *insist* that reproduction garments be labeled!

Leta Goodyear made this costume from an old shirt silk. Soft ivory color matches old French lace. Jacket back has carefully constructed bustle. All sewing that shows is done by hand. Leta studied dressmaking and tailoring, and she costumes dolls because she loves it. We supplied old fabric for this F.G. doll.

COSTUMING COSTS

Costumes for dolls made by a courturier who supplies the antique material may run as high as $250. The ivory-silk costume on the A.T., page 31, was expensive. The small 12-inch Gibson Girl, page 63, cost $150 to be costumed. Medium-size doll costumes run about $200. Cost varies with the skill of the courturier, the supplier of materials and how work is done. If the doll has original underclothing, socks, shoes, a hat or bonnet, the cost can be less.

A costumer charges for what is done. Unless told otherwise, a doll will be costumed from hat to shoes.

There are fine dressmakers who buy good-quality,

Pleated silk dress was sold by Countess Maree Tarnowska for $140. It is a simple style, with plain bodice and short puffed sleeves with pink bows. Inset lace is used at waist, down bodice and around neck. Knife pleats go around skirt. Tiny blue flowers are embroidered designs in silk.

Marine-blue moire reproduction dress and bonnet from Spain. Both pieces sold for $200. Fabric is antique, but dress design does not enhance a doll. We could not find a doll the costume looked good on. Antique lace is beautiful, but pattern is too large. Handwork does not compare to work found in the United States.

modern silk fabrics and produce a beautiful costume at a more reasonable price. We often provide fabric we have saved for years, which makes the cost less.

High-priced courturiers have a reputation for authentic costumes of authentic fabric. Many have won awards at UFDC competitions.

A doll will only be dressed once while we own her, so we have it done to perfection. A beautiful costume makes these works of art more beautiful.

Do It Yourself—There is no inexpensive way to costume dolls unless you have antique fabrics and are your own costumer. It may be worthwhile to take lessons from an accomplished seamstress to learn how to sew, rather than paying to have many dolls costumed by an expert. You can learn from studying costumes in this and other books.

Antique fabrics are not easy to find. Sometimes you may have to buy an old dress for $150 to get enough fabric to make a doll costume.

Some reproduction costumes are not as expensive. In our search for reproduction costumes, we have found different prices in different countries for costumes. English dresses of antique fabrics, without underwear or bonnets, average about $135. Dresses and bonnets made of moire silk in Spain were priced at $200. In Canada, $100 bought a fine handmade costume. One of my neighbors made a doll costume from my antique fabrics for $35.

As you can see, there is wide variation in cost and results. You must be your own judge.

Crescent Bru wears beautiful silk dress. Some beading remains on sleeves. This doll and dress were in a museum for many years, which accounts for their excellent condition.

French Doll Costumes

In this book, we show many French costumes. We include descriptions of original costumes if we do not have photographs.

Some costumes are falling apart, but we feel it is important to copy them while they still are usable. We have tried to label costumes as we see them. In labeling a costume *original*, anyone can be wrong, so we have been cautious. As collectors and researchers of dolls in original costumes, we see more than most people. Some mother-made costumes are original. Many dolls came without clothing, and a mother-made outfit was the doll's first dress or costume.

Refer to photographs for ideas and feel free to duplicate old costumes. By doing so, you will help preserve priceless, authentic designs.

RARE DOLLS

Dolls by A. Thuillier (A.T.) and H-dolls are so rare we cannot establish a pattern for their costumes. Occasionally at UFDC conventions, rare dolls are exhibited in original clothing.

An A.T. in original dress was sold in Paris in 1983. She was dressed in silk and lace, with a flat straw hat decorated with flowers. The dress was a typical French type with a long waist. The skirt had five rows of ruffles, each edged in lace, and the low waist and sleeves were tied with ribbons and roses. A long, jacketlike garment was edged in the same ribbons and lace. The bodice was gathered and made of frail fabric, and the jacket back had a bustle.

Our H-3 doll, page 44, is dressed in delicate, antique silk lace. The dress is probably original, and it is beginning to deteriorate in places. The lace is in fine condition, except on sleeves.

Another of our H-dolls wears a fitted blue dress. The doll came to us in it, and it fits so perfectly, we assume it is original. The skirt is knife pleated, and the cummerbund is pleated. The bodice has vertical pleats, but there is no other decoration. The dress is threadbare in the back, as if the doll had been moved around on a shelf.

BRU DOLLS

The Bru Co. made dolls from 1866 to 1925. During those years, the company stressed beauty and quality, not mass production. Although rivals, Bru never made the quantity of dolls the Jumeau factory produced. We have not found labels in Bru clothing.

Bru Baby Dolls—Open-mouth Bru baby dolls had the same type of body as other Bru dolls. The bent-limb baby doll was not made until the 1900s. A few Bru baby dolls are found in original costume. One nursing Bru we saw wore a long, white-eyelet cotton dress. The dress had no fullness. Sleeves were straight and edges scalloped. The square bib had two rows of cotton ruffles. Large eyelet designs were used on the lower part of the gown.

Left: Jim Fernando created this work of art for our A.T. doll. Dress is antique pink satin, and lined skirt is gently gathered with overskirt of fluted georgette and one of flowered French lace. Pink-georgette overskirt and sleeves have three rows of shirred salmon-pink ribbon. Three rows of gathered lace cover blouse front inside fake wescott. Dress is two pieces and opens down back. This doll is shown on the cover.

Carefully fitted, bustled polonaise with ruffled skirt is perfect for this F.G. doll. Sand-gray silk taffeta is beautiful on her. Everything is lined with tan muslin. Steel-cut buttons and buckle are used as trim. Coral velvet adds color to outfit, and silk lace is used at neck.

Back view of sand-gray taffeta costume. You may think this color is dull for a costume, but it is beautiful on this doll.

Paper under lace of H-doll's dress, shown on opposite page, shows the pattern. Background lace is so delicate it is almost invisible.

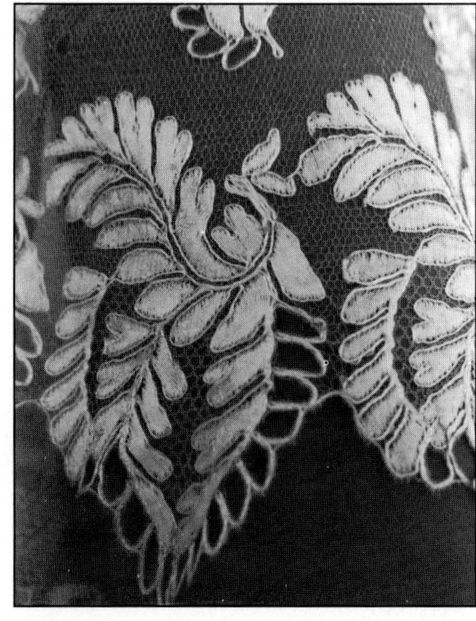

Left: H-3 doll gowned in antique Spanish silk lace. Dress is simple, gretchen-waist, Kate Greenaway style of stone-green sateen with 3/4-length puffed sleeves and full skirt. Skirt and sleeves are edged with another design of silk lace. Full ruffle of lace circles neckband. Dress is loosely lined with thin cotton and is open in the back from bodice to hem.

Bru dress of blue-silk taffeta is decorated with fancy antique braid and dorset thread buttons. Dress is two piece, with box-pleated skirt. Skirt has dust ruffle underskirt.

Back view shows bustle and interesting coat endings.

Close-up photo of drawn work on doll on opposite page.

Another Bru baby doll we saw in a museum wore a white bonnet that tied under the chin. The doll had a wool diaper that pulled between the legs and buttoned. Edges of the diapers had a finishing of ruffled, scalloped, embroidered cotton fabric. Blouse sleeves were finished in the same edging. The bib covered the shoulders and went down over the top of the diaper.

Singing Bru—There is another open-mouth Bru we have always wanted to call a singing Bru. She had the look of an older child. Our doll's original clothes consisted of a pale-green, wool-challis dress. The skirt had four large, inverted box pleats. Two rows of inserted lace decorated the skirt, and lace was lined with yellow silk. Lace-covered yellow silk formed the bodice, with a strip of skirt fabric from neck to waist in the center front. Elbow-length sleeves were trimmed with lace over yellow silk. A wide ruffle was sewn where sleeves met the bodice. Decoration was simple, yet stunning. A wide band of skirt fabric came over the left shoulder and appeared to tie at the waist under the right arm. A huge bow was not actually tied, but sewn together to give less bulk. Ends of the tie were applied lace and yellow silk.

Circle and Dot Bru—Our little Circle and Dot Bru, shown on the opposite page, wears an old, handmade dress. It is low-waisted and tied with a ribbon. The bow is carefully shaped, and the front and back are tucked. *Drawn work,* which is done by pulling threads, then cutting and sewing a design, is used.

Comfort's Clothes—Dress of blue-silk taffeta is worn by Comfort, as shown above on the left. It is decorated with fancy, antique braid and dorset thread buttons. Dorset thread buttons were made over a metal washer and wound with thread until buttons were covered. Sometimes designs were worked in the thread. The dress is two-piece, with a box-pleat skirt. The skirt has a lace dust-ruffle called a *balayeuse.*

Right: Circle and Dot Bru wears old, handmade linen dress that was once white. Every stitch on this costume was hand-sewn. Dress is low waisted, with pink-velvet ribbon. Bow is carefully shaped, and ends are fringed. Front and back have 14 hand-stitched vertical tucks. Between groups of tucks are three rows of drawn work that go down the back. Drawn work is used on sleeve ends and triangular collar. Gathered skirt is attached under the cummerbund and is hand-sewn. Skirt has three horizontal tucks with border of drawn work. Dress has back closing of pearl buttons. This dress could be classed as homemade and was made with love and skill a long time ago.

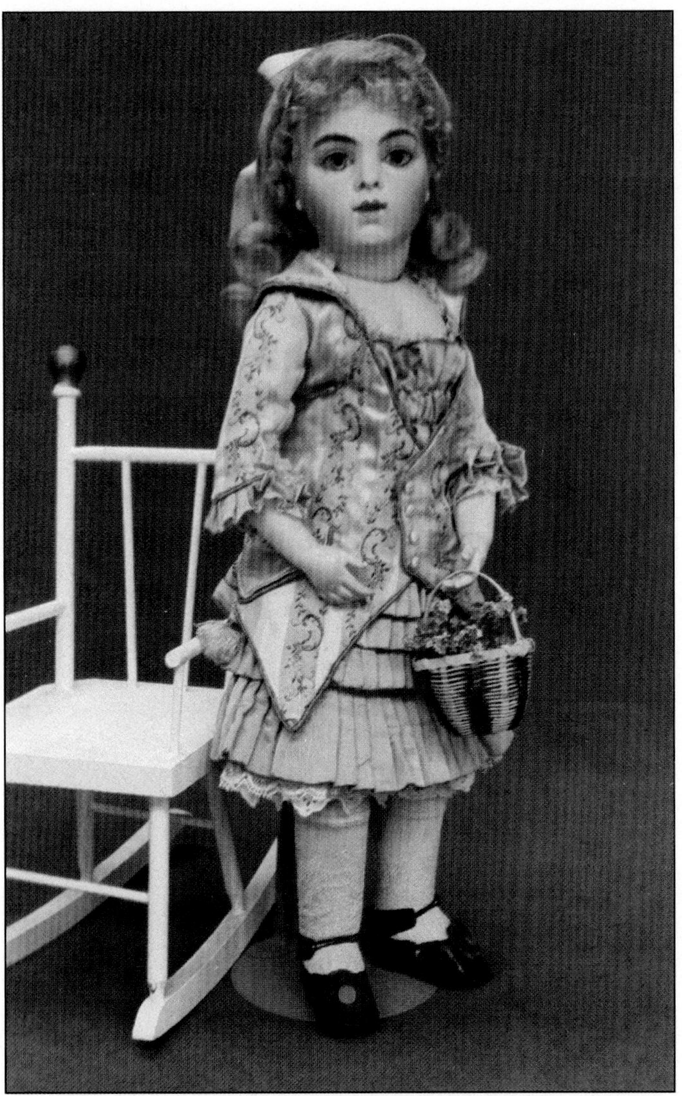

Left: Original Bru costume. Skirt has four rows of knife pleats, and brocaded jacket is piped in green and ends in points. Bodice is puckered silk, and buttons are tiny.

Below: Close-up photo shows false pocket with double piping and tassel decoration.

Sometimes deteriorating parts are removed from old doll costumes. We believe lace from neck and sleeves was removed from one Bru Jne 9 dress and new lace added. The dress is a delicate shade of pink satin, with designs of cream plush, which is similar to velvet. The dress has a low neck and gretchen waist. A row of lace and a balayeuse show below the skirt at the hemline. It is an 1891 style.

Bébé Bru Cherish—Our Bébé Bru Cherish, shown above, wears the most beautiful Bru costume we have ever seen. It is in excellent condition for its age. Colors are faded, but it is a wonderful dress to copy for a Bru waiting to be dressed.

Black, Brus—There are black Circle and Dot Brus and black Bru Jnes. One of our black Brus still wears her original full-length skirt and blouse. The skirt and head scarf are silk taffeta. The blouse is white-cotton eyelet, with large bloused sleeves that have a pull string at the elbow. Plaid is blue, yellow, black and white. Bru-marked shoes match the skirt, and socks are yellow. She has never been played with and wears her original costume!

In studying Brus, we found they were dressed in wool, linen, silk, taffeta, cotton satin, silk brocade and dotted Swiss. Other fabrics may have been used. Styles varied so we cannot say one design was used exclusively for Brus. Our favorite Bru costume is worn by Cherish.

Bru Shoes—Bru dolls in our cabinet wear shoes with the markings *B* in script, *Bru Jne Paris* and *M.B.* Shoes are made of white, turquoise, brown or black leather and trimmed with buckles and rosettes. Most shoes had straps attached at the back of the shoe that wrapped around the ankle. Other Bru styles include a pair of marked, side-button shoes, a pair of slippers without straps and a pair of shoes with a strap fastened in the middle with elastic, similar to Jumeau shoes.

JUMEAU DOLLS

Costumes of Jumeau dolls are numerous and varied because the Jumeau factory started making dolls about 1842 and was still producing dolls in the 1950s. Another reason for the variety of costumes is the number of dolls produced by Jumeau. In 1883 alone, the factory made 110,000 jointed, composition dolls with paperweight eyes.

Back view shows intricate work on jacket, pleating and gathering.

Early dolls made by the Jumeau factory were the lady type, with bisque heads and leather bodies. They were dressed in the fashions of the day by individual women in Paris who designed French fashions for adults.

As early as 1859, Jumeau advertised dressed dolls of all kinds. In 1871, he advertised nude dolls, dressed dolls and dolls with trousseaus. An 1877 advertisement stated dolls were dressed in linen or silk in the latest Paris fashions.

Commercial Costumes—It appears Jumeau dolls were dressed in two grades of costumes in 1885. Commercial dresses were made in the Montreuil factory and consisted of a chemise with plain underclothes. Shoes and socks were made there. Many dolls were boxed and shipped in these simple outfits, and parents were expected to buy other outfits.

Couturier-Dressed Jumeaus—Other Jumeaus were couturier-dressed. These dolls wore beautiful lace-trimmed underclothes, elaborate hand-sewn dresses in soft, well-chosen colors and hats or bonnets to match. Sometimes they had specially made shoes to match a costume. Occasionally dolls had wardrobes of clothing, including jewelry.

All this was accomplished by sending a doll to a dressing shop on Rue Pastourelle. Mme. Jumeau made all the decisions about dressing the dolls. She had as many as 50 women working for her in the shop, cutting patterns and sewing costumes. Besides the women in the shop, there may have been as many as 200 outside workers, who took dolls home to costume them. These women were "piece workers" and were paid for what they did.

SFBJ Dolls—Jumeau joined the SFBJ (Société Française de Fabrication de Bébés et Jouets) in 1899. Dolls were still manufactured under the Jumeau name. In 1921, it was reported in *Playthings* that SFBJ employed 2,800 people and produced 6 million dolls that year.

SFBJ had its own costuming department. Mme. Bonneaud created the costumes, which were current styles or regional costumes. Costumes were *factory type*—they were cut in large numbers and assembled in order. Clothing was made as efficiently as body and head parts.

Other Jumeau Dolls—Some Jumeau dolls came with trunks that were filled with large wardrobes. Dolls were made for export and dressed to appeal to the country they were going to. Jumeau sent dolls to South America, the United States and Australia. To appeal to more buyers, they made black dolls, brown dolls and yellow dolls, then dressed them for various countries and regions.

Jumeau Shoes—Jumeau shoes were marked by indenting or stamping. We have shoes marked *E.J. Déposé, Bébé Jumeau Paris Déposé* and *Paris*, a drawing of a bee, and the word *Déposé*.

Shoes were made of leather or fabric. Fabric shoes were canvas, with silk or satin covering. Shoes were often covered with dress fabric. The most-popular one was a brown slipper with one strap. It fastened with a button in the middle.

Other Jumeau shoes were slippers with elastic pulled over the instep from button to button. Some Jumeau shoes had an additional piece of leather over the center of the instep, with two buttonholes in it. This piece fastened to a button on each side of the shoe. On the toe of most shoes was a rosette and four rows of gathered ribbon, each one smaller than the one below.

Long-Face Jumeaus—Long-Face Jumeaus are found in many costumes, and many have been changed or re-dressed. One Long-Face Jumeau, page 50, wears a child's tucked white dress. Another we saw wore a dress made for a museum many years ago.

The Long-Face Jumeau with brown hair and green eyes, page 51, wears an original costume that was handmade. Brown Jumeau socks and shoes are original.

Left: Long-Face Jumeau in child's dress decorated with white work. Rows of minute tucks with inset eyelet and eyelet edging decorate dress. Child's dress of the doll's period is considered by most collectors as authentic. This doll is 31 inches high.

Right: Two dolls from Strong Museum wear original costumes. With time to look at and study these costumes, even a beginner would find it easy to identify them as original.

One Long-Face Jumeau we saw in a museum had an arm band on her colorful costume. Her dress came to the top edge of her lower leg. The skirt had a cream background with printed red rosebuds and moss-green leaves. It was gathered on a waistband. The short-sleeve jacket was moss-green satin, and jacket edges laced across a bodice of salmon pink. Sleeves were finished with matching salmon-pink ribbon. She wore a short salmon-pink apron, and salmon-pink slippers to match. Socks were red knit, which were common on Jumeau dolls. The costume went well with the doll's blond-mohair wig.

Another Long-Face Jumeau we saw wore a dress of lace over tucked satin with a low velvet sash. Her bonnet was tight fitting, with a handful of delicately tinted flowers across the front.

As you can see, there are many correct ways to dress Long-Face Jumeau dolls.

Other Jumeau Costumes—To give you an idea of the variety of costumes and materials used for Jumeau dolls, let us describe some costumes for you.

In the Margaret Strong Museum, in Rochester, New York, a pair of Jumeau dolls wear costumes reminiscent of the late 1700s. These dolls may have been costumed for an exhibition of some kind. They are shown above, on the right.

The 21-1/3-inch boy doll wears a tricorner hat of molded beige felt. His hip-length jacket is red satin, with silk embroidery of red flowers, white flowers and green leaves down front edges. His cuffs are antique beige with a French-lace ruffle. The beige-satin vest is hand-embroidered around the edges and has two decorated pockets. A fluff of matching lace is used at the throat. Red-satin pants are snug and button at the knee. The knee cuff is embroidered and fastens with a bow of red satin lined with beige satin. He wears brown Jumeau socks and red slippers.

His companion is more modestly dressed. Her threadbare, light-blue costume is silk brocade. The upper sleeve is puffed and goes into a long, tight cuff, ending in a ruffle of dress fabric at the wrist. The outer dress is coatlike and comes to the same length as the underdress. The dress top has a self-fabric ruffle at the neck and a lace collar down the back, around the waist to the front. Tight gathers of beige satin form the waistline. The skirt is made of graduated layers of French silk. The doll wears brown Jumeau socks and one-strap shoes to match her dress. This unusual pair of costumes can be copied.

Our Jumeau, Melody, page 52, wears an original

Right: This brown-hair, Long-Face Jumeau wears a handmade, original costume. Yellow silk taffeta is shredding. *Plastron,* the panel down the front, is shirred cotton lace and silk taffeta. Box-pleat skirt has overskirt of cotton lace. Sleeves have a pleat at the turned-back lace cuff, which gives sleeves fullness. Imitation jacket fastens at neck with small ribbon tie. Cummerbund is gathered, folded lace and has a large bow for a bustle, which appears to have been added later.

Left: Close-up photo of front of costume shown on opposite page shows decorative braid and cord buttons.

Right: Back view shows bow, cord buttons and lined streamers. Concealed closing is tiny brass hooks, which is typical of French costumes.

costume that is typical in style and design of a couturier. The dress is gray-green silk faille. The basic fabric has a satin stripe and satin ovals of the same color. There are three box pleats on each side and two double box pleats in the center back. The front shows use of decorative braid and cord buttons. The back of this original Jumeau dress has a bow, cord buttons and lined streamers. A concealed closing of tiny brass hooks indicates the dress was made by a costumer. The dress is lined in stiff cotton, and the skirt has an added pleated balayeuse on the inside. The balayeuse is edged in the same lace as used on the sleeves and neck.

In the Strong Museum, we found a fashion doll by Jumeau dressed as a rich woman from the Middle East. Silk was shredding, but the gold lace of the sleeves was almost perfect. The undertop and full, bloomerlike lower part of the garment were pale-yellow silk. The vest was deeper yellow, decorated with gold sequins. The front top was embroidered in blue, orange and yellow. The long, gold-sequin belt had beaded edges. The waist belt was gold sequined and decorated with turquoise and red beads. She wore the same color beads around her neck. Her cap, which was similar to an inverted pot, was embroidered and trimmed with hang-down coins. There was a string of coins around her shoulders.

An open-mouth, light-brown Jumeau we saw in a museum was dressed in an African costume. Her full-length skirt was deep teal, and wrist-length sleeves were edged in black. Her apron was black with black lace. Color was added to the costume

Left: Jumeau costume of Melody. Skirt is styled with 12 radiating pleats. Mandarin collar is salmon, edged in lace and centered with bow of decorative silk braid. V-shape of pleated peach silk is used at center front. Tiny pleats of cream silk run from shoulder to center waist. Pleats of coat sleeves form cap and V of decorative braid and lace. Dress has jacket, called a *polonaise*, with bustle made of lined streamers of dress fabric caught up and topped with bow of matching braid.

Wire-eye Steiner in original dress. Dress is simple, with ruffle on bottom and gathered front piece added to basic shape. Fabric is polished cotton.

Back of original Jumeau dress or chemise shown on opposite page. Lace at bottom has fabric under it to show pattern.

with a yellow-gold shawl at her shoulders. It was fringed in red, with red rickrack. Her headdress was yellow-gold, with gold beads for decoration. She wore large gold-hoop earrings.

Some Jumeaus are found in embroidered, pleated linen outfits. Some are dressed in fine wool challis; many are dressed in satin. Lace, net and decorative cord were used to finish outfits.

We have a labeled commercial dress by Jumeau, shown on this and the opposite page. No one argues the originality of this doll, with its label still on the costume. It is a commercially made frock of white cotton.

Child dolls wore children's dresses and dolls with ladies' bodies wore ladies' dresses. Jumeau dresses for child dolls came to the upper edge of the lower-leg or just below the knee joint.

JULES NICHOLAS STEINER DOLLS

The Jules Nicholas Steiner Co. made a variety of dolls from 1855 to 1891. Dolls made by Henri Alexander, May Brothers and Edmond Daspres are considered made by the Steiner Co. because they were all part of the Steiner Co. after 1891. A few dolls remain in original clothing, and we have found variety in their clothing.

We found a picture of an early walking Steiner with an original two-piece costume. The dress was made of thin cotton and trimmed with lace around the skirt and separate jacket. The skirt was full length.

A labeled Steiner that kicks and cries, wearing an

Right: This original Jumeau dress on 17-inch Jumeau is in perfect condition. Dress is white cotton and belt, which has two rows of red stitching, is centered with a red *Jumeau* label. Large box pleats run from yoke to bottom of skirt. Three rows of lace run down center of box pleats, and two rows of lace run around bottom. Sleeves are elbow length and made of small vertical pleats. Shield-shaped yoke is red silk, with lace and red embroidery. One-strap brown-leather shoes are marked *E.J.5.* This doll is shown on cover.

BÉBÉ JUMEAU
DIPLOME D'HONNEUR
BÉBÉ JUMEAU
5

Left: Reproduction dress on Steiner doll. Original dress was photographed, taken apart and copied. Bonnet was made the same way.

Right: Close-up photo of doll shown on opposite page. To be in this condition, the doll may never have been played with. Everything seems like new. Even tiny beadwork is in perfect condition.

original dotted-Swiss long baby dress, was sold at a Theriault auction in November 1983. The dress was white, with blue cotton under it. It had a boat neck edged in lace, and the bodice fell from the neck in gathers. The skirt was gathered in a waistband. A front panel of the skirt was made of horizontal strips of inset lace, dress fabric and rows of frilled lace at the bottom.

Costumes in Catalogs—In a 1901 catalog, we found eight dolls made by Steiner. Phenix Bébé had a commercial dress with the word *Phenix* on the front of the belt. The dress was printed fabric with a large fluted collar that came to the belt. Skirt and sleeves were finished with lace.

Another doll wore a plain, pleated skirt with a natural waistline. Puffed short sleeves had ruffles over the shoulders. The bodice was gathered at the neck and waist. There were no other decorations except a bow on each shoulder. The hat had three wires around the stand-up brim, which made a semicircle around her face.

One costume had smocked bodice and cuffs. Small ruffles over the shoulder tapered to the waist. The doll wore no hat.

Another doll wore a plain dress with a large, lace-trimmed square bertha. There was a bow at the natural waist. Sleeves were puffed at the shoulder, with long, tight lower sleeves.

Our Steiner—In our collection, a petite Steiner wears her original French costume and is shown above and on the opposite page. The costume is typical of the late 1880s.

We found an A-series Steiner in a light-pink cotton-sateen dress with matching bonnet. The dress had deteriorated, so we had an exact copy made, and it is a true reproduction. The original dress and bonnet were photographed, taken apart and copied. The pattern was made available to doll makers and was done by Martha Treyz, a pattern maker, when she was 88. The doll is shown above, on the left.

The Steiner reproduction dress shows *gigot* sleeves, which are full at the top and tight at the bottom. The undecorated brettelles are wide over the shoulder and narrow at the waist. The full skirt has three tucks around the bottom, and the dress is lined with cotton.

Right: Petite Steiner wears her original French costume. Lower skirt is knife pleated, with V-shape front and back and coat sleeves. Dress originally was pink satin, decorated with black cord, beige ribbon and tiny silk fringe. V at front is filled in with puckered silk, outlined with beige ribbon, black cord and tiny fringe. Neck is covered with fine beadwork. Tiny pleated ruffle fits tightly at neck and around sleeves. Ribbon comes from two places in the shoulder seam and ties in a bow halfway down the sleeve. Cummerbund is separate, decorated with ribbon, braid and fringe and fastens in back with hooks covered by a large bow. Doll wears part of *Au Nain Bleu* paper label on her back. This may indicate she was dressed by this doll shop, famous for its fine dolls and costumes.

Feather-stitching and wings are unique on this SFBJ doll.

SFBJ in hand-sewn costume. Lace decoration is unusual.

Tiny tucks decorate yoke and sleeve, and ribbon runs through inset embroidery. We left old ribbon in.

Commercial Chemises—We know many dolls came in commercial chemises, but we seldom find one in good condition. One of our Steiner dolls, page 83, wears a chemise of coarse cotton. We found this same dress on a doll in an 1891 catalog, but we cannot tell if the doll is the same Steiner.

Another of our Steiner dolls, shown on opposite page, wears one of our favorite dresses. No description can do justice to this original Steiner dress. Fabric is thin, with insets of embroidered net.

An early Steiner doll, page 89, wears a lovely, deteriorating costume. This original silk dress cannot last much longer. It is good to record this simple pink-satin dress.

From studying Steiner costumes in our collection, those in museums and others in books and catalogs, we can draw certain conclusions. The original costumes of Steiner dolls, made from 1880 to 1900, were plain-color satin or sateen. Dresses had a natural waistline and gigot sleeves with different widths of brettelles over the shoulder. Skirts were full and unpleated. Costumes were decorated with self-fabric bows and tucks. Steiner costumes were less decorative than Jumeau or Bru outfits.

SFBJ DOLLS

SFBJ dolls, made by Société Française de Fabrication de Bébés & Jouets, were produced in great numbers. In 1912, the company advertised it produced 5 million dolls a year. Dolls were produced in the Vincennes factory and sent to Paris for costuming. They were dressed in the latest costumes by dressers, many of them fashion experts. Women all over the world competed in designing outfits for these dolls.

In 1922, Mme. Bonneaud was chief fashion designer for SFBJ. We think she designed costumes for some SFBJ character dolls still found in original clothing.

Four SFBJ boy dolls in original costumes were sold at a Robert W. Skinner Inc. auction in 1983. See page 1. They were well dressed, and the costumes were colorful. These four SFBJ boy dolls have the same number—*235*.

On the cover of the November 1983 edition of *Doll Reader* was a picture of a pair of SFBJ boy dolls in original costume, with the number 237. One was dressed in his original wool sailor suit, the other in brown velvet.

Right: Hand-embroidered, handmade, white-linen, original Steiner dress. Insets of net are embroidered, sleeves are decorated with tiny tucks and yoke is finely tucked. Bretelles are lace trimmed, with ribbon inserts where they attach to shoulder. Bottom of dress is finished in scallops and edged in embroidery.

Sleeve decoration of doll shown on right in full-length photo includes buckle.

Reproduction outfit of silk taffeta is falling apart. Silk is decorated with cotton lace, ribbon and silver buckle. Low cummerbund is sewn on. Dress has coat sleeves decorated with silver buckles and lace.

Close-up photo of dress on opposite page shows tight sleeves are puffed and full at shoulder. There is no other decoration except ribbon bow.

In our collection, we have a No. 235 SFBJ boy doll in his original box, page 91. He has a closed head and molded hair covered with flocked red hair. His eyes are blue, and he has an open-closed laughing mouth.

We saw a crying SFBJ boy doll at the Strong Museum, and he was dressed in a powder-blue wool suit. The jacket was trimmed with white braid and had three bone buttons down the front. Full-length sleeves had braid trim and two buttons. Under the jacket, he wore a cotton blouse with a ruffled collar. Over-the-knee pants were creased and had two bone buttons on each side.

The doll had molded hair that could have been flocked hair at one time. It showed no evidence of flocking except the molded hair was not colored.

There may be more SFBJ boys in original costume than any other dolls. Boys did not play with dolls, and girls did not care much for boy dolls.

SCHMITT DOLLS

Schmitt and Sons of France was listed as a doll maker from 1877 to 1891. We found no mention of clothing or dressed dolls, yet Schmitt dolls in original clothing are found. We have Schmitt dolls in our collection in original clothing.

Our early lambskin, wigged Schmitt, shown above in middle photo, wears one of the finest reproduction outfits in our collection. The silk taffeta is falling apart, but the doll appears never to have been undressed.

Another antique Schmitt costume, on the opposite page, is made of a unique combination of fabrics. The simplicity of the frock is enhanced by the use of textures.

The third Schmitt is dressed in a pink coat-style dress. It buttons down the front with three fabric-covered buttons. Each pleated pocket has two buttons. The round collar, cuffs and front of the coat are edged with narrow lace. Her shoes match.

Another Schmitt in our collection wears clothing of an undetermined age, but not antique. She has a well-made silk brocade jacket and a pleated, lined gold-satin shirt.

Our 31-inch Schmitt, page 4, has a costume with so much handwork that no one would attempt to copy it. The jacket is silver-gray satin with box pleated ruffles of appliquéd white satin in unique patterns. Only pictures can show the beauty of this dress.

Finding two dolls in similar outfits does not set a pattern for dressing of all antique Schmitt dolls. Look at the three dolls in hand-sewn costumes—each is different.

Right: Schmitt costume with yoke and long, tight 3/4-length cuffs of red velvet. Full skirt of high-waisted dress is red sateen and striped ecru faille. Skirt is made more bouffant by three rows of tucks near bottom. Sleeves are puffed, and red-velvet yoke is used in front and back. Dress has back closing with old brass hooks. Dress is completely lined with cotton sarsnet and is hand-sewn.

Gown of Gibson-Girl doll is nainsook and cotton satin. Six tiny tucks go across front and back. Sleeves are puffed, then tight in forearm. Tiny pearl buckle is used at waist, and bottom is trimmed with ribbon.

German Doll Costumes

German-doll costumes are not as beautiful as the ones created by French doll makers. Study reprint catalogs available from Marshall Field's, Butler Brothers, Sears and other places. They show German dolls with fancy, frilly, lace-decorated dresses and big bonnets. Dolls often wore simple one-piece shirts or chemises. Only a few dolls were dressed in silk and satin similar to French costumes.

What illustrations do not show is the poor fit of dresses and underclothing. Dresses were covered with ribbon, bows and inexpensive lace, which did not launder well. Few costumes have survived.

Mothers and grandmothers re-dressed dolls as they were played with. Often several garments were made to go with Christmas dolls.

Child dolls, called *character dolls,* were usually dressed as children. As you can see from the photos in this section, several costumes are original. We found several regional costumes on dolls dressed as they came from Europe.

In this section, we show reproduction costumes for antique German dolls. There seem to be more handmade dresses on old German dolls, with less frill and decoration, as compared with French costumes.

Some photos show what dolls were wearing at the time they were made. Study and use this information and these designs any way you can.

SIMON AND HALBIG DOLLS

The Simon and Halbig Co. was large and probably began making dolls in the 1870s. It was still producing dolls in 1926. Heads are usually marked *S(number)H.* The company added the name of other companies for which they produced doll heads. Simon and Halbig heads have even been found on French dolls!

Simon and Halbig made brown dolls and Oriental dolls. We find a few dolls in original clothing. Simon and Halbig dressed dolls in regional costumes and in costumes of various countries or various occupations.

Our Oriental doll by Simon and Halbig, page 69, wears a palette of primary colors. This doll was shown in a 1910 Butler Brothers' catalog. She is still in mint condition. The doll on her right is an Armand Marseille Oriental boy doll.

Left: Baby girl in highchair is dressed in lightweight cream wool. Pink ribbon is drawn through lace to make beltline and is used on short sleeves. Four vertical tucks on front are centered with lace and pink ribbon. Dress was probably made by the owner's mother. Child doll on right wears the same type of dress in white silk, decorated with French knots. Both dolls came from the same family. Girl doll on left wears an original commercial dress. Dress is faded green with white-eyelet yoke. Yoke in front is edged with dress-fabric ruffle.

German dolls in boxes. When German dolls came dressed, they were covered with ruffles, lace, bows and ribbons. Dresses were made of inexpensive fabric and materials. Costumes did not last long if doll was played with. Dresses fell apart when laundered.

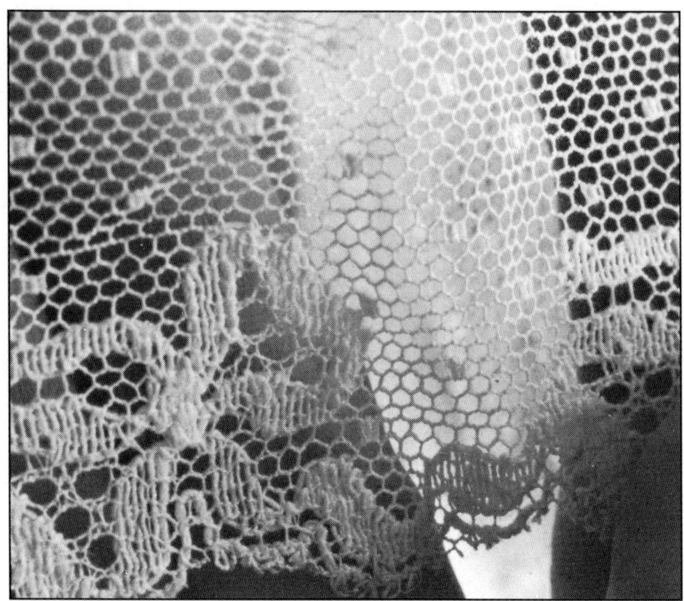

Old handmade lace is unusual as this close-up photo of dress on opposite page shows.

Blue-silk dress is made with separate skirt. Long jacket buttons with brass buttons. False yoke is square, with rim of pinked ruffling.

Back of blue-silk suit shows jacket shaping, silk gathered to make bustle and pointed bottom.

Typical white-cotton dress often worn by German dolls. This one was worn by a French Jumeau doll. Dress has berthalike ruffle around shoulders, edged in hem-stitching and cotton lace. Sleeves were gathered in narrow band, and hem-stitches and lace were added. Low-waisted skirt is decorated with inset lace that is the same on both edges. Inset lace is used on yoke with three lines of hem-stitching on each side of inset.

Right: Kley and Hahn doll wears aqua cotton-sateen dress decorated with fine, bow-design lace. Bodice is plain and opens down the back. Ruffled, lace collar and lace ruffle on bottom of skirt add decoration. Aqua band adds shadow line where lace is attached. Sleeves are snug, with slight puff at shoulders and ribbon ties at waist. Doll is shown standing next to a catalog reprint.

DRESSED DOLLS

Back of XII doll's dress is as interesting as front, with extra ribbon and more zigzag of lace and ribbon.

More Simon and Halbig dolls in our collection were dressed by mother or grandmother. Most do not wear original commercial costumes.

The Simon and Halbig child doll, page 62, wears a simple dress. It is made of white silk and decorated with French knots. Another girl wears a commercial dress, and her costume is original. The dress is faded, mottled moss-green, with a white-eyelet yoke. The yoke is used only in front.

There are many pictures of dolly face dolls wearing picture hats with ruffles and frilly dresses with wide berthas in old catalogs. *Dolly face dolls* are German dolls with open mouths and teeth, and plump cheeks.

One doll we saw had a full, mid-calf skirt with ruffles and lace frills. The upper part of the dress had wide bretelles and puffed sleeves. The outfit was trimmed in lace, and the wide picture hat was covered with ruffles and lace. A string of flowers went to the waist. There were two bunches of flowers on her hat. The doll was advertised in 1908.

Many costumes were handmade. The one shown on page 73 is one example of a handmade costume. It is fine, translucent, white cotton. Horizontal tucks and lace decorate a yoke outlined in a gathered white frill and edged in lace. The doll was left in the dress for many years, and it is too frail to take off. Her stockings are falling off. Dresses were longer in the 1880s. It is possible a doll costumer made the dress because it is so well-made.

Another doll we have is the smiling child of Simon and Halbig, page 97. The dress was probably made after the doll was produced.

The Simon and Halbig 929 doll, page 153, is gowned in a rust-red cotton frock. Every stitch is handmade. The older the doll, the more likely it is to have handmade clothing.

The doll on page 80 is dressed in brown wool and red decoration is cotton. When we say Simon and Halbig *dolls* are dressed in a particular style, it is misleading. Many times it is only the *head* that was made by Simon and Halbig. Their heads were used by other doll makers, such as Kämmer and Reinhardt, Heinrich Handwerck, C.M. Bergmann, Dressel, Hambuger and Co. and maybe others.

KESTNER DOLLS

The J.D. Kestner Co. made dolls and toys in

Left: Unmarked XII child doll wears wheat-colored, princess-style dress. Color brings out brown in her eyes and darker wheat-color of her hair. Heavy silk has check pattern in the weave. Narrow pleating goes around hem, and pleats are lined with sized cotton. Flounce of lace-edged beige was added and is longer than pleats. Lace trim on upper part of garment is attached in zigzag pattern. Double pieces of fringed, muted-pink ribbon were added between every-other zigzag.

Back closing with brass buttons and buttonholes. See full-page photo of doll on page 80.

Embroidered headdress and string of tiny beads decorate Oriental hairstyle of larger doll on opposite page.

Germany. As early as 1845, Kestner was listed as selling dolls. At that time, dolls were sold wearing a chemise, shoes and stockings. Early Kestner dolls wore mohair wigs that were made by sewing hair in strips, then sewing strips to gauze caps.

Kestner was one of the few companies that made the entire doll. They made other kinds of dolls, such as wax, Celluloid and papier-mâché dolls.

Four famous dolls were made by Kestner—the Kewpie, Hilda Baby, Gibson Girl and Bye-Lo Baby. The company made hundreds of designs of baby and dolly faced dolls, along with the early turned-head style. Kestner dolls are still popular and expensive.

We find no evidence of later bisque-head dolls with original clothing. There are no marks or styles we can look at and say, "That is Kestner's."

Some Kestner dolls were dressed by commercial dressmakers after they were imported to the United States. Others were sold without clothes. Dolls were dressed by the child, her mother or a relative. We have appraised Kestners with costumes the owners felt were original. Upon examination, the clothing looked homemade.

Large Kestner Googlies are not often found in original costumes. One we felt certain was original was a *241-0.* It wore a two-piece romper suit of pink stripes, with a top of white-cord fabric. The pointed collar was large and points came down almost to the belt. A belt of the same fabric fastened with a round metal button with prongs bent under. These metal buttons were often used on inexpensive dolls of the 1910-to-1914 period. Sleeves and pants were striped. Pants were gathered at the waist and fell to the lower calf and were hemmed at the bottom. The doll had a straight, Dutch-boy hairstyle.

Our Little Boy Blue was made by Kestner, and he wears a sailor suit. The sailor motif for boys and girls was popular from 1890. If you are dressing a German child doll from this period, try a sailor suit. Boy dolls are not plentiful and patterns for them are hard to find. Another doll in our collection, Miss Kestner, wears an original, handmade lace dress designed for her.

Right: Original Oriental costume on Simon and Halbig doll has underdress of muted green, pink and pale yellow. Red kimono is printed with black designs. Kimono lap is cadet-blue satin, and sleeves are bordered with same blue. Bright headdress is embroidered and beaded. Kimono has one box pleat in back and large yellow bow. Boy doll is Armand Marseille doll. He wears simple reproduction outfit of pants and top.

Fabric for this Kate Greenaway dress is antique silk with satin stripe and minute jewel spots of satin. Decoration is antique linen chain. Skirt is full and falls from yoke. Sleeves are full and gathered at wrist.

One unusual little Kestner, shown above, wears a Kate Greenaway fashion.

Another Kestner doll wears a mother-made dress. If this was the first dress this doll had, we consider it *original*, even though it did not come on the doll. If the dress was made about the same time as the doll, but not *for* her, we call it *contemporary*.

Our Kestner Gibson Girl, page 63, wears a typical Gibson-Girl outfit with a turned-up straw hat. Gibson-Girl dolls were sold without clothing. They were dressed in the fashions that Charles Dana Gibson made famous with his drawings.

In one museum, we found a Kestner lady doll, No. 162, with a complete doll's trousseau. She had 16 costumes and at least 14 hats. Her costumes included walking suits, day dresses, evening dresses, a coat trimmed with fur, a bathing suit and a riding habit. Shoes varied with each outfit. The doll had straw or fabric hats, trimmed with ribbons, bows, feathers or flowers. These would be appropriate for 1900-to-1912 German lady dolls. Clothes were made by the mother and aunt of the girl who owned the doll.

The complete wardrobe of the Kestner lady doll gives us an idea of the pieces of underclothing popular at the time, such as fancy and plain petticoats, corsets, corset covers and drawers. Cotton and silk were used for petticoats, and petticoats were made in many colors. The wardrobe included tan lisle stockings.

In checking dolls, books, catalogs and other sources, we do not find evidence of commercially dressed Kestner dolls. So how do you decide how to dress one? We suggest you dress a Kestner as other German dolls made around the same time.

ARMAND MARSEILLE DOLLS

Armand Marseille made dolls for his own company from 1865 to the late 1920s, and he made dolls for other companies. Not many Marseille dolls have survived in original costumes. They were play dolls, and mothers let their children play with them.

I received one for Christmas. Mine came with inexpensive underclothing, socks and shoes. My aunt purchased the doll and bought patterns for two dresses, a kimono, nightgown and underclothing. She purchased several pieces of cotton for dresses. My mother gave me the doll, patterns and fabric, and after Christmas, she made the clothes.

In our collection, we have a little A.M. 390 dressed in her original Volendam costume, which is a regional costume. Other dolls were dressed in regional or occupational costumes.

We have one pair of German dolls in original costumes, page 13. We have verified the authenticity of their costumes by matching the dolls with dolls in the Butler Brothers' 1911 Christmas catalog. The back of the costumes are as interesting as the fronts. Color is brighter in back. These costumes would be fun to copy.

Right: Armand Marseille's Lucy wears checked-cotton everyday dress. Mothers made these dresses for play dolls because they took the stress of children's tea parties and laundering. My mother made practical dresses for my dolls. This reproduction dress is well-designed, well-sewn and the kind the doll may have worn.

SINGER

Original German doll costume.

Heubach doll wears a machine-made nightie. Outside is wool; inside is soft and fleecy. Rickrack decorates round collar and front placket, and it has a sewn-in label.

Our Armand Marseille Oriental doll, page 69, wears a reproduction outfit. It is a simple pants-and-top costume.

A Googly we saw in original clothes, marked *A.M. 323*, wore a red-felt top with a pointed white-felt collar. The top came down over the red-and-white-check bloomers. Her short curls were topped with a bow of the same red felt.

Most Armand Marseille dolls were dolly face and dressed in commercial, frilly dresses of tarlatan, which was an inexpensive, gauzy fabric. When these costumes were washed, they fell apart. Homemade dresses were made to be played with and laundered.

HEUBACH BROTHERS' DOLLS

The Heubach Brothers Co. made many German dolls, and they specialized in character faces. *Character doll* means the face was modeled after a real person. Earlier dolls represented idealized children instead of a real child. Most Heubach dolls were the dolly face type.

Around 1908, a change to character faces was noticed. Advertisements began to read, "Dolls with real, childlike faces," "Dolls modeled from life" and "Human expressions modeled by well-known artists from living subjects." We look for these dolls today—dolls with pouting, crying or laughing expressions. They look almost real.

Right: Original costume, including underclothing and shoes, of Simon and Halbig 119 doll. Design is simple, and skirt is full. Bodice is decorated with tucks and inset lace, then outlined with frill and more lace. Doll and costume are from early 1880s.

There is no record of anyone designing costumes for these dolls. We know costumes were mass produced of inexpensive materials. We found no evidence of silk, velvet or satin being used. Dolls were dressed as children, usually in outfits that could be played with.

Little boys wore inexpensive sailor suits, machine-knit tops and pants. Wide-collared cotton blouses were worn with below-the-knee pants. Pants were trimmed with two buttons on the outside of the leg.

Some people are familiar with Whistling Jim's rompers, which were made with variations. They were usually blue or blue-striped fabric with a plain yoke and pleats that made the blouse and ended in elastic-legged pants. A belt fastened with two white buttons.

Heubach girls were dressed in cotton. Some wore white lace-trimmed dresses. Others wore simple cotton dresses with eyelet trim. Dresses were crude and simple, but effective.

Only a few hats remain with dolls. Straw hats often found on Heubach dolls could have been a later addition. Knit caps that match suits can be original. Large tams or berets that match suits or sailor hats are original. Many Heubach dolls had molded hair, and hats did not stay long with a doll.

The only shoes we consider original are paper shoes with cardboard soles. These shoes had a plain silver buckle with shoe paper drawn through the buckle. Socks were plain and usually made of inexpensive cotton knit.

Some character faces were put on bent-limb baby bodies. Babies were dressed in white-cotton, lace-trimmed baby dresses or knit outfits.

Dress a Heubach character doll as a child in play clothes. Do not use patterns for French bébés because it is incorrect.

KÄMMER AND REINHARDT DOLLS

The Kämmer and Reinhardt Co. was in existence from 1886 until after 1925, and it made K(star)R dolls. The company is most famous for their character dolls, especially the 100 series. Heads were made by Simon and Halbig for this series.

Early dolls were modeled by Ernst Kämmer and later by Karl Krauser and other artists. Character dolls were modeled from real children and named for the child model.

Many dolls were commercially dressed, probably in the factory. One advertisement shows dolls in simple play clothes.

Boy and girl dolls wore dresses. Girl dolls were dressed in short-waisted chemises with a ruffle over the shoulder and no sleeves. Boys wore pleated dresses with short sleeves and a belt. One boy's dress we saw had a high neck with a collar. Another had a dress with a square neck, decorated with wide braid. Braid went down one side of the dress and was used on the belt.

Other articles of clothing for K(star)R baby dolls, besides long dresses, included a sack, bonnet, bib, cloak, flannel skirt and diapers.

In a reproduction Kämmer and Reinhardt catalog, baby dolls are shown dressed in white lace-trimmed dresses and frilly white bonnets. Some dolls wore knit sweaters and bonnets, and some wore bibs. Advertisements state dolls are in charming "walk clothes," which were inexpensive and marketable.

Several photographs in the catalog show K(star)R 117 dolls in different costumes, but they were simple. One doll wore a straight playdress with a square neck and belt. Two coats trimmed with artificial fur were shown with leggings. One beret appeared to be knitted. Other play dresses included jumpers, a print dress with an apron, a white-collared dress with plain bodice and a print skirt. Shown in the same group were two boys. One wore short pants buttoned to the blouse, and the other wore rompers that went over a blouse with buttoned shoulder straps.

Another photograph showed a K(star)R 117 with dressy clothes. Some dresses were shown without sleeves, some with embroidery and some with a frill around the bottom. A few dresses had tiered ruffles. One little boy doll wore a smocked blouse with button-on short pants. There were pages of K(star)R 117 dolls dressed only in a slip or underwear combination. Across the front of each dress was the label *Mein Liebling*.

Other K(star)R character dolls were dressed in regional costumes of bright colors. See page 92. We know these costumes are original, and we have a couple in our collection. A K(star)R 101 in original regional costume was exhibited at the UFDC convention in 1983. It was similar to the one in our collection shown on page 92.

The *Pouty One*, Gretchen K(star)R 114, wears an original outfit in mint condition. She is shown on the opposite page. She came from Europe in this regional costume. It is faded and the string-gathered apron is yellow with age, but it is still a fine example of costuming.

The graphite-blue, cotton-sateen skirt has wide box pleats and is edged in two rows of red-and-blue

Right: The Pouty One, Gretchen, wears an original costume in almost-perfect condition. Skirt is faded and string-gathered apron is now yellow. Blue skirt has wide box pleats edged with two rows of braid.

This old K(star)R 115 is shown on page 102 in reproduction dress. Photo shows her in old gingham costume, which better suits this character doll.

Groups of four tiny tucks were used on front of this bodice. Two layers of eyelet are ruffled at neck of this gretchen dress.

decorative braid. The once-white apron has four rows of tucking and finished on the bottom with eyelet. The blouse is finished with a row of inset lace and gathered lace, which is the top of the slip. The wescott is black velvet with an added section that flares out over the skirt. The vest is lined and banded with the same blue cotton as the skirt.

The December 1912 *Ladies' Home Journal* showed pictures of K(star)R 114 boy and girl dolls and patterns that could be ordered for a complete wardrobe. Patterns included dresses, coats, a boy's suit, rompers, pajamas, nightshirt, robe, school dress and other items. Clothes were simple designs and shown in cotton stripes, plaids and polka dots.

Another K(star)R 117 child wears her own pink cotton costume shown on the opposite page. It appears to be a commercial dress.

Right: Kämmer and Reinhardt child doll wears dress with shield-shape yoke of inset lace, edged with ruffled cotton lace. Slightly puffed sleeves are gathered at wrist and edged in lace. Bodice is puffed or bloused, which was the style in the early 1900s. Belt is sewn in and fits snugly at her waist. Skirt is full. Extra tuck at bottom makes dress stand out. Dress had so much starch, three washings could not remove it all.

Deutsche Volkstrachten

Detail of exquisite work on sleeves of large K(star)R doll.

The two little girls shown on page 99 are from the same K(star)R 101 mold. They model two different costumes. The black child wears a costume made by its child owner. Machine-stitching is chain-stitch, indicating it was done on a child's sewing machine or an old adult one. The other child wears a commercially made dress we think was made for her.

A K(star)R 115 is shown on page 102 in a reproduction dress. We put her back in her original gingham costume, even though it is faded. See page 76. Groups of four tiny tucks run down the front of the bodice. Two layers of eyelet are ruffled around the neck of this gretchen dress. We label this dress *original, mother-made.*

Monday, the K(star)R Googly, is dressed in blue and bronze satin. See page 151. Dolls were dressed in fabric left from other garments. The dress is homemade, probably as old as the doll, and may be her original costume.

Miss Naughty, a flirty-eye child doll in our collection, wears a commercially made dress. The simple frock is typical of the ones German child dolls wore.

K(star)R 109 dolls are not often found in original costumes. See the two dolls on the opposite page. The small doll on the left wears an inexpensive regional outfit. Vivian Iob copied the outfit in antique materials for the large doll on the right. The blouse was a child's blouse from the 1900s.

There is variety in the costumes of Kämmer and Reinhardt dolls. Patterns appeared in magazines for dolls purchased undressed. There were dressed in original regional costumes. Many dolls were dressed in variations of children's clothing.

K(star)R dolls are in demand today. We find people dressing these dolls in long or full-length elaborate dresses. We have not found K(star)R dolls dressed in these costumes in our research. They were dressed as children, mostly in cotton play clothes.

Left: Small doll on left is K(star)R 109 doll. We kept her dressed as we found her. Her white-cotton blouse hooks down back. Her wescott is black satin with tiny brass buttons. Faded red skirt, with two rows of black braid, is commercially made. White-cotton apron is lace and braid trimmed. Large doll on right is a large K(star)R 109. She wears an outfit copied in antique fabrics made by Vivian Iob. Blouse was a child's blouse of the 1900s, and the Irish-linen apron was a child's apron.

Getting the Doll Ready to Costume

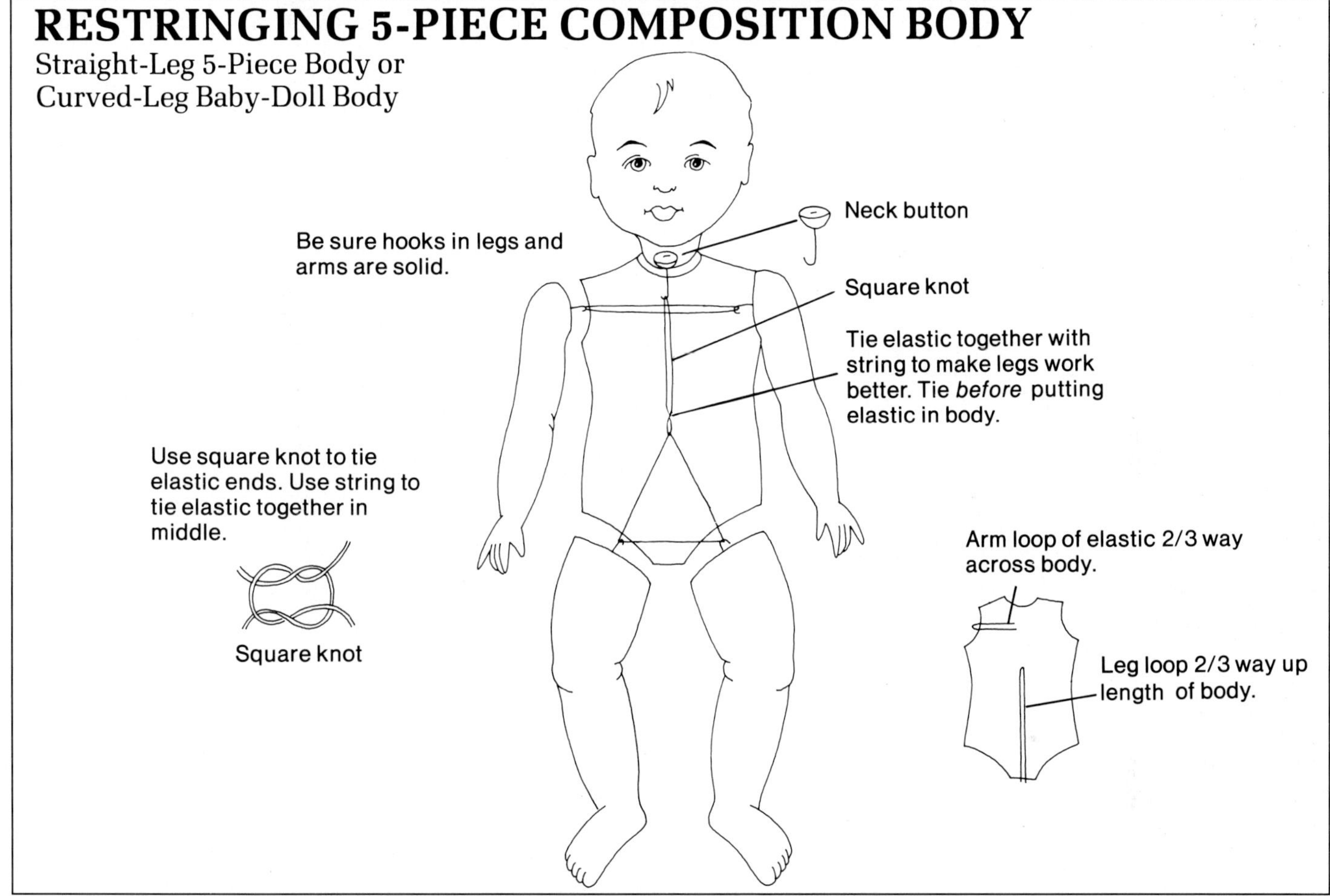

If you have a doll without clothes and you want to costume her, make any necessary repairs first. Do not make repairs that are *not* necessary. Do not repair bodies except in cases where parts that show are worn and unsightly or joints are broken. Never paint over *any* markings on a body.

If a body must be restrung, do it *before* costuming. Restringing does not change a doll's value. If a leather body needs patching to keep cork or sawdust in, patch it. Clean bisque at the same time.

This is not a repair book, and we only touch lightly on the subject so doll collectors can do minor repairs. If your doll needs extensive repairs, take it to someone with a reputation for repairing dolls. If you want to try to do the job yourself, Marty Westfall's book *The Handbook of Doll Repair and Restoration*, is an excellent resource.

CLEANING BISQUE DOLL HEADS

Clean bisque doll heads until they are bright and shiny. Cleaning will not injure a bisque head. Colors on bisque heads are fired in and part of the bisque. Do *not* wash papier-mâché or composition heads or get water on composition bodies. These bodies have water-soluble finishes, and water damages them.

In preparing to wash a doll's face, remove the wig if it is loose. If you do not want to remove the wig, turn hair up and wrap aluminum foil around it. If the face is not too dirty, a towel will keep hair from getting wet. We use an all-purpose cleaner, such as *409*.

Left: Susie sits on her trunk, dressed in dress of harsh brown fabric with red-cotton decoration. Fabric does not seem a good choice for a doll dress, but may have been all that was available. Dress is hand-sewn, even buttonholes. Two vertical lines of red cord run down front. Center-front panel is seven vertical pleats tacked down. Puffed collar is brown and edged with red. The same treatment is used above the row of sharp pleats that go around hemline.

You need cotton swabs and padding to go under the doll, such as a folded towel or several pieces of heavy terry cloth. Follow these steps when you clean your doll.
1. Put the doll on the padding. This protects the doll so it does not get rub marks or scratches on the face, and it absorbs excess moisture.
2. Cover the upper part of the body with foil, plastic wrap or another towel to keep water off the body.
3. Lightly spray the face with the cleaner and wipe with a wash cloth dampened with cleaner. You will be surprised how clean this makes the bisque. Wet a cotton swab with cleaner, and clean nostrils and lips. Put some cleaner in dirty hollows, such as ears. Turn the doll over and clean the back of her neck.
4. Clean eyes of French dolls that have paperweight eyes with cotton swabs.
5. Wet a clean cloth with warm water, and wipe the head. If soil remains, use more cleaner where necessary.
6. If the doll has sleep eyes, do not get any cleaner in the head through eye holes. Use a cotton swab, and wipe the eyes in the *open position* only. Use light pressure and a little cleaner. Dry the head with a towel. If the wig is off the doll, cleaner will remove dried glue around the top of the head. If the head is off the doll and it has paperweight eyes, use a small brush on the head. Dip the brush in cleaner, brush the doll and rinse the head under the faucet. Dry the same way you dry a dish.

REPAIRS ON BISQUE HEADS

Many people collect dolls on a budget. Sometimes a doll with a large V broken out of the neck and a body in pieces can be purchased at a low price. With gentle work and an authentic costume, you can have a doll worth collecting.

You can do many small repairs yourself. A broken piece on the neck may not show after a doll is dressed and the wig is in place. If you want a perfect, invisible repair the first time, send it to a company that specializes in doll repairs. Repairs are expensive.

Do Your Own Repairs—We learned to do repairs by reading and practicing. Before we repaired our second doll head, we read the book *Repairing and Restoring China and Glass, The Klein Method*. See *Resource* section, page 158. Klein sells equipment and materials. Follow the steps below to make small repairs on your bisque doll heads:
1. If the head is still on the body, remove it by cutting elastic.
2. Carefully remove hair and pate. If the doll has sleep eyes, put a wad of soft paper in the head to keep eyes from moving during repair.
3. Clean the pieces—we prefer to clean the whole head. Any place you glue must be clean and dry *before* gluing. We use a toothbrush and some hot water with bleach and soap. Put loose pieces in a pan of water while you scrub edges of the head where the repair will be made. These edges are always dirty, and when glued, a black line shows. Bleach removes dark coloring. Scrub edges of pieces in the pan, rinse and dry thoroughly. We use a towel, then a hair dryer.
4. The next step is tricky. Anchor the head with rolled up towels so it stays in place while you add pieces.
5. First, test pieces in the hole. Put them in place, and mark them with a pencil in two places. We make a mark from the broken piece across the crack to the head. When lines match up, we know where to put the piece.
6. We use a fast, strong glue. Use a small amount around the broken piece, push it in place and match pencil lines. There should not be any excess glue to squeeze out. If there is extra glue, remove it with a scalpel. Be careful not to move the placed piece. The joint will show no matter how careful you are. If you replace many pieces, or some pieces are missing, follow the same procedure, but use filler.
7. To make filler, we use plaster mixed with white glue. A drop or two of water may be added to this mixture to thin it. Apply the mixture with a palette knife, smooth it with a wet brush and sand it after it dries. You can buy commercial fillers. Sometimes you can glue paper over the hole on the inside. This helps hold plaster mixture in place.
8. If you fill in an area where a piece is missing, you must paint the area to match the rest of the doll. This takes an artist's touch. Professionals spray paint on with an airbrush, so no edges show where they stop painting. An airbrush is the only way to get professional results. Whether you touch up the repair with an airbrush or by hand, use Duncan bisque stains, which are water soluble. A mixture of Duncan colors for flesh tones will match the doll's color as closely as anything you will find. Duncan paints are available at ceramic stores and studios. If you do not use an airbrush to apply paint, use a soft facial sponge. Some people use sponges to apply cheek blushing.
9. Never refire an old bisque head. You will fire off original paint, then the head will have to be repainted. A refired and repainted head is of little value.

REMOUNTING SWIVEL HEADS ON SHOULDER PLATES

Some dolls have leather bodies with a shoulder

Right: Steiner chemise of coarse cotton decorated with pleats and inexpensive lace. Colored cotton was put under the lace to give it color. This is the original dress the doll wore when it was made.

TWO NECK BUTTONS FOUND IN FRENCH DOLLS

Stiff spring
Wood button
Wire hook

Wood washer
Stiff spring
Wood washer
Wire hook

REMOUNTING SWIVEL HEAD ON SHOULDER PLATE

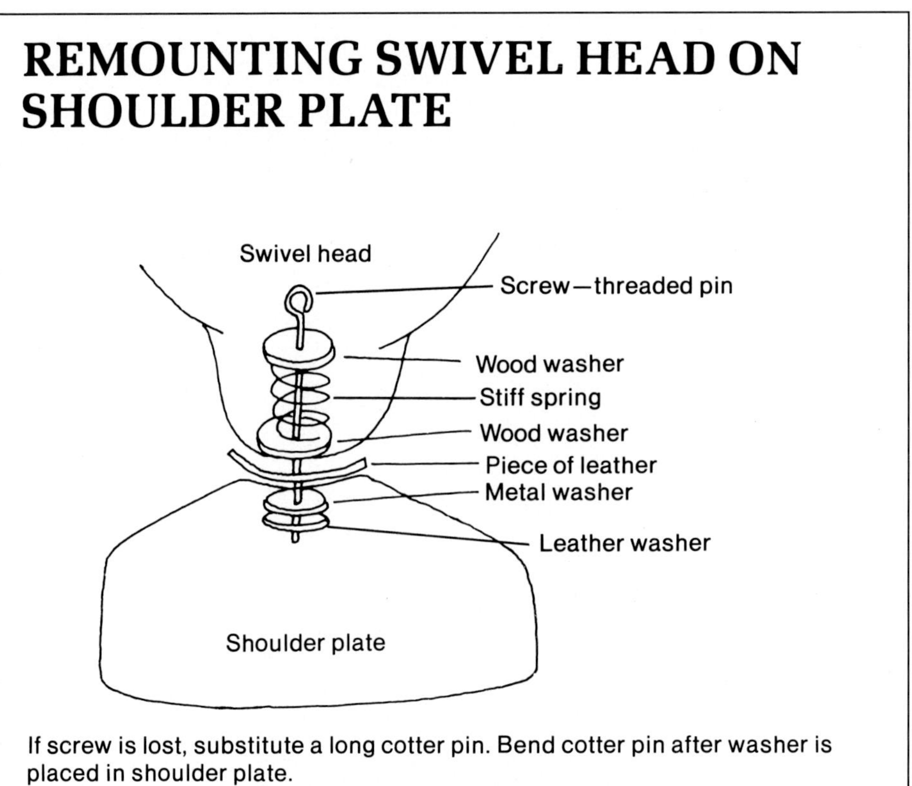

If screw is lost, substitute a long cotter pin. Bend cotter pin after washer is placed in shoulder plate.

RESTRINGING FRENCH SCHMITT BODY

This body has ball joints in shoulders, elbows, hips and knees.

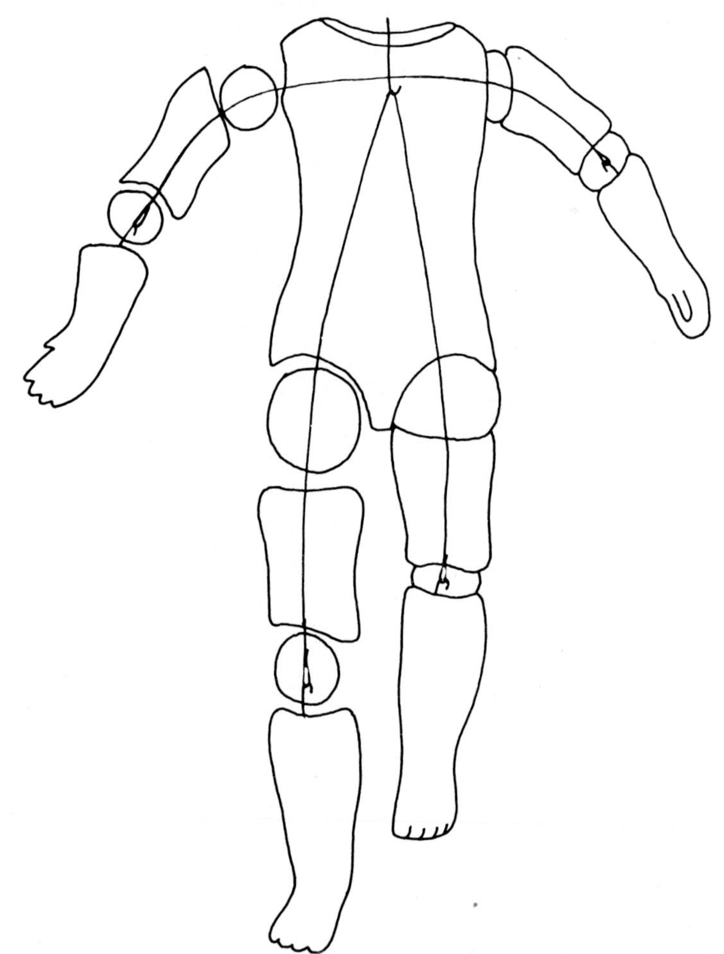

plate and swivel head. In their original assembly, these dolls had an arrangement made for fastening the two pieces together. Refer to illustration shown above as you read these instructions.

Manufacturers used 2- or 3-inch threaded pins with a top similar to a screw eye. It went down from the inside of the neck, through a round wood washer, a stiff spring, then another wood washer and the neck hole. The neck socket was covered with leather or kid. The screw went through the shoulder-plate hole, a leather screw, then a metal washer. This was held together by a tiny screw.

To reassemble this arrangement, remove the wig and pate from the doll. Two people working together are better than one to do this job. Securely hold the head upside down. Push with the other hand on the spring so most of the screw pin comes out the neck hole. The other person puts on the shoulder plate and washer, then puts on the screw to hold it together.

If the screw pin is lost, substitute a long cotter pin. Bend the ends out under the bottom screw. Springs and washers can be purchased in a hardware store.

This arrangement can be used on any swivel head and shoulder plate. It is used on reproduction dolls when necessary.

RESTRINGING DOLLS

When you restring a doll, you replace worn or broken elastic in a jointed doll body. There are hundreds of different bodies on French and German dolls. Even in our extensive work with dolls, we occasionally find a body that is different. There are almost as many stringing methods used as there are doll bodies made. We will cover the simplest and easiest methods for collectors to use.

We suggest you first restring a medium-size doll of little value. You can test the method and build your confidence. It is really an easy task.

Sizes of Doll Elastic—The size of elastic we use depends on the size of the doll's body. You can use another size elastic if you do not have the correct size. We have even used doubled, light elastic in emergencies, but it is better to have the right size. Round elastic is used for restringing dolls.

Elastic for restringing dolls ranges from thin to thick. There is a larger elastic than this for very large dolls.

- Size 1 for dolls 6 to 12 inches.
- Size 2 for dolls 12 to 20 inches.
- Size 3 for dolls 20 to 30 inches.

Tools—You will need the following tools to restring your doll:

- Elastic of appropriate size.
- Stringing hook. A coat hanger wire with a hook on the end will do.
- Hemostat. Two are better than one.
- Pliers with pointed ends, such as needle-nose pliers.
- You may need a wood head button and some *S* hooks.

See the *Resource* section, page 158, for information on where to buy materials and equipment.

RESTRINGING FRENCH DOLLS

Refer to illustration on this page as you read these instructions. The following steps are designed to help you restring the doll as efficiently as possible:

1. Put the doll on several folded towels or a padded surface. This keeps the doll from getting scratches on her nose or color worn off her face, and it keeps parts from rolling away.
2. Assemble necessary tools and equipment. Make a stringing hook by straightening a coat hanger. Unless you are stringing large or very small dolls, make the stringing hook about 16 inches long. Shape a hook on one end, and bend the other end for a handle. Stringing hooks can be purchased from doll-supply stores. Hemostats are useful in doll work, so buy one or two. If you buy two, get two different sizes.
3. If the doll's old elastic is still intact, cut it apart.
4. Lay out the body pieces. Be sure the right arm is on the right side, the left arm on the left side and so on. It is annoying to finish stringing a body and find the left hand on the right arm.

RESTRINGING FRENCH-DOLL BODY

Typical French Composition Body

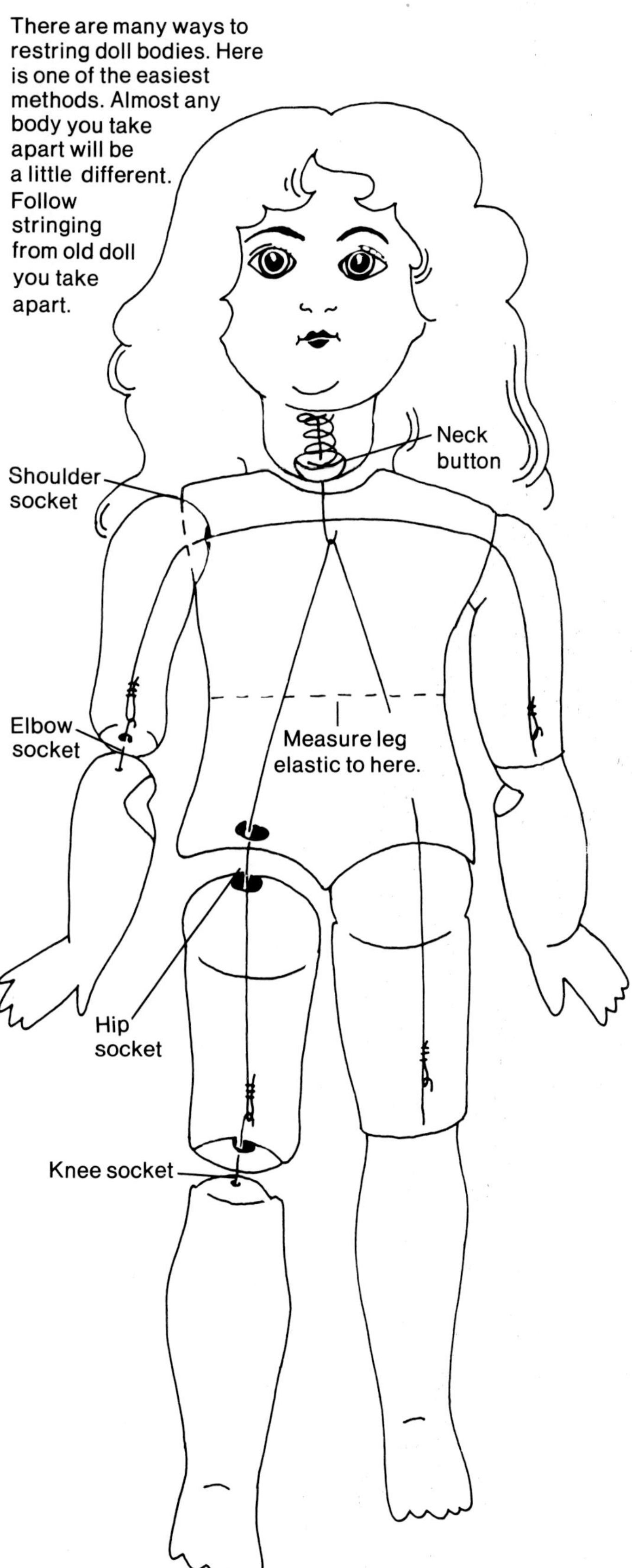

5. Hook the legs first. Measure from the hook of the lower leg halfway up the torso, and double this. Make a little loop on each end of the elastic by winding thread around it. Some people tie a knot. Hook one end of elastic to one lower leg hook. Thread the other end of elastic up through the upper leg, in the torso leg socket, out the other torso leg socket and down the upper leg. Hook elastic on the hook that protrudes from the lower leg. Elastic should be loose.
6. With the stringing hook down through the head-socket hole, hook elastic and pull up loop from legs. Clamp the hemostat to hold elastic at the neck. Make sure elastic has good tension. If legs are loose, elastic may be too long. If it is loose, release the hemostat, untie one leg and tighten elastic.
7. Hook arms. Make a loop in the end of the elastic, and hook it on the lower arm hook. Thread elastic through the upper arm, into the shoulder socket, through the torso, out the other arm socket and down through the other upper arm.
8. Holding the doll tightly, pull elastic snug. Clamp the hemostat at the edge of the upper arm. Make a loop on elastic, and hook on the lower arm. Release the hemostat. Arms should be snug.
9. It is helpful to have someone working with you when you attach the head, especially with large dolls. Hold the hook of the neck button with pliers. Slip the hook gently into the loop of elastic at the neck socket. Holding the head, carefully release the hemostat, and gently ease the head into the socket.
10. If wig and pate were removed from the doll's head, it is easy to put the neck button in place from the inside. If there is no neck button, put in a new one. Often we restring a doll without removing the wig or pate. You will find the neck button inside the head. Hold the head up, and pull the hook down through the hole.

Or you can decide how to restring the doll as you take it apart. Cut old elastic at the knees, pull it out and check to see how it was attached. Follow the same procedure with arms.

RESTRINGING GERMAN BALL-JOINTED BODIES

German ball-jointed bodies can be restrung the same way as French doll bodies. The same method works for almost any kind of doll body. Differences are the separate hands and ball joints. Refer to illustration on this page as you read these instructions. A few French-doll bodies have ball joints.

In stringing a German ball-jointed body, begin at the lower leg. Go up through the ball joint, the upper leg, in through the leg socket on one side and out the other side. With arms, elastic is hooked over the hook mounted in the hand.

Sometimes legs are strung with double elastic. Double elastic is hooked over the lower leg hook on

RESTRINGING GERMAN-DOLL BODY
With Composition Ball-Jointed Body

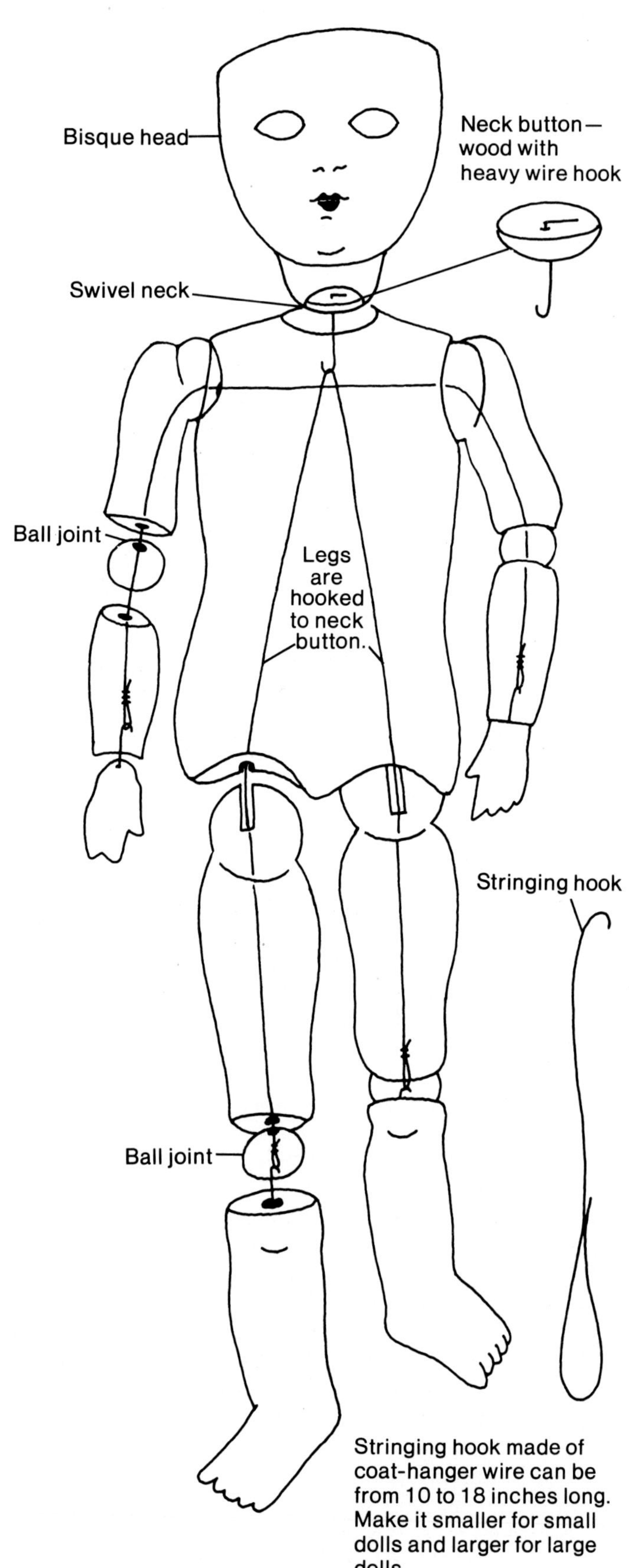

Stringing hook made of coat-hanger wire can be from 10 to 18 inches long. Make it smaller for small dolls and larger for large dolls.

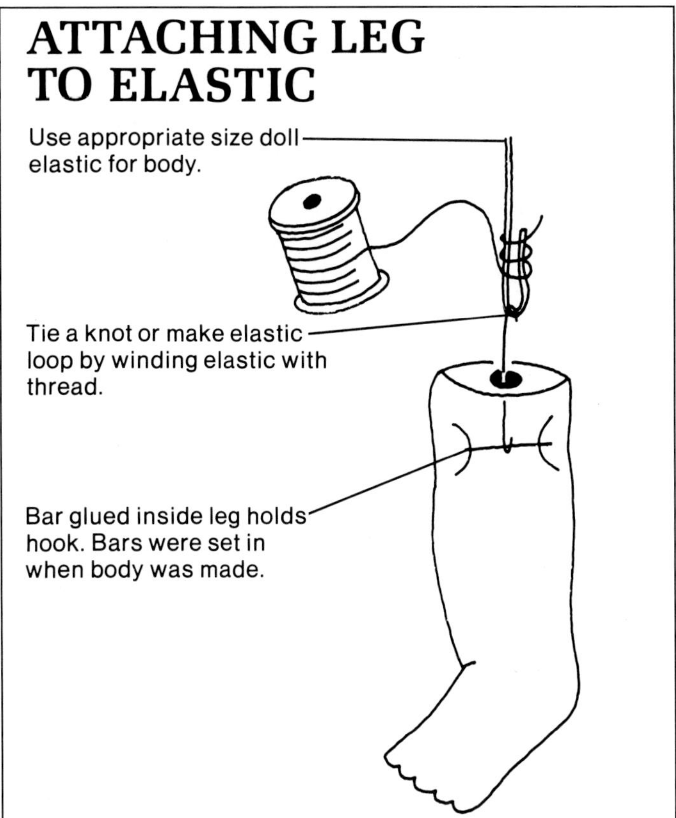

Hook leg elastic on leg hook, then push elastic through leg socket into torso.

each leg. Elastic is then drawn tightly and tied over a pencil at the neck socket. After you string a few dolls, you will find the method that is easiest for you. Every doll collector should be able to restring dolls—it is not that hard to do.

RESTRINGING FIVE-PIECE COMPOSITION BODIES

Directions for stringing five-piece composition bodies can be used for baby bodies. Refer to illustration on page 81 as you read these instructions.

Baby dolls with bent limbs have a hook embedded in the arm at the shoulder and a hook in the leg at the hip. Straight-leg dolls have the same hooks. Some Steiner dolls had this type of body, and these bodies are easy to string. Follow the steps below to restring five-piece composition bodies:

1. Make two elastic loops of the correct size for the body. One is for arms and the other for legs and head. Without stretching, the arm loop should lay across the top 1/3 of the body. This allows for a knot and enough stretch to hook both arms. Measure leg elastic from the crotch. It should run 2/3 of the way up the body. Tie ends of loops with a square knot.
2. String arms by hooking the arm hook into the elastic. Run the stringing hook from the opposite arm socket, and hook it into the elastic. Pull elastic through, attach a hemostat and hook in the other arm. If the doll is small, thread elastic through with a piece of wire.
3. Tie a string around the middle of the leg loop. This makes legs work better and not pull up. Hook the leg hook over elastic, and push elastic into the torso through the leg socket. Pull out the lower loop with the stringing hook or needle-nose pliers, and hook on second leg. Elastic will be loose.
4. Stretch the top of leg loop through the neck hole. Clamp with the hemostat, and hook on head. Gently loosen the hemostat, and ease the head into the socket. If the area is too small for needle-nose pliers, hemostat or stringing hook, use fine wire to string elastic. Some people tie on a piece of string, and thread it through.

REPAIRS FOR COMPOSITION AND PAPIER-MÂCHÉ DOLL BODIES

Leave major repairs on composition doll bodies to experts. Often collectors feel it is better to do nothing than to do too much. We want to remind you—*do not paint over* labels or markings anywhere on a doll. This destroys any chance of positive identification. Do not repaint a doll body to make it look good. This decreases the value of the doll.

Patching Holes—Patch holes around sockets, in the torso or leg area with spackling compound. Mix spackling compound with white glue. Using a palette knife, work the two ingredients together on a tile or can lid. Fill the hole with the compound, using the palette knife, and make it as smooth as possible. When dry, sand with a fine grade of sandpaper. Remove dust, and paint with bisque stain mixed to match body color. Spray with clear gloss acrylic if the body is shiny. The patch should be invisible.

Some people use spackling compound and white glue to rebuild fingers on composition bodies. Set a tiny piece of wire in the finger where it has broken off. The wire should be shorter than the finger will be. Build the compound mixture around the wire in the desired shape. Smooth the finger by sanding after mixture dries. Wire in the finger serves as reinforcement.

Using Bread Dough—You can use a mixture we recently discovered—bread dough, which models easily. Model the finger separately, and make it the correct size and shape to match the others. Put a drop of white glue on the spot of attachment and put the finger in place. Let the finger dry overnight, then paint it to match the hand. It should be sprayed. Ingredients and description for making bread-dough mixture are found on page 142.

Dough is excellent for small repairs and socket repairs. It is hard and durable. You can make a sharp edge or work on places, such as knees, where other compounds cannot be used.

We have repaired fingers on bisque hands with bread-dough mixture. It can be used to fill in a missing piece on a broken head. Bread dough is one of the best formulas we have found for use in dolls.

Plaster and White Glue—We use a mixture of plaster and white glue to repair composition bodies. Make a little pile of plaster, and add enough white glue to make a soft paste. Fill in holes, and smooth with a paintbrush dipped in water. To repair a large spot, make the mixture in a paper cup, and add a little water.

If you want a thinner mixture to use as a coating, dilute the mixture with a little water. Use as little water as possible to make a smooth coating. When it dries, it is hard. It may be the repair mixture you have been looking for. Sand smooth, then paint. It is strong enough to make repairs at the neck socket.

Painting—The paint we find most satisfactory for painting doll bodies is Duncan bisque stain, found in ceramic stores and doll shops. We use a mixture of the colors Dresden Flesh and Native Flesh. The mixture we use is usually 2 parts Dresden to 1 part Native. You must make your own mixture to match the bisque tone of your dolls so hands and arms showing below clothing are close to the color of the face.

We have our own rule about when to paint and not to paint a doll. This does not necessarily apply to other collectors. If hands are damaged or fingers missing, we paint after repairs. If a spot has been broken and must be filled in, we paint the spot to prevent further deterioration. We probably paint hands more often than other doll collectors because discolored hands do not show well in photographs.

Color should match the old body if you are patching a hole and painting a small area. Usually our mixture of Dresden Flesh and Native Flesh matches most bodies. Vary the mixture, and test a spot on the body where it will not be seen.

Old composition and papier-mâché bodies are water soluble, so paint soaks in. This makes the color different than it would be if tested on paper. Do not mix a large quantity of paint to use on other bodies because each body is a little different. Some very old bodies were almost cream color, while other bodies had a varnish that turned dark.

We use Duncan bisque-stain paint because it can be cleaned with water. These paints and colors may be used on new reproduction-doll bodies. If you must touch up a reproduction body, color is easily matched.

After painting, we spray the repaired area with a gloss acrylic or mat spray for added protection. We use Duncan clear gloss acrylic or mat bisque-stain spray. Spray the area once, let it dry, then spray again. It dries in a few minutes.

CLEANING LEATHER BODIES

Clean leather bodies that are not too soiled with saddle soap. Follow directions on the container. You can buy saddle soap in shoe repair shops and leather stores. We prefer not to clean leather bodies, so we leave them as they are. Most bodies will be covered with clothing.

REPAIRING HOLES IN LEATHER DOLL BODIES

You can repair small tears or holes in leather bodies with a patch. This keeps the doll from losing most of its stuffing. We patch holes with old, white glove leather. For a photo and step-by-step details, see HPBooks' *Doll Collecting for Fun & Profit,* by Mildred and Colleen Seeley.

Cut the edges of the hole even. If the doll needs more stuffing around the hole, use dacron or cotton. A pencil makes a good stuffing tool.

Stuff the doll, then cut a patch a little larger than the hole. Put rubber cement around the edges of the patch, and work the patch under the edge of the body leather. Depending on the size of the hole, use a darning needle or modeling tool to work it smooth. Cut a second patch. Make it large enough to cover the first patch and about 1/8 inch of the body leather. Use rubber cement to adhere one piece to another.

Let the cement dry a minute or two, then place the top patch over the first patch. Press edges down firmly, and try not to get cement on the body except where the patch is.

MINOR EYE REPAIRS

Any major eye repairs in bisque heads should be done by an expert or refer to Marty Westfall's *The Handbook of Doll Repair and Restoration* if you insist on trying it yourself. Minor repairs, such as regluing, can be done by anyone. Most people can set or reset eyes if there are no complications.

Suppose you are ready to costume your old doll and her eyes have fallen out. The first time this happens to any doll collector, she is horrified. If the doll has *set eyes*—eyes that do not move or sleep—it is a simple thing to repair. If the doll has *sleep eyes*—eyes that open and close—you may need an expert. If the doll has *flirty eyes*—eyes that move from side to side—the mechanism is complicated, and only an expert should try to repair it.

Loose Eyes—If eyes are loose in the head, handle

Right: Steiner satin dress. Inside jacket is fitted and sewn to the dress only at armholes. Neck section of jacket is covered with cream satin. Wide, low, dress neckline is bordered with silk-embroidered lace. Second row of lace goes over shoulder. Skirt is full and gathered, and waist is circled with rope of matching satin. Sleeves are cut on slant at wrist, and lace comes down over back of hand. Silk-covered rings are used as buttons at each cuff, and matching lace and cord go around skirt.

the doll carefully. Do not scratch or break the eyes. Lay the doll face down on a thick, folded towel, and remove the wig and pate. Often the wig pops off because glue is dry. If the wig does not come off easily, use a knife to loosen edges. If it still does not come up, dampen glue around the edges, and work the wig up, a little at a time.

Sometimes the pate is glued to the wig, and both come off together. If they do not, unglue the pate and remove it.

Now you can get into the head to get the eyes out. Examine the eyes. Are they both set in the plaster? Is the plaster broken in half? White glue will glue it together.

Hold the eyes in place in the eye sockets. Be sure the plaster holding eyes is right-side up. Take eyes out, and mark the top so you can replace them correctly. When eyes are out, clean the head. Refer to page 81 for information on cleaning bisque heads. Wipe the eyes with window cleaner so they are clean. Put white glue on each side of the head where the plaster will be used, and replace the eyes. Move them around until they fit exactly. Let eyes dry thoroughly with the head lying face down.

Sleep Eyes—If a doll has sleep eyes, you can do some minor repairs yourself. Otherwise let an expert do it.

Sleep eyes have a plaster hinge on each side of the head at the edge of the eyes. Sometimes plaster hinges come loose from the head. If you look carefully, you can see where they were attached. Replace the eyes, then put the plaster hinge in place. Be sure it is right-side up, in the exact place it came from. Put white glue on the spot, and put the piece back in. Do *not* get glue on the eye. Let glue dry before testing.

Sometimes cork that acts as a stopper for the eye weight comes unglued and causes the eyes to open too far. Usually the cork is still in the head. Glue it back in place. Examine the inside of the head because cork leaves a mark where it was glued. Cork is usually used in the chin area to protect the doll from banging by the eye weight, which adjusts how far eyes can open. If eyes are broken or gone, take the doll to a repair shop or put in set eyes yourself.

Set Eyes—Anyone can replace set eyes in a doll. Purchase eyes that match and fit your doll. They are purchased by *millimeter sizes.* Measure the eye from corner to corner, and add 2mm. This keeps eyes from falling through eye sockets. If a doll's eye hole measures 6mm from corner to corner, order an 8mm eye.

Purchasing eyes is not easy. They are handmade, and many do not match. Some eyes have smaller pupils than others, so always test them in your doll. The iris should touch the bottom lid and go under the top lid enough so part of the iris is covered.

Setting Eyes—To set eyes, you need plaster, a spoon, paper cup and eye-setting wax. Eyes, plaster and eye-setting wax are available at doll-supply stores. See the *Resource* section, page 158.

1. Remove a small piece of eye-setting wax, and roll it in your hands until soft. Make a coil about the size of a toothpick.
2. Put the coil around the eye socket on the *inside* of the head. Do the same with the other eye. Wax holds the eye in place and seals the crack around the eye opening so plaster will not leak.
3. Put eyes in place. Hold the head up, and move the eyes until they look correct. The doll should look at you. On large dolls, hold the doll in front of a mirror. Take time and be sure you like the placement. If all of the eye shows, the doll will have a scared or surprised look. If too much of the eye is covered, the doll will look sleepy or stupid.
4. Place the head with eyes in place face down on a towel. Have the head opening toward you.
5. Mix plaster to put over the back of the eyes. Fill a paper cup 1/3 full of water for a medium doll, more for a large one. Add dry plaster, 1 spoon at a time, until a mound forms in the water. Let it set for about 3 minutes, then mix. When plaster begins to thicken and coat the spoon, put a spoonful over each eye. Add more plaster if necessary and let dry.
6. Some people hold the eye in place with rubber cement before using plaster. Other people drip wax from a burning candle on the front of the eye. This is later cleaned off with nail-polish remover.

Types of Eyes—There are three kinds of dolls' eyes available. Some are a perfect sphere with a little handle where they have been blown. Others are almond-shaped. Old paperweight eyes are almond-shape with a clear bulge over the center of the eye. These are difficult to find.

Blown or round eyes are used for sleep eyes. Paperweight eyes are used on French dolls with set eyes. Almond-shaped eyes are found in very old lady dolls.

Never glue eyes with anything but water-soluble glue. It could ruin the doll because you would not be able to remove or reset eyes if you make a mistake.

With the materials we use, if you make a mistake you can soak everything with water and change it. If you need to remove the plaster holding eyes in an old head, soak with water, then lift with a knife.

Right: SFBJ 235 boy doll, in his original box, is dressed in shades of blue and wears a blue shirt with long sleeves. Shirt front has two box pleats, and shirt back has three. Shirt has white collar and cuffs, and a white handkerchief is tucked in his pocket. Blue-velvet, over-the-knee breeches are held up with four pearl buttons. Pearl buttons decorate sides of pants and are used on shirt front. Round cap is blue velvet decorated with strips of light-blue silk. Shoes are in fine condition.

Comité de la Vente des Poupées
ORPHELINAT DE BON SECOURS
PARIS

Janice Cuthbert's reproduction doll, Hilda, with reproduction dress and bonnet. Dress is made of antique pale-blue batiste and cotton lace, decorated with feather-stitching. Janice used silk ribbon as decoration.

Patterns and Color

PATTERNS

There are many different doll-body shapes and no answer to buying a pattern for each one. Early French dolls had straight wrists, but later French dolls did not. French wrists were chubby—a sleeve that fits a German doll will not fit a French doll. The hand may not go through the sleeve. French dolls had large hands.

The torso of a French doll was stockier than a German doll. A dress for an 18-inch German doll is too tight for a French doll. Some doll bodies had waistlines and a bosom, but most did not. Drawers made to fit the leg of a German doll will not fit a French one.

Patterns, though for the particular-size doll, do not necessarily fit all dolls of that size.

There are variations in jointed, composition bodies made by the French, and there are variations in German bodies. See the pictures of French and German bodies, pages 94 and 95. Arms are shorter or longer; legs are longer or fatter. Bodies vary in length and girth. Even head size varies. This makes necks and neck sockets different sizes. Each company did its own thing.

When you add leather-body dolls, you add a new dimension. German leather-body dolls do not have the same shape as French dolls with leather bodies. For example, clothes that fit a Bru doll do not fit other dolls. Commercial patterns do not fit either.

With reproduction dolls, there are not as many body variations. Body molds are difficult to make, and one company copies another. Companies usually pick a "typical" body type. For smaller sizes, they reduce the body. All reproduction bodies are reduced, decreasing about 14% with each reduction.

When making patterns for reproduction dolls, body sizes are more predictable. It is possible to buy patterns to fit a reproduction composition body.

Old dolls often have defects that must be camouflaged by the costumer. Sometimes shoulders on an old leather body are worn out, so the dress hangs limply. A costumer can cover this problem by adding inside padding. Often an elbow or wrist joint is ugly and worn. A costume with long sleeves hides this defect. Worn knees can be covered with a skirt or high stockings.

Some people feel a swivel neck is ugly where it

Left: Reproduction costume for K(star)R 101 copied from regional costume of another K(star)R 101. Skirt is antique watermarked taffeta. Blouse is pretucked white-cotton fabric, and red is silk crepe. Braid was made three different widths by adding red border. Costume by Jackie Jones.

Twill-covered composition body with unmarked head. Doll has good proportions for dressing.

Body of XI doll is short and stocky. Shoulders are wider than normal, and waistline is thicker.

fits into the body or neck socket. This can be covered with tight beads or lace at the neck.

The worst defects that need camouflaging are mismatched parts or bodies that are too big or too small.

Do not expect to find ready-made patterns to fit old dolls without adjustment. You must make adjustments or have someone make a costume to fit your doll.

PATTERNS TO FIT

Patterns we buy seldom fit exactly, so most costumers draft a pattern for each doll. They are able to look at an old dress—its shape and trim—and make a duplicate that is superior. We often see this when we judge reproduction dolls. This talent is a gift. Many people never knew they could do it until they began costuming dolls.

We have stressed how important an old costume is and how it is a part of a doll's history. A new costume is important—it must fit and enhance the doll. It must look as though it were made for that doll alone. The following four things make a reproduction costume worth investing in:

- Proper fit.
- Correct color.
- Correct style for the period.
- Pleasant appearance.

Usually underclothing is made first, then the dress is fitted over it. Be careful not to have too much bulk or heavy lines of underclothing showing through a fine dress fabric. Plan from the inside out, and fit each item. A doll does not move, so you do not need to plan for much movement. It will not grow or put on weight, so you can fit clothing exactly, and everything can fit as she is now. Garments will be her only costume, and she may wear them forever.

There is a shortcut to making a basic pattern. Doll dressers use tissues, such as Kleenex, pattern tissue paper or muslin to make patterns. You can make a pattern with aluminum foil. Lay the doll down on a firm surface with a thick towel under her. Always use towels or sheets as padding under dolls to protect faces from marring or bisque hands from breaking when working on them.

With underclothing on, take a single piece of foil, and press it over the chest. Mark the neckline with a pencil, lift off the foil and trim excess. Replace the foil, then shape it around the shoulder. Mark where the shoulder seam will be, lift off and cut. Replace the foil each time to be sure the line is correct. Fit the arm, and cut out the shape. If there is excess foil at the waist, fold a dart. If it is a lady doll, fold another dart a little below the arm at the bust. Cut foil along side seams to the waistline.

Mark foil with a pencil, then pinch and shape it until you have a perfectly fitted bodice. It seems easiest to use foil over the whole bodice section, although you only need half of this to make a pattern. After

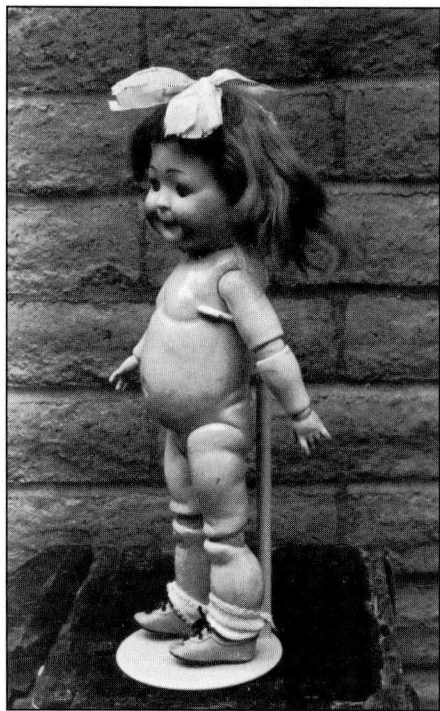
Most patterns will not fit over the fat tummy of this Googly 173.

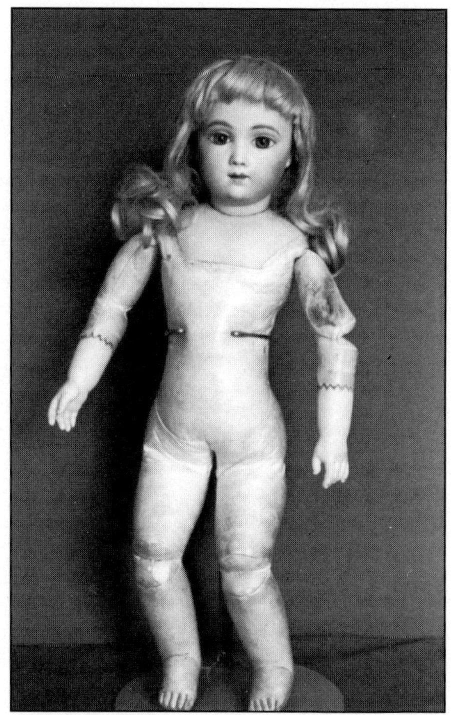
Leather body of A7T Snow Angel, shown dressed on page 31. Her proportions are good for dressing, except for her small wrists.

you fit the bodice foil, remove it and look at it. Be sure armholes are the same size. Add a little extra room under the arm so it is not too tight. Fold bodice foil in half from the neck down, and cut on the fold. Do the same for the back.

Pull out the darts and leave creases. Lay the foil piece on a folded piece of non-woven interfacing fabric, such as *Pellon*. Trace all lines, and add a 1/4-inch seam allowance. This makes the bodice fit the doll exactly. Decide where the dress will open, and add extra fabric for the closing. Test the pattern on scrap fabric before cutting fine fabric.

Make the sleeve of foil. Work around the arm, then cut the foil in half. Shape sleeves the way you want. Consult costumes of the period.

This method can be used to test or adjust ready-made patterns. Cut the ready-made pattern from foil, fit and make necessary adjustments. Shape the back the same way.

Fit inside garments as carefully as outside ones. This assures the outside costume will look better. *Be sure to leave enough room for a doll stand.*

When making the first foil bodice, check where the waist will be. If the garment is long-waisted, shape the foil to the desired spot.

Make other pattern measurements. The waist and wrists are the only other things that fit tightly.

Measure the waist and hips, and take 1/4 of each measurement. Measure from the waist to bottom of the skirt, and add enough for a hem. Use these measurements to draw 1/4 of the skirt, then add the shape you wish. This method of pattern making is for the creative person. Sometimes if you make the bodice fit, you can use other patterns for the skirt.

PATTERNS TO SIZE

A *pantograph* is a machine for enlarging patterns. It is usually large, bulky and difficult to work with, but many pattern makers use it successfully. A small one would be more helpful in making doll costumes.

Some patterns are printed on graph paper. This makes it easy to increase or decrease a pattern by making larger or smaller squares on another paper, then drawing what is in each square. If a doll is 10 inches and the pattern is 20 inches, make the squares half their original size. This is good for simple patterns. If the original is not squared, draw squares on the pattern. This method does not always work because some dolls twice the size do not have twice the waistline or twice the wrist measurement.

There are some easier methods. Many copy centers can expand or reduce a pattern several percentages. Sometimes it is necessary to shrink a pattern twice to get the size you want.

You can use a printer's camera. It costs more, but you can get your pattern the *exact* percentage you want, larger or smaller. This is done in print shops.

SUGGESTIONS FOR USING PATTERNS

Some old patterns have no seam allowances. To draw a seam allowance on a pattern, tape two pencils side by side. With the inside pencil, follow the pattern line—the other pencil will draw a 1/4-inch seam allowance.

On patterns with notches to show placement, cut notches so they stick out, not cut in. This saves cutting weak places in the seam. It allows you to let a seam out to enlarge an area of the garment if necessary.

IDEAS

The following ideas may help you measure dolls and fabric, and sew and finish your costumes.

- When measuring for pleating or gathering, use *three* times the actual measurement.
- Use spray starch on soft, old cotton to make sewing easier and clothes look better.
- Stay-stitch, then baste fine fabrics.
- Sometimes threadbare clothing can be lined with net or tulle to extend wearing life.
- The rough side of lace is the right-side.
- To store a dressed doll, wrap it the way you would store fine fabric. A clean white towel or white sheet keeps fabric from deteriorating.
- Lining and garment can often be sewn as one.
- Before gathering, make three rows of stitches using the longest stitch on your sewing machine. To make gathering neat, pull all three rows.
- Use tissue paper under seams of delicate fabric to help fabric slide and keep it from getting caught in the machine.
- To make lace curve, such as on the front of a bonnet, run long stitches along the inside edge. Gather slightly, and press the outside edge in a circular shape.
- Needles, called *sharps*, in size 8 or 9 are best for fine sewing. For fine lace or chiffon, use a size-10 sharp.
- In antique stores, you may be able to find old silk thread. Buy it and use it when you can match colors. Otherwise use polyester or 90/100 cotton thread. On heavier fabrics, use 50/60.
- A good source of fabric for tiny all-bisque or dollhouse dolls is an old handkerchief. Many antique handkerchiefs are available and some are embroidered in fine designs.
- Sometimes antique dealers find boxes of old, wide hair ribbons worn by girls during the 1912-to-1918 period. If ribbons are still strong, they have many uses on small dolls.
- Smocking was popular on children's and doll's garments. New smocking machines do some of the work for you. They can be purchased in some quilting stores.
- Use the teeth of a comb to crimp ribbon for shoe rosettes. Stitch rosettes together before removing them from comb. Spray with hair spray or gloss spray. Different-size teeth make different-size rosettes.
- When sewing fine fabric, such as silk, regular pins make holes, so use silk pins or needles.
- New markers for sewing leave marks for about a day, then disappear. They are available at sewing counters.
- On miniature dolls, use *liquid thread,* which is a type of glue. Glue is accepted in competition.
- Make or trace patterns on non-woven interfacing. It is easy to use and more accurate.
- Take time with priceless old fabrics. Test a pattern on scrap or muslin first. It is better to find out before you make a costume that it does not fit or that you do not like it.
- If an old costume is lined, line the new one. Before selecting lining fabric, consider the outer fabric you are using.
- Pad a lady doll to fill out the chest if necessary. Often shoulders are worn and stuffing gone. A little padding makes shoulders look better and match in shape.
- When cleaning old ribbon or lace, let it soak in cold-water wash, rinse and wrap around a jar to dry. You will not have to iron it. This works for many flat items. Let them dry on a flat counter or up and down on the refrigerator.
- Use fabric from men's undershirts for stockings.
- Use cans and jars as hat blocks for shaping and making hats.
- Keep ribbon in small, self-sealing bags.
- Roll old silk in a piece of white sheet before storing.
- Pin the hem on a doll's dress as you would a person's dress. Using a spool with a pencil in it as a gauge, mark the length desired around the hem.
- Use a large needle, a corsage pin stuck through a piece of cork or heavy cardboard to make small bows. This is easier than trying to hold them and sew at the same time.
- Some people use glue along raw edges when they cut a buttonhole. The buttonhole-stitch is neat and even over this slightly hardened surface.

Right: Smiling Simon and Halbig doll wears commercially made dress of cotton. Fabric is similar to organdy. Dress is plain, with lace hearts across front. Puff sleeves and neck are edged in lace. Dress was made after doll.

COLOR

The study of color is fascinating. Color theory can be applied to art, interiors, clothing and psychology. It is intriguing to see how color affects us and what it does to our daily lives. It is the same with the colors we choose for dolls.

Psychologists feel color conveys emotional messages and has an effect on behavior. White sends out a message of purity. This may be why many German children and baby dolls were dressed in white. Or it might have been the ease of washing white clothes.

Bright primary colors indicate strength, such as colors chosen for Superman. Usually strength is not something we wish to convey in our dolls, so we do not use many primary colors when selecting costume materials.

Some colors, such as peach or light blue, have a calming effect. Many hospital rooms are done in these colors. A doll dressed in subtle tones may have a relaxing effect on doll admirers. Grayed colors give comfort and relief from tension and have a calming effect.

People select colors they like for themselves from colors that are available. Some colors are fads. The Color Association of the United States (CAUS) advises manufacturers on colors for cars, appliances, sheets and other consumer goods. CAUS predicted cheerful, happy colors, such as rose, blue and pale green for 1984 and 1985. These colors were selected from the *LaBelle Epoque* costume exhibit at the New York City Metropolitan Museum of Art. Will this affect doll dressing? Yes, because these will be the colors, shades and tints available to costumers in fabric and trim.

If we look at our dolls in original costumes from 1880 to 1900, we find colors used were deep violet, sapphire blue, smoke, mauve, ivory, rose, aqua, steel gray, plum, mocha, muted pink, camel, burgundy, teal and winter wheat. These are soft, muted colors and convey a feeling of relaxation and gentleness. When costumes were new 100 years ago, colors were probably brighter.

Dressing dolls in correct colors is not easy. Some people have a natural talent for using color. Others must study color theory and application. Some people never discover the correct color for their dolls.

In reproduction dolls, we see many levels of talent. Often poor painters cover their dolls with bright costumes with ruffles, lace and bright colors. They hope the buyer will be impressed with the costume and not notice their poor workmanship.

These soft, muted colors make a lovely combination for a bonnet or costume.

A costume and its colors should bring out the beauty of a doll's face. Certain colors go better with one doll than another. Test a variety to see what goes well with cheek, hair and eye color. Wrapping a piece of fabric around the doll helps you decide. Often a doll's eyes are the key to color selection.

COLORS FOR COSTUMES

Many colors are used for doll costumes. Some colors enhance a doll, while others do not look good and detract from the overall appearance.

Red—Reds are often used in small amounts on dolls. With red, use a plaid containing red, navy, white, dark green and bits of cream or ecru.

Orange—This is not a common color for doll costumes. It is prettier when it is salmon or russet.

Right: Two little girl dolls from same K(star)R 101 mold model different costumes. Black child doll wears child-made skirt with large stitches of double thread. We wanted to show at least one child-made costume because many dolls were dressed by their owners. Sitting child doll wears commercially made cotton dress with striped design, decorated with eyelet flounce at bottom and armholes. Eyelet goes down center front of dress, and dress has back closing.

HANDY SUPER
CHALK CRAYONS
Unexcelled in quality
UNITED STATES CRAYON CO.
CHICAGO, ILL.
MANUFACTURERS OF
CRAYONS, TAILORS' CHALK and STENCIL INKS

Yellow—Pale shades of yellow are often used on child dolls. Bright lemon-yellow is not the best color with bisque. It is better to use it on the skirt or areas away from the face. Butter yellow, brass, gold, cream, ivory and wheat are better than true yellow. When using yellow, use shades of brown, gold, purple or pink with it.

Green—Soft green, moss green and pale green are good colors, especially on brown-eye dolls. Emerald green is seen more often in ladies' fashions. Pistachio or lime green are hard to use on dolls.

Blue—Blue ranges from sapphire-blue, misty blue, cadet blue, graphite and gray-blue to ice blue. There is shading toward green—aquas, teal, blue-green and peacock. With blue-greens, use a tint of the same color or pink because both are beautiful on blond dolls.

Violet—Purple, plum, mauve, smoke, amethyst, heather and grape are better shades for dolls than true violet. Use lighter or darker tints or shades with these colors. Some shades of pink work well.

Black—This color was often used on French fashion dolls. It is not an exciting substitute for a color. Brighten black with a primary color—red, blue or yellow. Black trimmed with beige or cream is good on black dolls. Grays—pewter, charcoal, smoke and pearl—were often used for coats and capes of lady dolls.

White—White was used frequently on dolls. Baby dolls and toddlers were dressed almost entirely in white. Bows or embroidery in pastel colors were often added. Many German child dolls were dressed in white dresses. French child dolls often wore embroidered white dresses.

Color wheels are good tools for costume classes.

THE COLOR WHEEL

Most people who dress dolls have not had an art education. Anyone can discover new colors and color combinations by using a color wheel. For people who are afraid of their own judgment in color combinations, a color wheel is the solution. They can be purchased at an art store. We recommend the Grumbacher color wheel shown below.

Primary colors—red, yellow and blue—are often used in advertising. They are found on Oriental dolls. See the doll in original costume, page 69.

Secondary colors—orange, green and violet—attract attention. They are made of equal amounts of two primary colors—red and yellow, blue and yellow, and red and blue.

All colors can be darkened by adding black. This makes a *shade*. They can be lightened by adding white, called a *tint*.

Do not bother to make a color wheel. Purchase one with its intricate mixing of color and many windows as a tool for your doll dressing. A color wheel is helpful in sewing classes. It helps build confidence in a person's ability to choose colors.

Many people like monochromatic color schemes on doll clothes and bonnets. *Monochromatic color schemes* are made from the same color, with the addition of black or white to one color. We like this color scheme because it does not detract from the beauty of a doll's face.

Complementary colors are opposite each other on the color wheel. These colors are often used in plaids. Many doll costumers use them because of their strong contrast. An example would be orange and blue, red and green, or violet and yellow.

Analogous colors are beautiful on dolls. These colors appear next to each other on the color wheel. With the Grumbacher wheel, turn it until it shows you how colors look together. Hold pieces of fabric against the wheel to see what you need or what you have that will go with it. Test color combinations to see how they look on the doll by draping them on her.

In studying old dolls, we find many colors combined with beige lace. Some color schemes are monochromatic, with added combinations of textured fabrics, such as satin and wool challis, faille and velvet or silk taffeta and lace. Sometimes a dress and bonnet are one shade or tint and decorations of flowers, ribbons or beads are several tints or shades of the same color.

Right: Bru Jne costume made of old materials. Jackie Jones did the pleating and fitting on this monochromatic costume. This Bru has a lady-shape body with snugly fitted corset underneath two-tone silk-brocade-and-crepe outfit. Workmanship on bonnet and costume shows Jones' talent.

Wig of reproduction doll made by Janice Cuthbert.

Doll Wigs and Styles

Styles of doll wigs are fascinating. We have studied wigs at auctions, museums, private collections, in books, reprints of old catalogs and on dolls in our collection. Many old catalogs were reprinted in 1976 during the Bicentennial. Some catalogs are still available from Hobby House Press. See the *Resource* section, page 158.

There are not enough dolls by one doll maker, either French or German, to say a particular doll maker used only one kind of wig. We will share with you what we have found and prefer not to guess at what we have not. We will look at some dolls by maker and some by time because this is the way we found them.

Styles of wigs are important because a change of wig can change the look of a doll. We will show you original wig styles so you will know and be able to recognize an original style. It will help you recreate a hairstyle similar to an old style.

Keep a wig in the same style as it was originally, if possible. Many dolls made in 1880, such as Brus and Jumeaus, wore a wig with hair pulled off the face and a fringe of short, curly bangs across the front. Some hair from the sides was pulled back and up, then tied at the crown.

Many wigs had center parts, bangs and curly hair at the sides. Some had a band of hair that went over the head, making front curls or bangs.

We have studied dolls with original wigs and looked in old catalogs. Human-hair wigs were long, and long curls are *always* human hair. Wigs with long curls were made after 1890. Wigs with side parts were made after 1900. Many earlier dolls had short, fuzzy wigs of lambskin or wool. Some boy dolls had short hair that was animal skin. These wigs are part of doll history.

There is not much information or reference material on the history of doll wigs and styles. The only sources of information are dolls or photographs of dolls. Even with these resources, it is not always possible to tell if a doll's wig was changed or not.

We look at several French dolls and discuss different wig styles. We have not seen all French wig styles. As with any part of doll study, you learn something new every day.

Bru Wig Styles—Everyone wants to know what kind of wigs Brus originally wore. We have found only mohair wigs on Brus that could be termed original. They came in shades of blond and auburn.

Many old dolls had mohair wigs that were

Left: Kämmer and Reinhardt 115 wears pink-cotton reproduction dress. This dress is hand-sewn and has small embroidered roses and shows fine workmanship of today's dressmakers. Doll's character seems lost in pink. Some K(star)R dolls came from Europe dressed in regional costumes. Others were dressed in everyday cotton dresses. See page 76.

changed to human-hair wigs. We have found two styles intact. One of the most well-known styles is the Bru wig with hair drawn back from the front and a soft fringe of tight curls around the forehead. A small amount of hair is pulled up from the sides. Front hair is tied on top of the head, and soft curls fall to the shoulders around back and sides.

In the second Bru style, hair comes down from the center of the head in heavy front bangs and below-shoulder soft curls. See page 101.

One black Bru wears a short, kinky black-mohair wig with no style. Bru Brevetés always wore sheepskin wigs. See page 19.

Steiner Wig Styles—We have 10 Steiner dolls in original wigs. Mohair wigs are platinum, blond, red-blond and chestnut. Two dolls in our collection may have original human-hair wigs. Wigs are the same brown color, with waist-length sausage curls.

Our blond-mohair wigs were woven on a loom and had center parts, but no bangs. Two wigs were sewn with the hair coming down from the center of the head in all directions, with whispy bangs and shoulder-length curls.

Jumeau Wig Styles—Many Jumeau dolls wear a Bru-style wig. Look at the Jumeau in her original box, page 55. One E.J. Jumeau has a blond wig with stitching across the front and curly bangs and curls around the face and back of the head. The hair barely touches the shoulders. A Tête Jumeau in our cabinet wears an identical wig.

We know Jumeaus wore human-hair wigs. One doll, Melody, page 54, has gold hair that reaches almost to the bottom of her skirt. It may have been in long curls originally.

Schmitt Wig Styles—Older French Schmitt dolls had sheepskin wigs. See the Schmitt in original costume, page 60. Another one wears a blond-mohair wig, page 61. Hair comes from the center of the head with a slight curl. A small, pale bisque Schmitt has short curls all over the top of her head, and hair is mohair.

Thuillier Wig Styles—Many Thuillier dolls, called *A.T.s*, wore wigs of blond mohair. Colors range from platinum to yellow-blond. Wigs are sewn on a net base. They have heavy bangs almost to the brows and soft curls on the shoulders. A.T.s are not numerous. We have only been able to find 30 A.T. dolls in books, museums and collections to study, so this small number does not make a good survey of all possible hairstyles.

Marque Wig Styles—Marque dolls wore a variety of styles—each doll had a different wig style. Some wore human-hair wigs, and some wore mohair wigs. Each wig was designed to fit the era of the costume. Our boy Marque has a Dutch-boy hairstyle, which is a straight cut with straight bangs. The wig is red human hair. Our girl Marque wears a center-part, blond, human-hair wig. She has slightly curly hair that hangs to her waist.

F.G. Wig Styles—No particular hairstyle can be identified with Gaultier dolls. These dolls were put together by several companies, and each company apparently created its own styles.

Other Wig Styles—German dolls wore many styles and different qualities of wigs. Some wigs were only a patch of hair with ends stuck on with glue. This was found on small, inexpensive dolls.

Boy dolls and some baby dolls had animal-hide wigs. We have a boy Googly with a fur wig. One doll has a turned head with long hair, but the wig is a piece of hide and it is coarse.

We looked in our cabinet to see what hairstyles German dolls wore. Our K(star)R Marie 101 wears a mohair ramshorn hairstyle. Hair is braided on the sides and wound over the ears. Our 131 Googly and our A.M. Googly have curls all over. See page 151.

A Marshall Field's 1914 catalog shows wigs dolls wore and wigs that were sold separately. The most expensive wig was described as a "side parted, first quality sewed doll wig, made of pure angora, with long curly locks, blond, dark brown, tosca." Another wig had hair coming from the center of the head in all directions. Length was slightly below the ears.

At the same time, wigs were bobbed with bangs or long, wavy curls. Many dolls had wavy hair with frizzy curls at the end. About 60% of the dolls had dark hair. Tosca, a gray-tan, was a popular color at the time.

The Kämmer and Reinhardt doll catalog from Waltershausen, Germany, shows 11 replacement wigs for the K(star)R dolls. The illustrations on the opposite page show these different styles. One K(star)R 117 doll was shown wearing many different styles of wigs. In the catalog picture, ribbons in a doll's hair were referred to as *silk hair knots*. They were part of the hairstyle. The different wig styles included:

- Center part with medium-length, vertical curls.
- Center part, smooth on top, ending with mass of long soft curls.
- Mass of short curls all over head.
- Side part, with hair slightly wavy, no curl on ends.
- Straight bobbed style.
- Center part with braids.
- No part, with ends rolled up or under.
- Short, kinky hair.
- No part, long bob.
- Short with bangs and vertical side curls.
- Side part with waves and ends turned under.

HUMAN-HAIR WIG STYLES

From the 1890s through early 1900, human-hair doll wigs were popular. As we study dolls, we find

WIG STYLES

Wig styles used on K(star)R 117 doll. These would be appropriate for any Edwardian-period German doll, from 1895 to 1920.

several important styles, as discussed below. There were four shades of hair—blond, light brown, medium brown and dark brown. From 1914 to 1916 the color tosca was used.

Human-hair wigs were made over a net crown. Hair was usually sewn by strips to the net. Most wigs had ribbons anchored in them.

The style we find most often on dolls is the center part with fine corkscrew curls and curled bangs. A similar style was parted in the middle with no bangs. Hair was smooth on top. Curls were long and reached almost to the waist. Silk bows tied first and second curls together.

The gretchen style is not often found. Hair is parted from center front to center back and drawn smooth, with two long braids. Braids were tied with ribbon. This is the kind of wig worn by one of our K(star)R 109 dolls. Our Steiner doll, page 97, wears an original style of this wig.

Another style similiar to the one described above had braids rolled up and tied with a ribbon over or in back of the ear. A center-part wig had braids wound around the head fastened with a ribbon on top. Another wig style had hair pulled back and braids wound in a knot at the back of the neck.

These are the most common wig styles we find today on antique dolls. The wig with long curls was the most popular.

CARING FOR AND PRESERVING WIGS

An original wig is an important part of an old doll, so try to preserve it. If you cannot save it, replace it with the best wig you can find. We prefer an old wig to a new one.

Wigs were made from lambskin, wool, fur from animal hides, angora goat (mohair), the longer, stiffer hair of the Tibetan goat and human hair. We will discuss caring for the two most common ones—mohair and human hair.

Many old wigs were made of mohair, which is fine, soft hair and a good texture for dolls. It was available in different shades of blond, brown and even black.

Mohair wigs could not be combed or played with. The hair is about 3 or 4 inches long. To make long hair on a doll, locks of mohair were tied in to make curls longer. This means locks are tied in partway down the length of the first locks. Wigs with long mohair curls were found on expensive dolls because tying was a lengthy, expensive process. This type of wig construction was not made for children to play with or comb.

When children tried to comb mohair, the comb caught. The child combed harder to take out the snarl, and this pulled the hair out of the wig. Look under a wig to see if locks are tied in.

Working with a Wig—We prefer to work on a wig on the doll. You can tell what must be done to it as you work. Before you costume a doll, set it on your lap and work on her hair, or leave her on the doll stand and work on a low table.

We use a rattail comb, a dog's steel comb and a corsage pin. Take the knots and snarls out of the hair one strand at a time. Work from the end of the hair, back toward the head. Gently comb the hair with the comb. We sometimes use a dog's steel brush. Steel tines are set in rubber, so when they come to a snarl, tines go over it instead of pulling out the hair.

Mohair can be curled with the low-heat setting on a curling iron. It can be sprayed and set with hair spray, curlers or clips. Human hair can be treated the same way.

Most mohair wigs have a base of sized cotton. This comes apart and shrinks if hair is washed. We prefer *not* to wash any wig.

Washing a Wig—If you feel there is no hope for a wig without washing it, wash it but do not expect much. Use the following process for mohair and human-hair wigs.

Remove the wig from the doll's head. Old glue is usually hard and crisp, and the wig comes off easily. If the wig has been glued with white glue, soften this by lightly spraying water around the edges. Gently work a knife under the edge. The wig base is similar to a skull cap.

Prepare to wash the wig. We use shampoo or cold-water wash. Use cool water because it will not shrink the base of the wig as much. Sometimes you can swish the wig up and down in the water without getting the base material too wet. Try to do this.

When you finish washing the wig, rinse it at least twice. If the entire wig is wet, rinse under cold running water.

Place a hard wad of paper on top of a glass jar. Use a jar about the size of the head, and make a paper wad about the same size as the curve of the head. Put a piece of aluminum foil over the paper, and place the wet wig over the foil-covered paper. Dry the wig with a hair dryer or leave it outside in the sun. Once when we dried a wig outside, a bird tried to steal some of the hair for her nest!

The wig base will shrink and be difficult to get back on the doll. Sometimes you can snip or make a cut in the base rim to give you enough extra room for the wig to go on. Sometimes two small cuts are better. Before doing any cutting, check to see if there are tucks in the back of the wig base that you can unstitch to allow more room. Be careful not to cut any hair.

We save all old wigs, and use parts on other wigs. It is not difficult to match colors of old wigs because few colors were used.

Wigs can be dyed. New wigs can be dyed, but you lose the curl and have to do it over. The gold hair of the Simon and Halbig doll on page 97 and the Kämmer and Reinhardt 115 doll on page 76 were curled human-hair wigs that we dyed. We left their hair straight to add variety to our collection.

On some small German dolls, wigs were made by inserting hair through a hole in a piece of cardboard or in a hole in the head. These wigs are usually poor quality and little is left of them. It is better to replace these with a new wig. If you feel a wig is worth saving, follow directions for working with mohair wigs on the previous page.

Pates—A *pate* is the cardboard, cork or plaster piece found under the wig of a doll. This piece rounds out the top of the head where the porcelain is cut off. A good pate is necessary to make the head round. Save old cork pates from dolls.

Almost all French dolls had cork pates. If you have a French doll that needs a pate, trim a piece of cork. It is more authentic than Styrofoam. French Steiner dolls had cardboard pates instead of cork.

You can purchase pates in all sizes. Some people use a Styrofoam ball cut in half. On French dolls, an egg shape is needed. Use about 1/3 of an egg, cut the long way. Cut a small edge off around the egg-shape piece to allow the center to set down into the head 1/4 inch.

Protection—If you use water to set a doll's hair or to remove her wig, wrap a towel or foil around her body. Do not get water on a leather or composition body. The finishes on these were not made for washing.

Do not permanently replace a wig until costuming is complete. This saves wear and tear on it. Often we remove a wig while the doll is being costumed, even if we will not do anything to it.

Styling a Wig—After you wash and comb a doll's wig, you must restyle or curl it. Human-hair wigs can be set the same way you set your own hair. In many ways, a human-hair wig is better to work with. It is stronger, longer and cleans better. You can use setting gel, hair spray, curlers, pins and a curling iron.

Mohair wigs can be set with curlers and pins, or you can use a curling iron if you are careful, and you can use a hair dryer. We comb the hair out and put every curl in place. Then we put a net over it and use hair spray. It is surprising how long the hair stays in place if you put the wig on *after* a doll is costumed.

If we are sending a doll to be costumed or doing it ourselves, and she wears a wig, we put a plastic bag over her head. This allows you to pull the clothing over the hair without messing it up. Do this each time you dress or undress a doll.

REPAIRING WIGS

Usually a wig is repaired, washed, made or purchased along with costuming. Do not glue a wig on a doll until the costume is finished and on the doll.

Study the doll, and try different styles and different colors. It is surprising what a wig change will

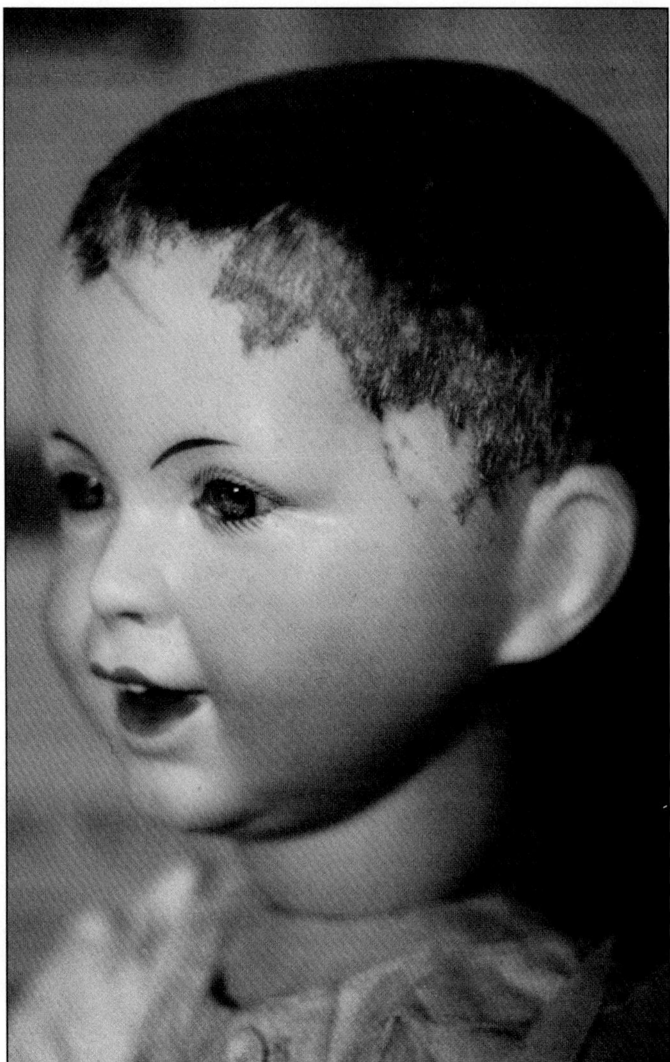

Flocked auburn hair of this SFBJ boy is flaking off. Little can be done to preserve it.

do for a doll. We prefer the old wig when possible.

Many old mohair wigs have been combed so thin there is little left of them. You may have an old wig that almost matches the one you are using. Most of these wigs had hair that was sewn on a strip, then strips sewn on a gauze cap. Sometimes you can cut a strip of hair from one wig and add it around the back of the neck over the old cap on the other. It can be stitched or glued on to fill out the old wig and make it passable.

In the same way, extra hair can be added to the front. If a wig is sparse on top, take some hair and put it through a small circle of cardboard. Put the hair and cardboard under the wig cap, and pull hair through a hole at the crown of the wig cap. Glue hair underneath. When dry, spread hair out in all directions over the old wig.

Another trick that works well with old wigs that have a lot of hair in the back is to reverse the wig. The front hair must be restyled. Sometimes we put on a cap or hat to cover what is not covered.

There are many wigs on the market today. Your pocketbook must go along with your selection. Some wigs are very expensive. We have shown old styles but many new styles are available.

Making a Wig—If you wish, you can make your own wigs for small dolls, and it is fun and inexpensive. We do not recommend that you make wigs for large dolls, unless you learn how to do it from an expert.

Replace lambskin or sheepskin wigs that are falling apart with the same type of wig. These wigs are not available on the market, so you will have to make them or have them made. The procedure is fairly simple. Buy a piece of sheepskin from a place that sells it for wigs. See the *Resource* section, page 158.

To make a wig pattern, cut a piece of foil in a circle. Press it down over the doll's head to the natural hairline on the back of the neck and to the hairline on the forehead. The doll's pate must be in place before making a pattern.

Take tucks in the foil to make it fit. Four tucks are usually enough. Use a pencil to mark the foil where the hair will come. Hair should come to the natural hairline on the back of the neck, close around the ears and down a little in front of the ears. You can decide if hair should curve across the forehead or come to a slight peak in the center of it. Trim foil with scissors, remove it and make both sides identical. Cut out tucks, spread foil flat and you have a pattern.

Put the pattern upside down on the *skin side* of the sheepskin, and tape in place. Use a sharp scalpel, knife or razor blade to cut out the pattern. Try to cut only the skin, not the wool.

Try the wig on the doll. If it fits, use adhesive tape on the inside to tape together tucks that were cut out. Tape two tucks and try the wig on the doll. Cut out more sheepskin if necessary. Tape another tuck and fit again. Keep working on the wig until it fits perfectly.

Another type of wig for *small* dolls is a glued one. It is so easy to make, you can do it from these general instructions.

Cut curls from old or new curly or straight mohair. Human hair is more difficult to work with. For baby hair, we have used long fibers from material used to make bath mats. This is available in craft and fabric stores. Some people use this fabric the same way we use sheepskin. Look at the picture of Baby Millie on page 15, and you can see this method is excellent for baby or clown dolls.

Put the doll to be wigged on a stand. Tape or glue her pate in place. Cut a piece of plastic wrap large enough to cover the doll from head to toe. Place it over the doll's head and clothing, including her shoes, to protect her from glue. Tightly draw plastic wrap over the doll's head, and put a couple of rubber bands around the neck. Mark on plastic wrap with a felt pen where you want the hairline. Lay hair out in piles, keeping even the ends to be glued.

Work from the hairline or bottom edge of the wig toward the middle. The length of the hair is shorter at the starting line and gradually gets longer, with longest hair on top. As you work, evenly distribute the hair so it is the same amount all over the head.

You will need a modeling tool or large corsage pin to press hair into airplane cement or white glue and a damp cloth to wipe your fingers. Put the doll on a table covered with newspaper, in case glue drips.

Use the shortest hair first. Have enough of this length to go 3/4 of the way around the head. Apply glue generously to the plastic at the bottom edge of the wig area, the hairline and around the head. Pick up little bundles of hair, and push blunt ends into the glue. Apply a layer of hair around the head, except the forehead. The doll will look bald with a fringe around the sides and back.

Apply more glue above the glued-on hair. Go across the forehead. Make this hair the same length as the first layer. Let the hair go down over the face so you can style it by cutting bangs or pulling front hair back. You can even set a row of curls across the front. Depending on the size of the doll, another layer of hair and glue may be enough.

There are many ways to finish the top. Hair can be set straight down into the glue. It must be long enough to go to the bottom of the first layer of hair. We use a Styrofoam pate on the doll, so the last layer of hair can be pushed down into the foam and glued. This makes a part or crown.

Glue hair only at the ends. Any hair not in the glue will fall out, so work carefully.

Let the wig dry thoroughly for a day, then cut rubber bands around the neck. Carefully trim the plastic wrap. If you have glued the hair to the pate, lift hair and pate together. If all the hair is glued to the plastic wrap, remove the wig and plastic, then peel off the plastic wrap. Cut it so it is shorter than the hair.

Put the wig back on the doll. Comb or work it as little as possible. Spray with hair spray, and trim ends where necessary.

Flocked Hair—Few boy dolls are left with flocked hair. Flocking was done as early as 1854, and was done for many years. The process was used to glue hair or cloth fibers on a bisque head. Several 20th century doll makers used flocking for short boy's hair. SFBJ, Heubach and Kämmer and Reinhardt often made boy dolls with flocked hair.

The doll's hair was modeled in porcelain, but not painted. As the last step of decoration, glue was applied over the molded hair. Bits of hair or fiber were blown on and stuck where glue was applied.

Today we find these dolls with flocked hair that is partially or almost completely worn off. Our SFBJ 235, page 91, has hair worn partly off on one side where it was not protected by his cap. Some antique dealers clean flocked hair off, and the doll appears to have white molded hair. There is no satisfactory way to repair flocking. It peels off in flakes each time it is touched.

Flocking for reproduction dolls is available in ceramic shops. The result is not exactly the same as flocking on old dolls.

MAKING WIGS FOR ALL-BISQUE DOLLS

Of all the dolls on the market today, all-bisque dolls are the most apt to be wigless or with little hair. Repair or replace these wigs with the same style as originally used.

In studying 3- to 8-inch all-bisque dolls, we found hair usually fell in these styles:

- Beehive—Long hair was curled tightly and wound around the head.
- Medusa—Tightly curled, long lock of hair glued in a tight wavelike direction, similar to a snake going around the head.
- Ramshorn—Center-parted hair with tiny braids wound around ears.
- Ringlets—Center part with long curls.
- Alice—Hair pulled back from the front and tied.

See illustrations on previous page.

Hair on most small dolls was glued directly to the head. Some small dolls have sleep eyes so a pate is used to fill in the top of the head. You can glue hair to the head, or use plastic wrap to cover the head and doll. See the wig-repair section, page 107.

To prepare a beehive or Medusa wig, use a small strand of mohair 8 to 10 inches long. Do not use real hair on tiny dolls because it is too coarse. Saturate the strand with hairspray and tightly wind it around a piece of large wire. Coat hanger wire will do. Fasten the hair at the beginning and end with tape or foil. If necessary, while hair is drying, spray again. Put in the oven at 150F (65C) for a short time to dry. If wire is straight and has no snags, hair will slide off when dry. If it does not slide off, unwind it and hair will go back into shape.

To make a beehive, trim a curl from the long curl, and glue it on the forehead. Cover the head with coating of white glue. Start at the center front and run the hair coil around the head in a spiral until head is covered. If one coil is not enough, use more. Glue should be tacky enough to hold hair in place. Adjust hair or make coils tighter with a corsage pin.

The Medusa style is done the same way, except coils are put on in a tight S-shape around the head. This kind of hairstyle was often found on small dolls.

For the Alice wig, glue hair long enough to cover the face in a circle around the head. Let dry, then pull hair up and tie on top of the head.

For long curls or ringlets, place hair over the top of the head and trim to ear length. Be sure it is glued on tightly. Add more glue at the bottom edge, and glue on long curls. Long curls are made by winding sprayed hair around straws, pencils or cotton swabs. Do not remove the curls until they are completely dry, then glue on the head. Make curls in proportion to the head.

You can make many variations, such as cutting long curls and placing them all over the head to make a curly top. If you want a part in the hair, sew hair on a tiny strip of bias fabric. Glue this across the head, then curl the wig or add curls. Add tiny braids. This same method can be used on lady dolls.

Flat-brim straw hat is worn by this Jumeau. We do not think it is her original hat.

Hats and Bonnets

Original hats and bonnets from old dolls are not often found. If a doll is found with an old hat or bonnet, preserve it.

There is little we can do about fading, which often happens with satin, sateen or velvet. Bonnets of these fabrics can be gently brushed or vacuumed.

Hats were usually wired to keep their shape, and may be out of shape from packing and squashing. They can be bent back into shape. Usually it is best to stop here—no one expects a 100-year-old hat to look fresh and new.

Often hats have matted flowers and frayed ribbon. Flowers can be pushed into shape. Bend stem wires back to their original positions, and bend leaves so they look natural. Some people use a felt pen to add color to leaves and flowers, but we prefer the muted shades of aged flowers. Ribbons can be pressed with the tip of an iron. Remove them, then iron until neat and replace.

Washing Ribbons—When washing ribbons from hats or clothing, put them in cool water with some cold-water wash and let them soak 5 to 10 minutes. Rinse them in fresh water. Wind wet ribbon around a clean glass jar, fasten with a pin or needle, and let dry. The ribbon will not need ironing when it dries.

Use the same procedure for lace. Usually there is only a small amount of lace on a bonnet. We do not usually take lace off, but we do press it with an iron. If possible, use a little spray starch to stiffen lace. We prefer the ecru color of aged lace and do not wash or bleach it. It is a matter of choice.

If lace, old ribbon or flowers must be replaced, use old materials when possible. It spoils a beautiful old bonnet to add new flowers or ribbon.

When you remove ribbon, note exactly how it was folded and tied. Sometimes it is best to make a note or sketch so you can replace it exactly. Be sure you take tiny stitches, and use matching thread.

Wool Hats—Press wool hats around the edges using a thin piece of cloth as a pressing cloth. Bend hat into original shape while it is slightly damp. Sometimes steam from a steam iron refreshes a hat and helps get it back in shape. Wash stocking caps in cool water and cold-water wash.

Straw Hats—Straw hats are often in good condition. Reshape them by using a steam iron or kettle of hot water. In extreme cases, remove the lining, and run the hat under hot water for a second. Reshape the hat, and put dry paper towels in it to hold its shape while it dries. We sometimes place the hat on the upturned bottom of a jar of the same size. This allows the crown to dry in a uniform shape.

Left: Antique sateen bonnet is Kate Greenaway style and in good condition. It has one wire in finely shirred brim and three rows of gathering with wire between outer two. Another wire is used around hood and connects to part that goes around the neck. Inside is lined with stiff buckram. An added bavolet is used at back neck of bonnet. Bonnet is decorated with ribbon and Spanish lace to match costume.

Sometimes dolls wear flowers instead of hats. This K(star)R wears a Colorado wildflower halo made for dolls.

Hat is covered with pink velvet, and back, or *crown,* is gathered. Band of folded pink velvet and ruffle of double velvet frames face. Flowers are same color. Two double bows of pink ribbon are used on each side. Bonnet is lined with stiff buckram and finished inside with silk. It is completely hand-sewn.

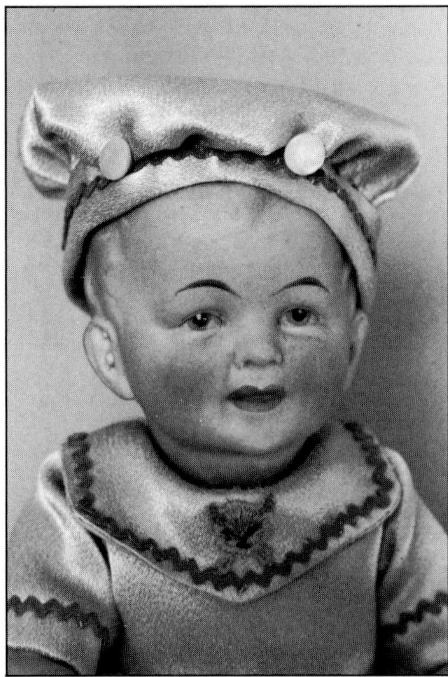

Heubach boy doll wears variation of French beret. This type of cap was worn by boys in Europe and is often seen on character dolls. This is a reproduction cap.

Hat brim made of pleated, stiff lace. Old flowers decorate back of brim and back of hat.

Weave of this straw hat is unusual, and flowers are faded.

Kley and Hahn boy doll wears old straw hat. Crown is flattened and brim turns up slightly.

Unusual antique bonnet worn by doll with sheepskin wig. Bonnet has five rows of wire and wide strips of white cloth to tie under chin.

Side view shows hat is similar to a bag and is gathered at top. It is finished with covered button. Brim is spread out and wired and made from starched, white-cotton fabric.

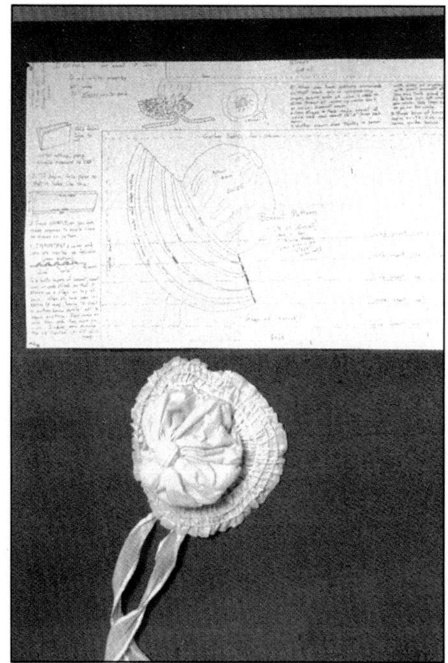

Pattern for reproduction bonnet made from antique bonnet.

Cotton Bonnets—Most cotton bonnets can be washed and bleached if they are white. Colored-cotton bonnets can be washed and rinsed. We have a problem with wired cotton bonnets because some wire rusts, and rust marks show on the fabric. Fast drying may prevent this.

Remove all ribbon and other decorations before washing. Press decorations and replace them after the hat or bonnet is dry.

Old hats and bonnets do not need to look new—they are old. You will soon appreciate the old look. In most cases, we still feel it is better to leave things as they are.

FRENCH HATS AND BONNETS

Most French hats and bonnets are variations of a few basic designs. *Chapeau* refers to any fancy French bonnet or hat. A bonnet can be a variety of shapes—tight-fitting, with or without a brim, often shirred over wire. A bonnet usually ties under the chin. Below is a description of various types of hats and bonnets.

Capote—Bonnet with a soft crown and stiff brim. This word was also used for a cape.

Kate Greenaway—This sunbonnet type has a *bavolet,* a gathered piece across the back of the bonnet to shade the neck.

Mob Cap—Gathered circle, usually trimmed with lace. A *biggin* is an extra-large mob cap.

Bolero—Hat with conical crown and small brim.

Picture Hat—Hat with wide, off-the-face brim.

Hood—Tight-fitting bonnet with no brim.

Beefeater—Soft, round crown and flat brim made by shirring fabric over wire.

Normandie Bonnet—Hat with a high, half-moon-shape puffed crown. There are many variations of brims.

Auto Bonnet—Tight, turned-back brim and slightly puffed crown.

Beret—Flat circle or pancake-shape, with a band to hold it on the head. It was shown in 1911 and may have been used before that. A large beret is called a *tam-o'-shanter.*

Poke Bonnet—Hat with a projecting front brim, high, rising small crown and ties under the chin.

Toque—Small, round, close-fitting French hat with or without a brim.

GERMAN HATS AND BONNETS

German dolls came with several different types of hats and bonnets in the 1900-to-1915 period. Hats were usually frail and poorly constructed, and they did not last. Many hats were traded from one doll to another.

Straw Hats—There were several straw shapes. The straw hat that tapered straight down from a rounded dome, forming a small brim, was common. The *Panama* was a straw hat with a brim that rolled back

Plain bonnet with stiffened, ruffled brim. Old pink ribbon for ties was used to make ribbon rosettes.

Reproduction mob cap is worn by this antique Eden Bébé. Cap and dress are ruby silk with white lace and pink china-silk bodice.

Five original German straw hats. We chose as many different shapes as we could find. Hats are decorated with ribbons and flowers.

Sand-gray Normandie-type bonnet is made in three pieces and carefully lined. Front ruffle goes away from face and is edged with beige silk lace. Coral velvet bow matches decoration on dress.

gently. It was commonly used with sailor suits. There was a Panama with a flat brim, turned up on one side and a flattened crown. The shaped, braided straw was flat on top, with a flat brim.

Other Hats—Flannel caps and tasseled stocking caps were used for boys. Many girl and baby dolls wore bonnets and brimmed bonnets made of dress fabric. There were many versions of the mob cap.

Before 1890, some shaped felt hats were used on child and adult dolls. During the period of the character dolls, from 1910 to 1916, dolls wore hats or caps to match their clothing. They were similar to real children's caps and hats.

Knit caps and bonnets were used for a long period, which could have started in the 1880s. It continues to the present.

Crocheted bonnets and caps were used for toddler and baby dolls. Patterns for them sometimes appeared in ladies' magazines.

Materials for Hats—Material used for German doll hats, bonnets and caps varied as much as the materials for French hats, but it was less expensive and flimsier quality. Dress fabric and inexpensive lace were commonly used for bonnets on dolls that came dressed from 1890 to 1916.

Right: Normandie-type bonnet is monochromatic mixture of maroon velvet, cranberry faille, deep-cranberry sateen ribbon and short feather. Pleated beige silk lace softens bonnet around face. All materials are antique. Combination of textures and colors enhances doll features.

Bonnet made of soft straw. We think it was a person's hat that was taken apart and made into a doll hat. Decorations are fairly fresh.

Unusual picture hat wired with six rows of wire. Hat is one-piece, large circle, drawn into shape with wire. Decoration is flower frill of self-fabric.

Red Riding Hood bonnet from Snow Angel's costume, by Jim Fernando, page 31. Antique satin is quilted, and double row of pleated lace decorates edge. Antique ribbon and one row of lace run around this.

Fabrics used were cotton, wool and velveteen. We even found a linen bonnet.

Caps, bonnets and hats were trimmed, but not in the same way as French hats. They were usually trimmed with ruffles and ties of self-fabric. Ribbons, ribbon flowers, plush flowers, lace and bows were used as decoration.

DESIGNING DOLL HATS

Before you begin designing doll hats, you must remember two important things:

- Do not put a fancy French hat on a German character doll.
- Do not let the hat subtract from the beauty of the doll by being too colorful or too elaborate.

Select materials that are dull and similar to old fabrics if you are not using old fabrics.

Doll Milliners—A doll milliner must be an artist. Work must be color coordinated and carefully stitched. Hats and bonnets are usually lined with buckram and inner-lined with silk or satin. Many hats and bonnets were wired to keep their shape. Decorations must be carefully selected from ribbons, bows, veiling, feathers and flowers.

Materials for hat making are available today. Check for suppliers in the *Resource* section, page 158. There is no reason new hats cannot be as carefully made and as becoming to dolls as old hats. The selection of style, color, fabric and decorations makes this possible.

Making a Pattern—We suggest you use aluminum foil to make the basic pattern for a bonnet. If the foil pattern fits, the bonnet will fit. Make the pattern over the wig on the doll that will wear the bonnet. You will find it easy to make tucks, darts and other alterations and to fold and unfold foil for a pattern.

Not all hats fit down over the head. If you want to make a pattern for one similar to this, you do not need exact measurements. Hats resting on top of the head are secured with a hat pin. They must be the correct proportion on the doll to look good.

Measuring for a Hat—To measure for a bonnet or pull-on hat, follow these steps to help you measure correctly:

1. Measure around the head. Put the tape measure high on the forehead and low in the back. This is where the bonnet should come to. From this same line, measure over the head from front to back, and measure from side to side over the head, starting at the bottom of the ear.
2. Draft a pattern, or use your measurements to see if a pattern you have is the correct size. Select trim that is a smaller scale. Most human-hat trim overwhelms a doll, so be sure trim is smaller.
3. Use buckram for stiffness in bonnets. Or use a stiffening spray made for hat makers when buckram is not suitable.
4. When you trim a bonnet, it must be attractive, elegant and in harmony with the costume. Trained milliners do a beautiful job, but there are many gifted,

Fancy variation of mob cap. Iridescent green taffeta is lined with peach, and frill is pleated.

Blue-silk bonnet for Bru Jne doll by Jackie Jones. See full-page photo of doll on page 101.

talented doll people who can design and make bonnets. They know at a glance what colors will blend to make the perfect ensemble. If you have any doubts, use your color wheel.

5. The shape of bonnets is important. Study the shape of the doll's face, then decide the shape of the bonnet to bring out her beauty.

Bonnet Construction—Bonnets are basically made of two parts—the *crown* and *brim*. Many variations can be created by varying the shape of either. Some bonnets are made only of a brim or crown. In addition to shaping the brim and crown, different fabrics can be used for variation, such as silk, lawn, velvet, plush, satin, sateen, taffeta and wool.

Ruffles, frills, trim and brims are added. Hats are decorated with self-fabric ruffles, inset lace, pleated laces, frilled lace and tatting. Feathers, fruit, flowers, ribbons and bows are used as decoration.

It is not difficult to take one basic pattern and vary it to create many bonnets. Bonnets will look different, and no one will recognize them as the same pattern. See illustrations on page 119.

The crown of the bonnet is the back section. Sometimes it is round and fits on the crown of the head. Often the crown is elongated and comes down to the nape of the neck. The crown can be a straight piece of fabric with one side gathered until it forms a circle. It can be empty, with no crown fabric at all.

An enlarged crown or circle can be gathered to make a cap by itself, called a *mob cap*. A *tam* or *beret* is an enlarged crown with a band.

A brim is even more versatile. It can be an almost-straight band over the head sewn to the crown in the back. Front corners tie under the chin with bows. The creative part comes with shaping the crown. It can be elongated in the back, or go together in the back around the crown. It can be puffed by the use of cords or wire across the top of the head. See illustration on page 119.

An additional piece, or second brim, added to the band around the face can change the bonnet. A second brim can be close to the face or go almost straight up in the air. The curve of the under edge of the second brim makes the difference. The narrower the inside curve of the brim, the more perpendicular it stands on the bonnet. The wider it is, the lower the brim will come. It is fun to test different brim shapes on your doll to see which shape is the most attractive. First, cut paper, then use it for testing.

Sometimes two brims are used alone with no crown. Brims are often decorated with radiating lines that draw attention to the doll's face. Many old French bonnets were made this way. Sometimes brims are decorated with lace, flowers or bows.

MAKING HATS FOR DOLLS

Make hats from dress fabric, straw or felt. Fabric and wires for shaping are available at millinery-supply stores. See the *Resource* section, page 158.

Today, many straw hats used on dolls are basic hats, dressed up with flowers and ribbons. Reshape basic hats with steam or hot water. If you are going to reshape a straw hat, have a form to dry the hat over. A glass jar, ball of foil or back of a dish works well.

Basic straw-hat shapes are available from Doll and Craft World and other doll supply sources. You can purchase straw braid to make a straw hat yourself.

If you want a hat in fabric matching a doll's dress, you must make it. Patterns are available, but most doll makers create their own patterns. Use spray sizing to stiffen fabric for hats and to prevent ends from raveling. Some fabrics can be dipped in a mixture of 1/3 white glue and 2/3 water. For less stiffening, use less glue. Some trim and edging can be glued instead of stitched for neater results. There are several brands of glue in tubes that can be used instead of thread. These are found on notion counters.

The basic shape of felt hats can be made by wetting felt with a mixture of 1/3 white glue and 2/3 water. Shape the hat over a form, such as a small jar, glass or bowl. Use foil between the glass and felt so the hat will not stick to the glass. Separate pieces for brims can be stiffened, set in shape, then put together with glue after they dry. We once made hundreds of tricorner hats this way, holding brims in shape with rubber bands as they dried.

Fusible mesh, found at fabric stores, is excellent for hat making. It is simple to bond one fabric to another for brims, edgings, braids and other treatments.

Beautiful hats and bonnets can be made of heavy lace or lace purchased by the yard. Make the desired shape, then dip pieces in the glue mixture used for felt. Line these pieces with colored silk, or weave ribbon in and out of the holes. You need a form to dry the hat on, such as a glass or bowl covered with foil. It takes experimentation and imagination, but you can do it!

HAT AND BONNET SUGGESTIONS

Below are some suggestions we can share for making hats and bonnets. They may save you time and frustration.

- Use a color wheel if you need help selecting trim for hats and bonnets. It is helpful if you are working with a group making bonnets.
- China silk was often used for hat linings and is still available.
- Pleat wide bonnet ties where they attach to the bonnet.
- Fasten medium-ribbon bonnet ties to hat with a half bow.
- Make tiny ribbon bonnet ties into ribbon rosettes by winding the ribbon back and forth, then tying a separate ribbon around the middle of the loops. Place these on both sides of the bonnet where the bonnet tie attaches.

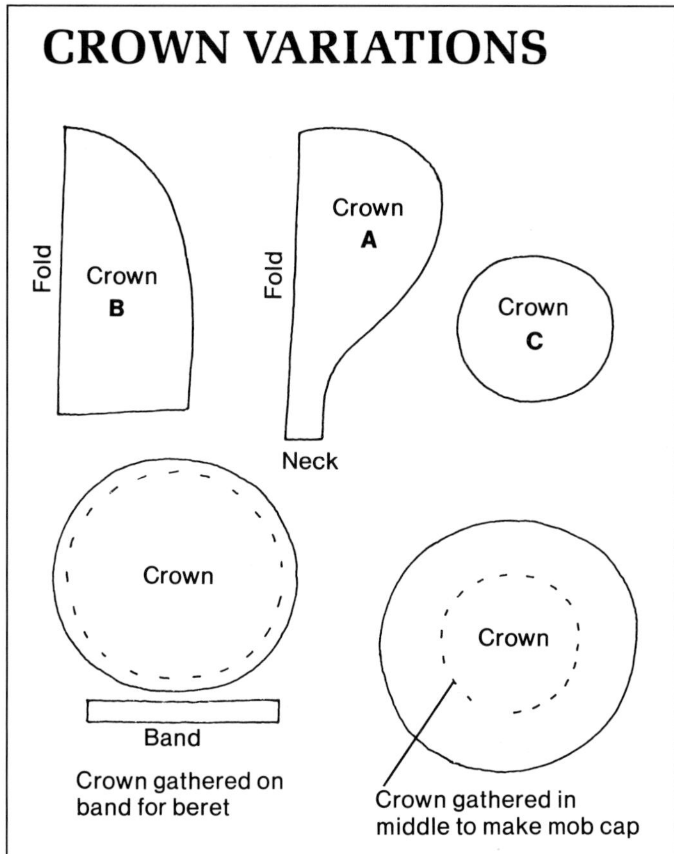

Use these different crown shapes to help you make a bonnet pattern.

- Create a rosette by making single knots in the center of each bow loop.
- Bonnet patterns can be increased or decreased at most copy centers. This saves time.
- Use glue on bonnets where stitching is not easy.
- Any needle will work for hat making, but long millinery needles are easier to use.
- If you are going to make many bonnets, buy the proper materials from a millinery-supply place.
- If you are going to make many bonnets, use a head block. Some people use foam or balsa wood. A head block makes shaping and pinning easier and more exact.
- Silk-covered millinery wire is better to use in a bonnet than other wire. Use special ribbon wire for making bows.
- Cording is often used on hats and bonnets. Cording is a bias strip of fabric with cord sewn inside. It is used to make soft, round edges.
- *Insertion* lace or eyelet is often used in soft-cloth bonnets. Both edges are the same on insertion lace. It is sewn on, then fabric underneath cut away. Lace can make a design, or colored ribbon can be sewn underneath it.
- Insertion lace can be pleated or gathered, then set on the bonnet.

BRIM VARIATIONS

Make pattern with aluminum foil.

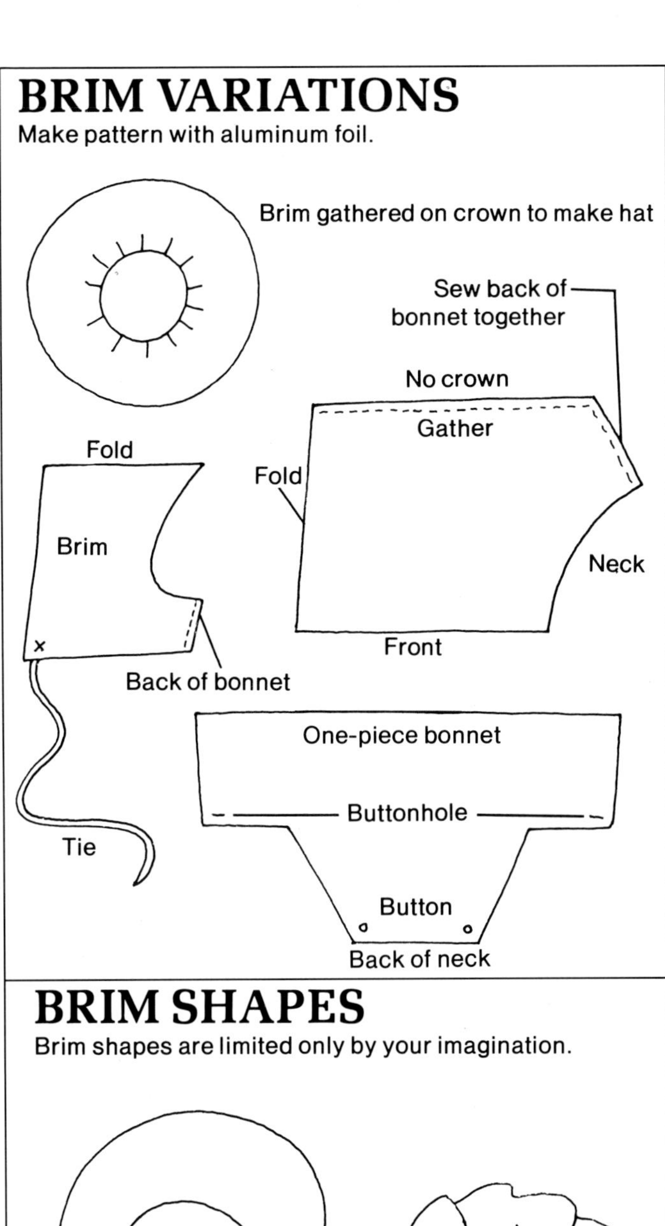

BRIM SHAPES

Brim shapes are limited only by your imagination.

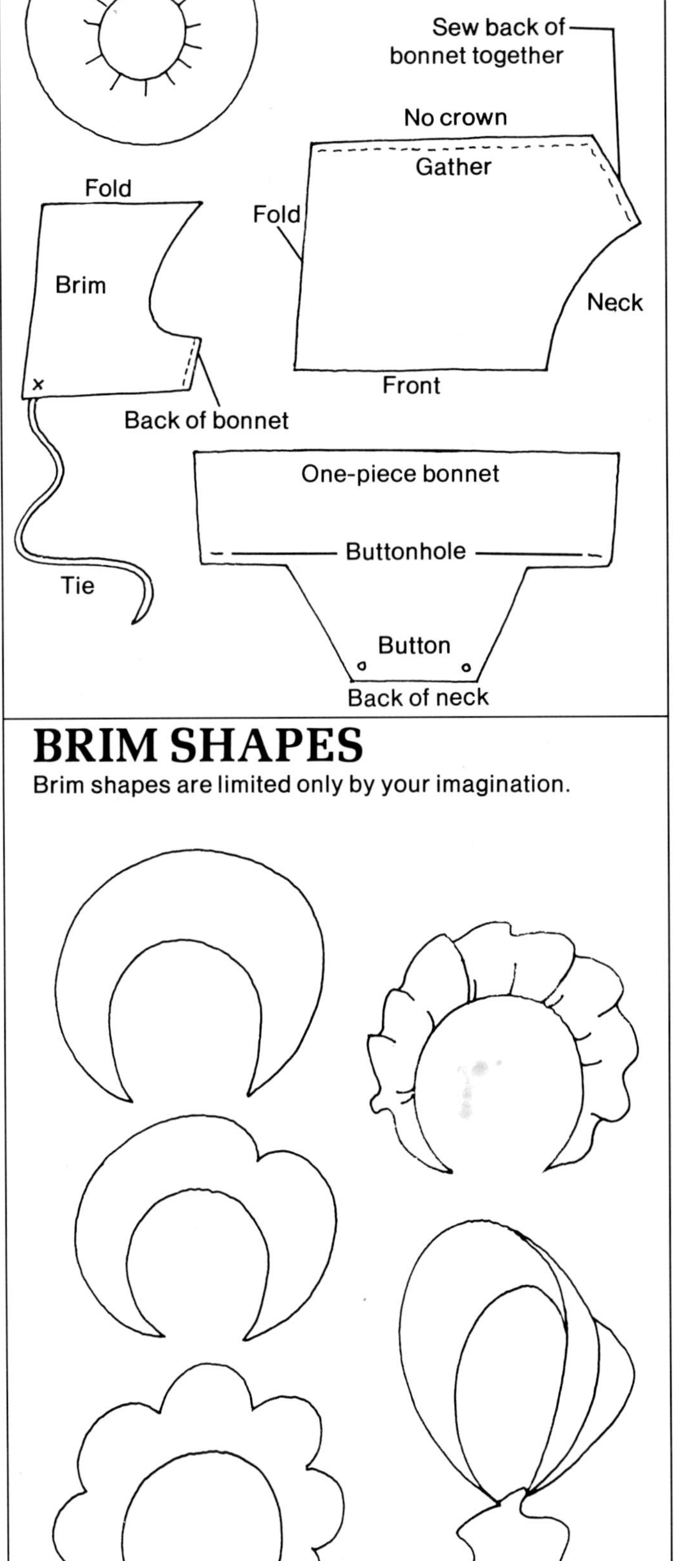

- Ribbons and bows are favorite bonnet trims. On French bonnets, the finest-quality silk, satin and velvet were used. On German bonnets, the least-expensive ribbon was used in large quantities.
- Shade ribbon on one or both edges. Roll the ribbon in a tight roll, and use a rubber band to hold it. Mark back and forth across the roll with a wide felt-tip pen until all edges are touched. To color both edges, turn over and do the other side. Another method of shading is to dip the roll in liquid dye. Put the dye in a flat container, deep enough to go up 1/16 of the ribbon. Dip the roll in and out until you achieve the effect you want.
- Fabrics for hats, such as silk chiffon, French silk veiling, millinery ribbon, imported brocades, straw cloth, and other items, such as hat wire, braid, glue, tools, silks, buckram, piping, ribbon, tulle, net, needles and flowers, can be found at millinery-supply stores. See the *Resource* section, page 158.
- Study hats in this book for ideas. They show authentic styles.

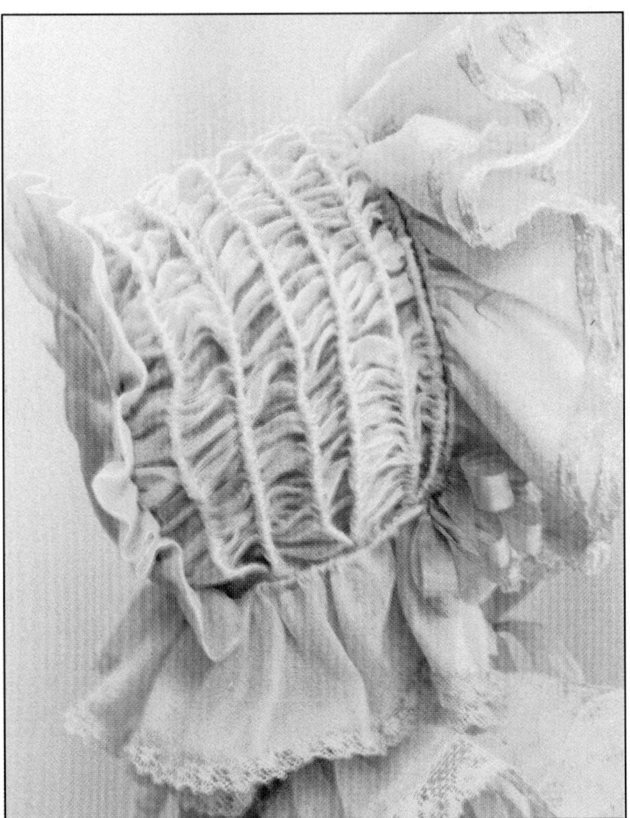

Hilda bonnet made of batiste fabric gathered on cord. All work was done by hand on this bonnet. Use this idea on other bonnet designs. Make cording by using cording foot on your sewing machine or make by hand. To gather main part of bonnet, sew through double-fabric thickness at even intervals, then pull cords to gather. Use a pattern, and cut out shape. Ruffles do not have to be hemmed if double fabric is used with fold at top.

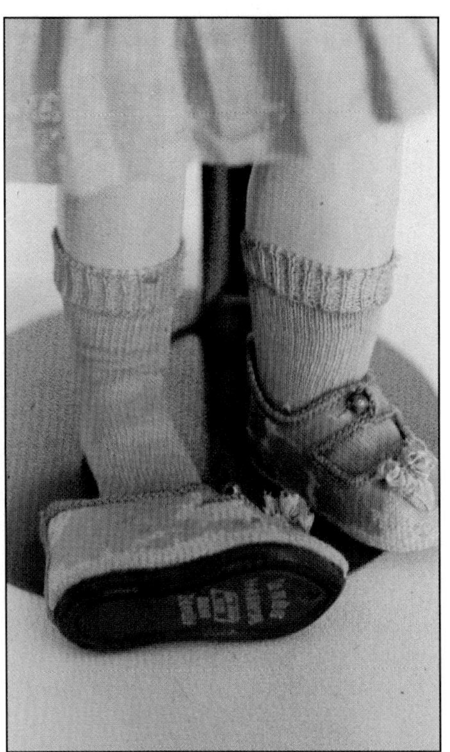

Bébé Jumeau shoes of heavy fabric covered with salmon-color silk which is worn off. Original socks were once salmon, but are now faded to non-color.

Shoes, Stockings and Underwear

Many doll costumers do not make shoes. They feel it is a different art, and it can be. Today, some people make and sell reproduction shoes and boots. You may be able to find exactly what you want from them, or they may have something to match a costume. More often, you will have to have shoes made by a professional or make them yourself. Shoes are not difficult to make, but they do take time.

Shoes must look good with an outfit. They must be from the correct time period.

Doll makers find it is easier to make shoes if they have a *last*. Originally, a last was a metal form used to make shoes. Doll makers use extra sets of lower legs or legs from the same-size doll as a last. Legs are set feet-up so you can work on them. If you are afraid you will get glue on the feet, cover them with foil or plastic wrap. You need a little room for socks or stockings.

Eras of Boots and Shoes—Shoes and boots did not come or go in one year, but overlapped. Companies that made certain shoes for dolls did not stop making them when fashions changed. What was in stock was used up. We cannot pinpoint a doll to a certain year by its shoes. The following dates give you an idea of the types of boots and shoes used during different periods:

1880 to 1890

Over this 10-year period, children and dolls wore boots with straps, buttons or elastic insets. Some boots had small heels. Shoes that laced up the front and low, leather shoes with ankle-high straps were made. There were also shoes with fabric tops. Boots and shoes were decorated with fancy bows, tassels and buckles.

1890 to 1900

Shoes for women and children replaced boots. Winter shoes were high and laced. Patent leather became popular for low shoes. Canvas shoes and suede shoes were worn. These shoes were less-decorated than shoes of the previous decade. Bows, buttons and cross straps were used. Small children's shoes came above the ankle and buttoned on the side. Most shoes had heels.

1900 to 1920

Children wore high shoes that laced or buttoned. Sandals with cut-out holes became popular for summer wear for boys and girls. The one-strap, patent-leather shoe was the most popular. Shoes were flat heeled.

Left: Miss Kestner wears an original lace dress with line of up-and-down tucks and lace in the bodice. Skirt tucks form part of design and are edged in scallops and bordered with more lace. Two different lace designs were used with the fine white cotton.

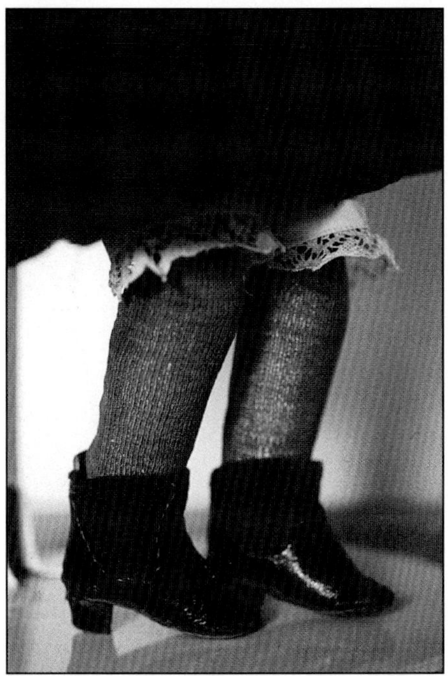

French boots with heels and elastic inserts.

Unmarked leather slippers decorated with round, silver buckle.

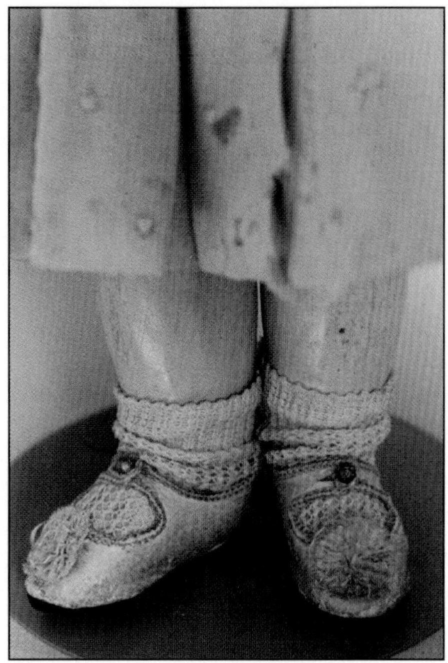

Another pair of pink-leather shoes found on Jumeau in original clothing. She wears original knit socks, and shoe toes are decorated with pink rosettes.

COMMERCIAL DOLL SHOES

Doll shoes you purchase from doll-supply companies are usually a plain design. You do not want more than one pair of plain shoes in your doll cabinet. There are some things you can do to plain shoes so they do not all look alike.

One plain shoe comes with a wide, clumsy strap across the instep. Cut off the strap to make the shoe a slipper. Change the front by trimming it to a new shape. Attach a ribbon to the back of the shoe, and tie it around the ankle. Fasten ribbon on each side and tie over the instep. Sew color thread around the top edge, and add new rosettes, bows or buckles to a plain shoe. Shoes can be dyed or tinted to match a doll's outfit.

It takes imagination to make a pair of commercial shoes match a special doll outfit. Try it—you may create a special pair of shoes.

Measuring Commercial Shoes—It is difficult to purchase shoes for dolls from a catalog. Knowing the size and shoe-sole shape helps.

Place the doll's foot on a shoe chart, or measure it from heel to toe. See illustrations on opposite page. Add 1/4 inch. Sizes usually do not correspond to the actual length of the foot. Not all shoes fit all dolls because some feet are long and narrow, some are thick and wide, and some are square.

Below is a chart that shows the size of a shoe and the length, in inches, of the doll's foot it fits. Use this as a general guideline.

Size	Length of Foot
1	1 inch
2	1-1/2 inches
3	1-3/4 inches
4	2 inches
5	2-1/4 inches
6	2-1/2 inches
7	2-3/4 inches
8	3 inches
9	3-1/4 inches
10	3-1/2 inches
11	3-3/4 inches

SHOE PATTERNS FROM DOLL SHOES

Many dolls come from the attic with one shoe missing. A large number are sold with one shoe. The chance of finding another shoe to match is extremely slim. The best use of the remaining shoe is to make a pattern, then make two shoes from the pattern. Even the best shoemaker cannot match old materials exactly.

TAKING SHOE APART

To make a pattern, you must first take the old

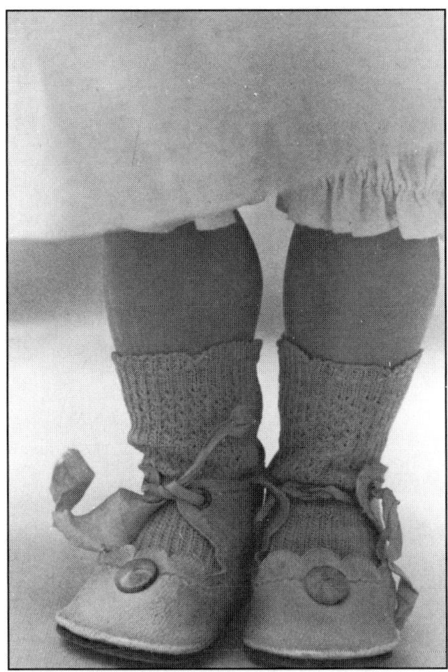
Well-made leather shoes worn by Simon and Halbig doll. Shoes have leather soles and are scalloped around top. Ties are ribbon, and front is decorated with buttons. Often French and German shoes were decorated on toe with dorset thread buttons.

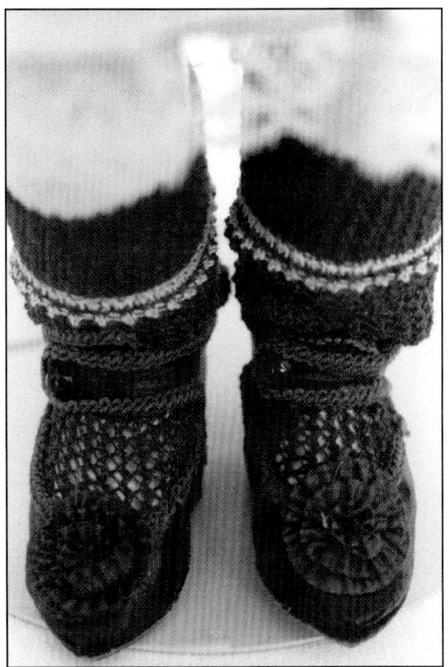
Shoes marked *E.J.* from Jumeau in original clothing. Mesh socks are often found on Jumeau dolls in original clothing.

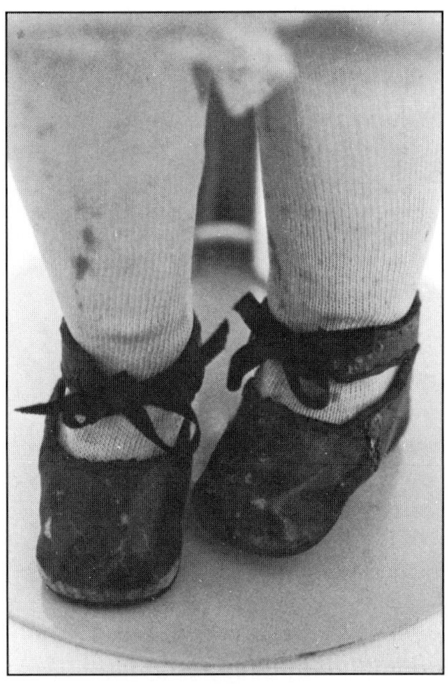
Circle and Dot Bru wears shoes marked with script *B.* Shoes had bow or buckle at one time and are made of stiff leather. Stockings are marked with iron rust.

shoe apart. Each shoe has an inner sole and an outer sole. Follow steps below to help you take a shoe apart:

1. Dampen the bottom of the shoe by setting it on a wet cloth or damp paper towel. Glue should be loose after a few minutes. If this does not work, hold the sole under hot running water for a few seconds. With a sharp knife, carefully work off the sole. It should come off in one piece.
2. Little tabs of the upper shoe are bent over and fastened to the bottom, and tabs are glued between the two soles. With the knife, lift tabs that are glued to the bottom of the inner sole. Remove the sole. Now you have three pieces.
3. Carefully rip out stitching at the heel. Press the pieces flat with your hand. Trace around the pieces, filling in any tears. Be sure all pieces are right-side out. Trace the pattern on new-shoe material. For the second shoe, turn the pattern pieces over, and trace on the shoe material.
4. Most doll shoes are made in three pieces. If the shoe has a seam across the toe, take this out. If it has an instep seam, remove it. Study the old shoe so you can put the new shoe together the same way. Be sure you know which piece is the top, or mark the outside of each piece so you can reverse it for the other shoe.

Use one of these guides to check the size of the doll's foot before ordering or buying shoes.

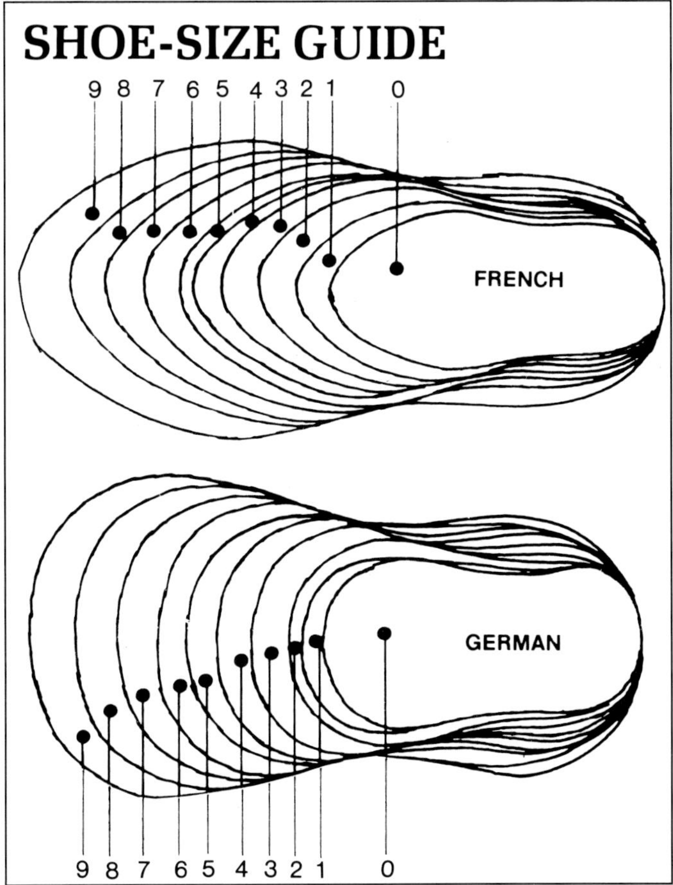

COPYING SHOE

You may have several dolls in your collection that wear the same size shoe, or your friend may have doll shoes that are the right size for your doll. You can make a pattern from these shoes without damaging them. It will not be as accurate as a pattern made from taking a shoe apart, but it will work.

It is an art to make a pattern from a shoe without taking it apart. You must work slowly and accurately. Leave shoe on doll as you copy it. Use a sharp pencil and aluminum foil. Follow the steps below to copy a shoe:

1. Trace around the sole.
2. Cut out this piece.
3. Make the inner sole by cutting another sole the same size.
4. Mark both pieces, such as left inner sole and left sole, then trace upside down for the opposite foot.
5. Using a piece of foil a little larger than needed, wrap foil, without wrinkles, around the toe to the back. Cover the top of the shoe.
6. Press foil tight with your fingers. With a pencil, mark where the sole meets the upper part of the shoe. Mark where the upper line of the shoe comes to, where the shoe fastens, the back seam line and all other seam lines. Check after each marking and cutting.
7. Carefully remove foil. Trim it so you have a piece that fits exactly over the upper part of the shoe. Test it so it is exact.
8. Spread foil flat. Add 3/8 inch to bend over to hold the shoe to the inner sole. Add extra material for the heel seam. Trace the pattern on paper, then turn it over and trace for the other foot.

Some shoes are more complicated than others. With patience, this method can reproduce almost any shoe.

Be sure the shoe fits the doll you are going to use it on. Try the pattern on the doll. If you use an already-made pattern, test it by putting the doll's foot on the sole pattern, page 123. There should be extra room around the edge and in the toe.

Doll's feet are stiff, not flexible, so any give must be in the shoe. Shoes for one 12-inch doll do not necessarily fit another 12-inch doll. Companies made different-size feet, so fitting a doll's foot is not easy. The usual pattern reduction does not necessarily work on shoes because feet vary too much. Usually if the sole fits, with a little room to spare, you are safe unless the doll has a fat leg. In this case, the strap will not fit.

MAKING PATTERNS

A creative doll costumer can make a shoe pattern to fit. Make the shoe the same way as copying a shoe. Use foil to make your pattern, as follows:

BRU BOOT

Sew flap to boot from point A to point B. Flap buttons on outside of shoe.

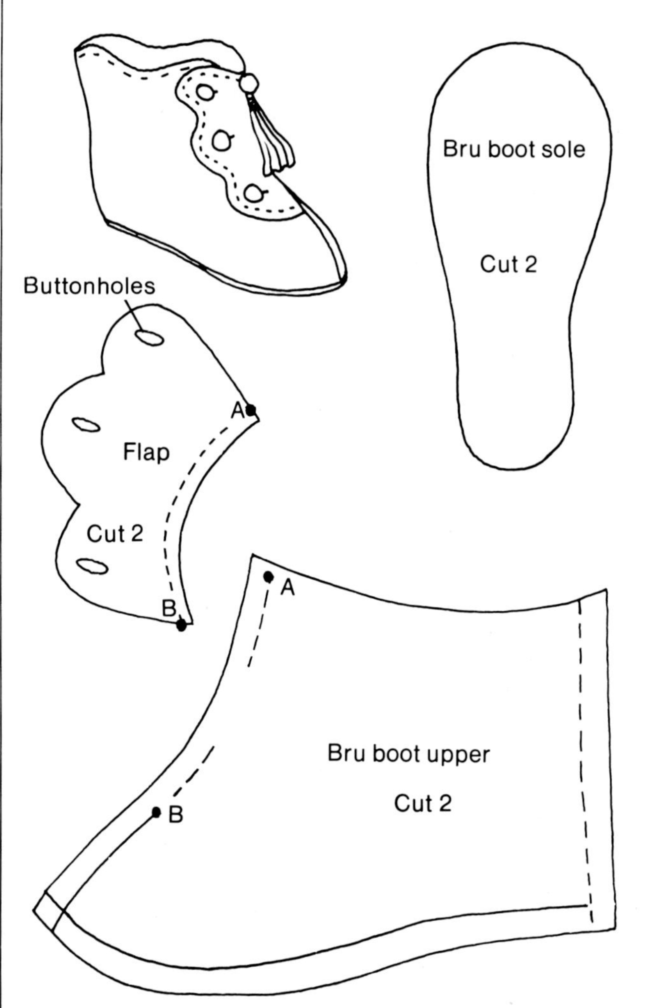

1. Trace the doll's foot. Add 1/8 inch or more around the outside edge for a large doll.
2. Cut the inner sole to the foot size.
3. With the sock on, fold foil on upper part of doll's foot.
4. With a pencil, mark strap placement, and mark the top of the shoe.
5. Cut foil, and fit it on the foot. Adjust for perfect fit.
6. Lay the finished pattern on paper, and trace around it. Add enough for seams and for bending inner sole for gluing top to sole.

Reverse the Pattern—When making patterns, tracing patterns or using a commercial pattern, *always reverse the pattern for the other foot.*

Designing Shoes—When making sandals, draw a design on both leather uppers before putting them together. Cut the design out with a sharp knife or scalpel. Punches make interesting designs.

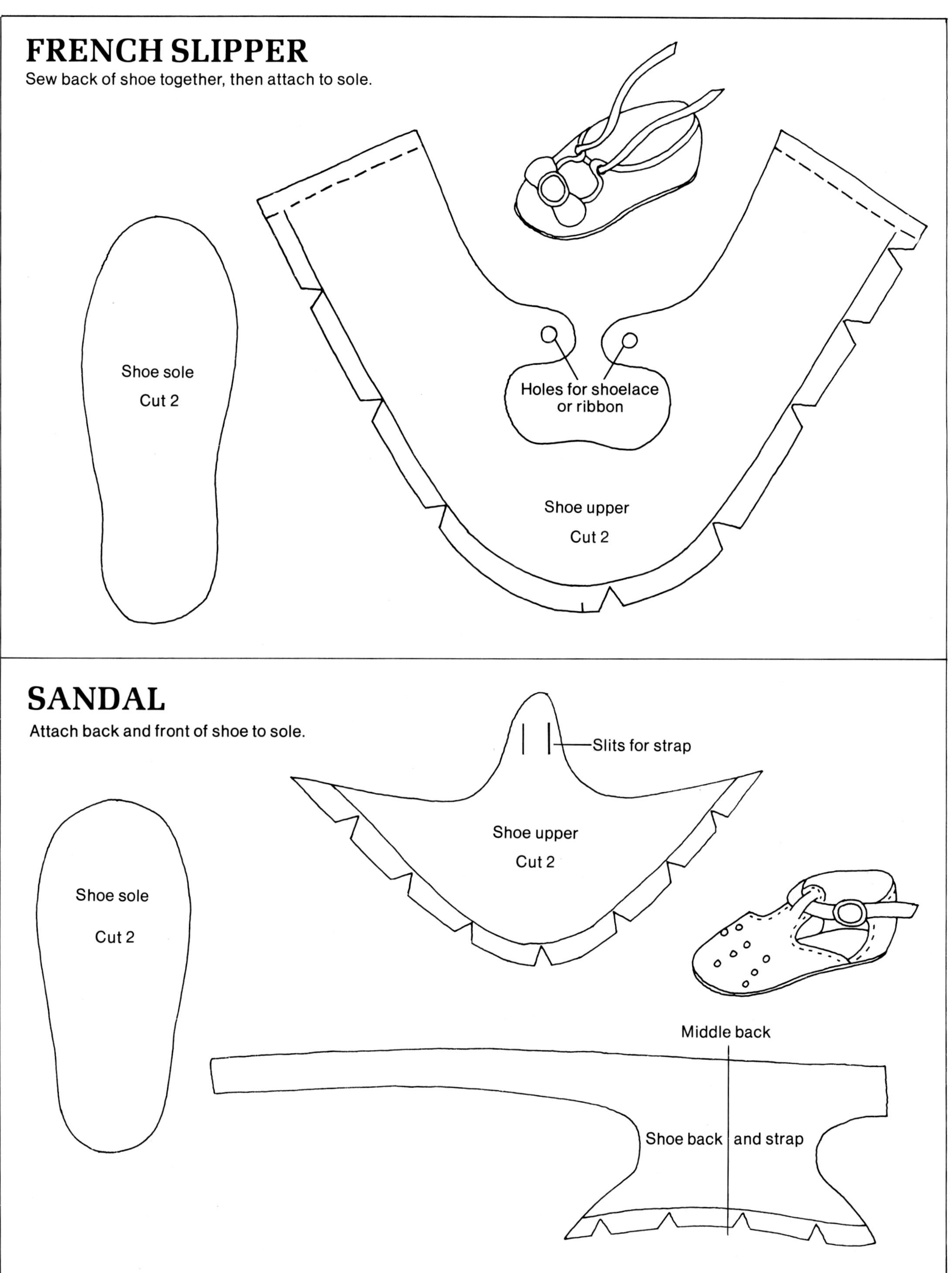
FRENCH SLIPPER
Sew back of shoe together, then attach to sole.
Shoe sole
Cut 2
Holes for shoelace or ribbon
Shoe upper
Cut 2
SANDAL
Attach back and front of shoe to sole.
Slits for strap
Shoe upper
Cut 2
Shoe sole
Cut 2
Middle back
Shoe back and strap

JUMEAU SLIPPER

Sew back of shoe together, then attach to sole.

Shoe sole
Cut 2
Hole for shoelace or ribbon
Fold
Place rosette on toe
Cut 2
Shoe upper

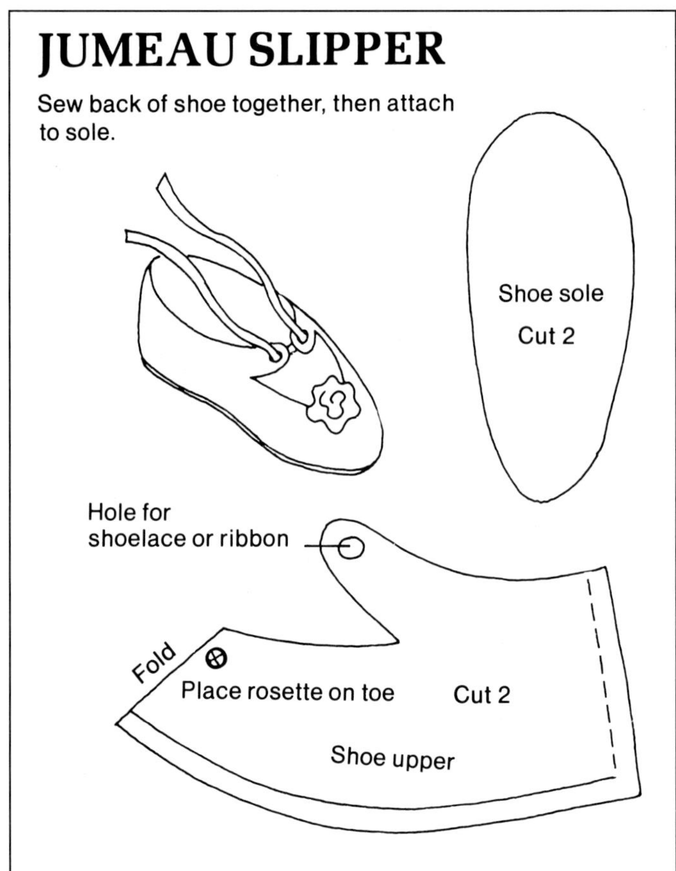

In leather stores, purchase tools with designs or letters on them. You can put your mark or initials on the shoe sole before putting shoes together.

MATERIAL FOR SHOES

Experiment before you decide on material for shoes. Leather is usually the best material to use. It can be purchased from leather companies. Choose leather that is lightweight, such as kid, thin calfskin or cabretta. We have used glove leather and chamois and found them too soft. Sole leather should be stiffer and thicker.

Use a cement for leather, or use rubber cement. On most shoes, we apply a thin coat of glue to *each* piece. Let glue dry a little, then press pieces together. White glue can be used.

Fabric shoes can be made of velvet, satin, silk taffeta, cotton or silk. They must be lined with a heavier material. Two fabrics can be bonded together with fusible mesh material that melts when heated. This is found at fabric stores.

Shoes can be made of almost any dress fabric if it is glued to heavier fabric. Super Suede makes nice shoes in many colors. Some plastics, such as shiny black for patent-leather shoes, works well. Leather is probably the best.

FRENCH ANKLE-SNAP SHOE

Sew back of shoe together, then attach to sole. Add heel.

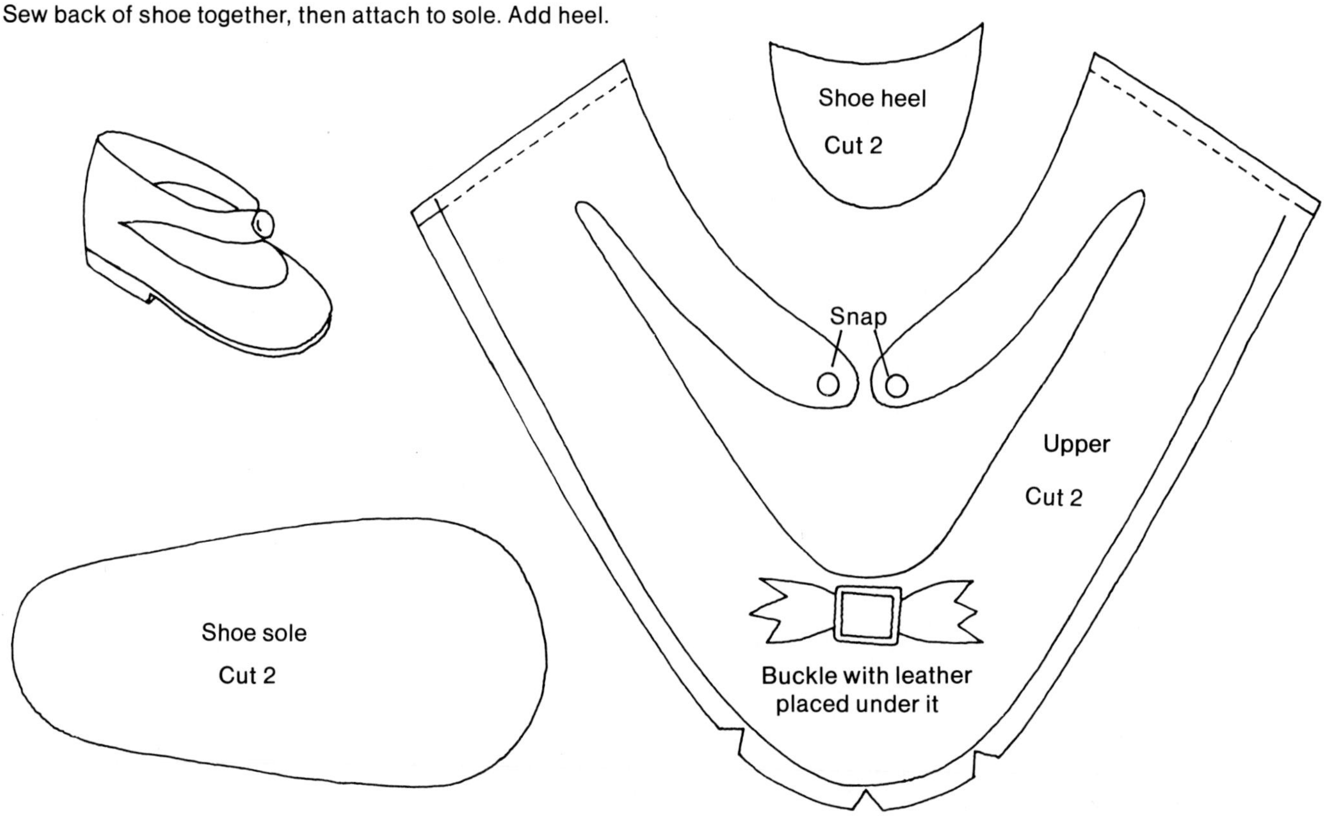

Shoe heel
Cut 2
Snap
Upper
Cut 2
Shoe sole
Cut 2
Buckle with leather placed under it

COMMON SLIPPER

Sew back of shoe together, then attach to sole.

Slipper sole
Cut 2
Slipper upper
Cut 2
Put bow on toe
X

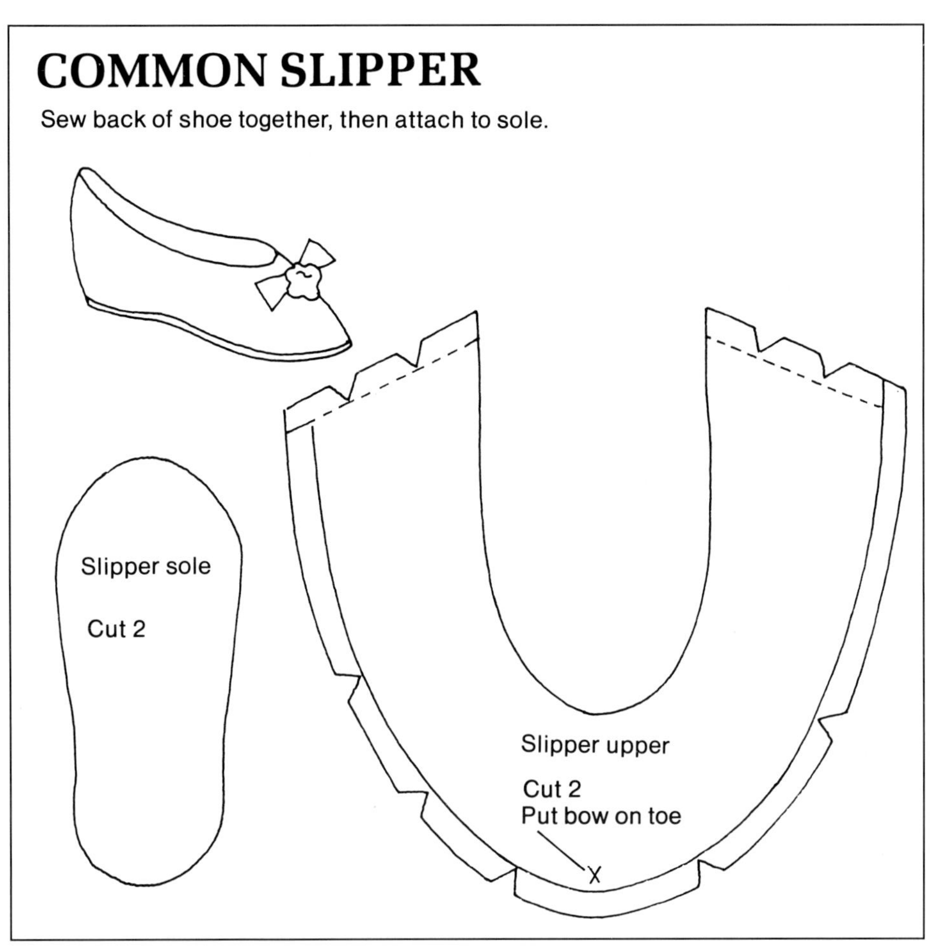

JUMEAU ANKLE-STRAP SHOE

Sew back of shoe together, then attach to sole.

Shoe sole
Cut 2
Button
Fold
Shoe upper
Cut 2
Cut pattern on fold.
Do not crease leather, but fold over gently.

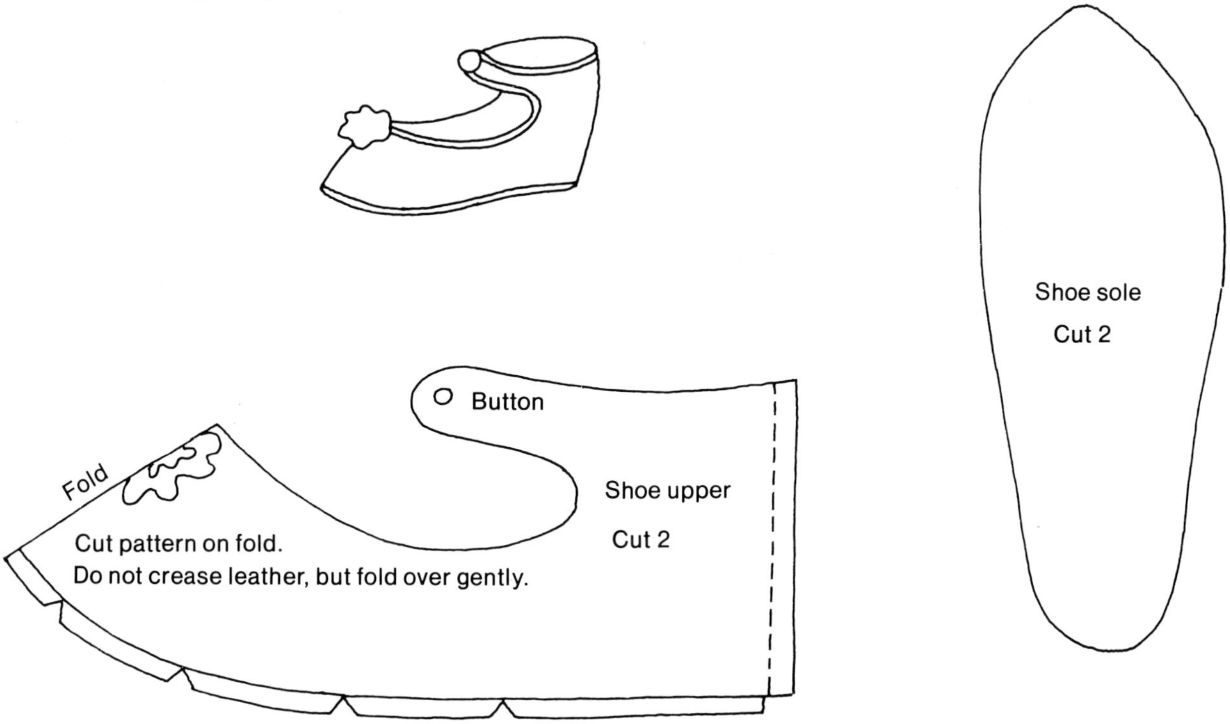

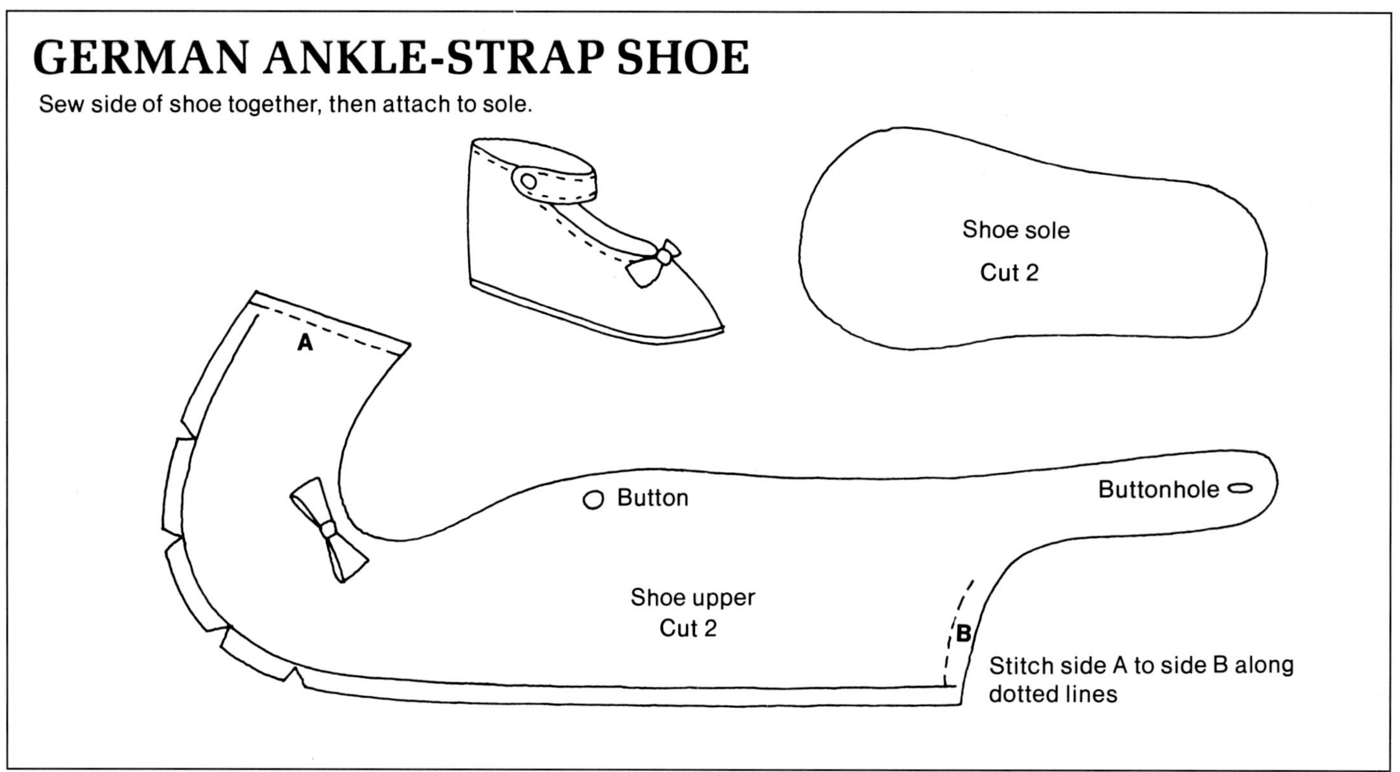

You can purchase eyelet-making kits from craft and fabric stores to make holes. Use a leather punch to make holes for ties or laces. An eyelet-setting tool is better than a leather punch. This tool sets a metal eyelet. Small tool kits, with a variety of hole sizes, are available in craft stores. Leather stores have larger kits.

Color raw edges of leather around the sole so it looks natural. Use liquid shoe polish, watercolors or felt pens.

Cut inner soles from thin cardboard. File cards are the correct thickness and are available in many colors. Cut the inner sole the same size as the sole. Posterboard is a little heavier—use it for larger shoes. See the shoe patterns on pages 124 to 128.

Choosing Decorations—Many decorations can be used on shoes. At one doll convention, we found someone selling antique glass buckles and metal buckles still on their cards, which had been imported from France. There were six different kinds. Tassels were often used and are easy to make. Tiny pompons were used on toes of shoes and are available in many colors at craft stores.

Make rosettes, commonly found on Bru and Jumeau shoes, by winding ribbon in and out of a comb. Spray ribbon with hairspray or matt spray. Run a thread through the edges to draw it up. These tiny circles are used one on top of the other in decreasing sizes until four layers are sewn together. See the illustration showing how to make other rosettes on page 130.

Carefully press and shape bows, then spray with gloss or matt spray. Sew bows on shoes. Make rosettes with rickrack, lace or cord. Tassels are made of thread, embroidery floss or crochet thread.

Flower-shape pieces of leather are sometimes used under cut metal flowers. Other leather shapes are used with buckles.

PUTTING SHOES TOGETHER

1. First cut uppers from suitable material, and cut the sole from heavy leather. Turn the upper pattern over, and cut the second shoe. This makes a right and left shoe. It helps if you have an extra pair of doll's feet to work on. Doll makers often have extra legs.
2. Cut soles from heavy leather.
3. Cut insoles from cardboard.
4. Cut a smaller sole of cardboard to use as filler between the sole and insole.
5. Punch holes and do any top-stitching *before* you assemble the shoe.
6. Sew the back seam or other seams.
7. Press the inside of the seam flat with your fingers. Sometimes rubber cement holds flaps back.
8. If the flat part of the upper that goes over the inner sole does not have Vs, cut them now. Some patterns do and some do not.
9. Bend and glue flaps from the uppers over the insole.
10. Glue in the filler piece to make the sole flat, and glue on the sole. Shoes with more pieces are more complicated. Make your first shoe an easy two-piece shoe.

PUTTING SHOES TOGETHER

Shoes with more pieces are more complicated. Start with an easy two-piece shoe.

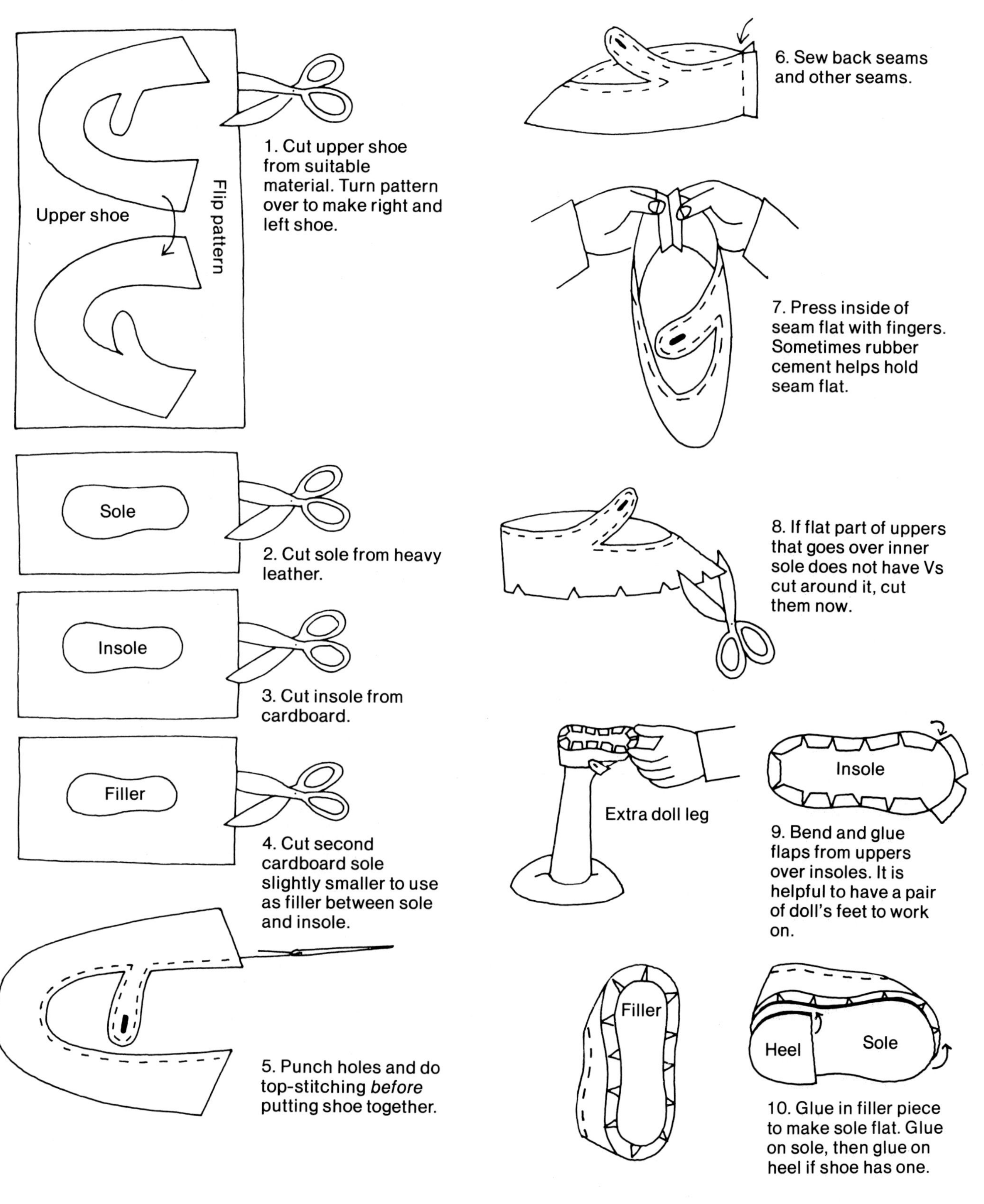

FLOWERS FOR DOLL SHOES

SHOE BLUETTE

You need baby rickrack for this project.

1. Cut ends of rickrack so both ends are in downward direction. See illustration.

2. Insert needle in each upper point with running-stitch. Leave all points on needle.

3. Pull thread through rickrack, leaving 3 inches free at each end.

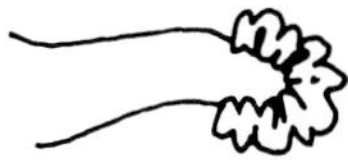

4. Tie thread together from both ends to form tight circle.

SHOE ROSE

You need regular rickrack for this project.

1. Fold rickrack in half, and hook Vs together.

2. Stitch through all upper points with running-stitch.

3. Draw thread tight, coil and tack through center.

Shoe bluettes and shoe roses can be used as decoration on shoes you make or plain ones you buy.

HINTS FOR SHOE MAKING

- Use a leather punch to make buttonholes on ankle straps.
- If you want to use shoe patterns again, trace them on index cards. It is easier to trace around firm board.
- Use your sewing machine without thread in it to make tiny holes to hand-stitch through on tops of boots and shoes. Stitches will be evenly spaced.
- Use tape to fasten a pattern on the leather for tracing. Do not use pins or needles because holes show.
- Dampen leather soles before putting on your initial or mark.
- The button on a single-strap shoe always goes on the *outside* of the foot.
- Glue on buckles or decorations for the front of the shoe. Old shoes had buckles and other decorations sewn on.
- Cut heels from thick cardboard, several layers of leather or balsa wood.
- Usually French-shoe toes are pointed and German-shoe toes are round. An exception is Simon and Halbig shoes—they are German, but some have pointed toes.

STOCKINGS AND UNDERCLOTHING

STOCKINGS AND SOCKS

French and German doll dressers costumed their dolls in stockings and socks. *Stockings* come above the knee, and *socks* fall between the ankle and knee.

Socks—French socks were made in solid colors to match an outfit, with stripes to add color or light beige to go with any costume. Some socks were made by the dressmaker, but most were commercially made with shoes. Many socks were good quality and have lasted 100 years.

The French bébé wore socks that were commercially knitted or crocheted with a little stretch in the top. Some were high enough to meet the over-the-knee skirt. Others were just above the ankle.

There is little left of German doll socks. They were made of inexpensive cotton mesh. Once it stretched out, it stayed that way.

Today, many German socks are full of holes, and often one sock is missing. Sometimes we find German dolls with shoes and socks glued on. This practice started as a way to keep play dolls' shoes and socks on and prevented the child from losing

Shoes from German dolls are not as good in material and workmanship as French shoes. Note pair of sandals. Three pair of shoes are made of stiffened fabric with cardboard soles.

them. Pins were used on leather dolls for the same purpose.

On some composition. bodies, socks stuck to the legs. This was probably caused by dampness. With care, these socks can be peeled off. After removing them, spray legs with gloss spray to protect them from moisture. New socks can be put on without fear of sticking.

Eras of Stockings and Socks—The following dates give you an idea of the types of stockings and socks used during different periods:

1870 to 1880

Stockings were white.

1880 to 1890

Silk stockings came in horizontal or vertical stripes, and in pink, turquoise and blue. They could be plain or elaborately embroidered and often had designs up the ankle, called *clocks,* in contrasting colors. Little boys often wore bright-color stockings—red was a favorite color. For everyday use, black or brown stockings were used. At the end of the decade, knit socks appeared on dolls.

1890 to 1900

Stockings in the 1890s were often black and made of cotton, silk or lisle. For dressy occasions, stockings matched a dress or shoes. Fancy striped stockings, decorated with clocks, were used for dress. Some were embroidered. Shear stockings were popular by the late 1890s.

1900 to 1920

All through this period, children wore black, white and tan stockings. Socks, both short and mid-calf, were more colorful.

MAKING SOCKS AND STOCKINGS

Today we use fabrics with stretch to make socks. Making socks and stockings is not difficult. Patterns and measuring do not have to be exact because fabric has some give. See illustrations on page 132.

The following ideas will help you dress your dolls with socks that fit and are correct for the period of dress:

- If you make stockings, make them high enough to go to the hip joint. This makes them stay up without wrinkling.
- Use a rubber band to hold up stockings if necessary.
- When dressing a doll with stockings, put them on before drawers.
- Use stockings with patterns up the ankle *only* for lady dolls.
- Use ribbed cotton stockings for child dolls. They are available at doll-supply stores in brown, black and white.
- Tint white socks or stockings with liquid dye to match a doll's outfit. Some people prefer socks or stockings to be lighter or darker than the costume.
- Baby socks should be white, ribbed cotton.
- Suitable stretch fabric for socks and stockings is still available today. This is the only time we recommend using modern fabric on an old doll.

Commercial Stockings—Most commercial stockings are a straight tube sewn across the bottom. There is enough give so stockings fit. Sometimes they are not finished on the top edges.

There is a nice sock with a shaped heel and toe on the market. These are found in the Doll and Craft World catalog. See the *Resource* section, page 158.

Making Stockings—Make a pattern for socks or stockings by measuring the length you want the stocking. Measure the widest part of the leg at the calf. If the stocking goes to the hip, slant to the largest measurement there. See illustration on page 132.

Another way to make a pattern is with foil. Fold foil around the leg from front to back, and trim where the two sides meet. Open the foil, and trace on paper for a pattern. Add seam allowance.

Today, you can find beautiful two-way stretch lace with small patterns that are perfect for stockings. Stretch lace comes in soft cream, ecru and white and is found in larger fabric stores.

Old fabrics, such as stockings of all colors, are fine

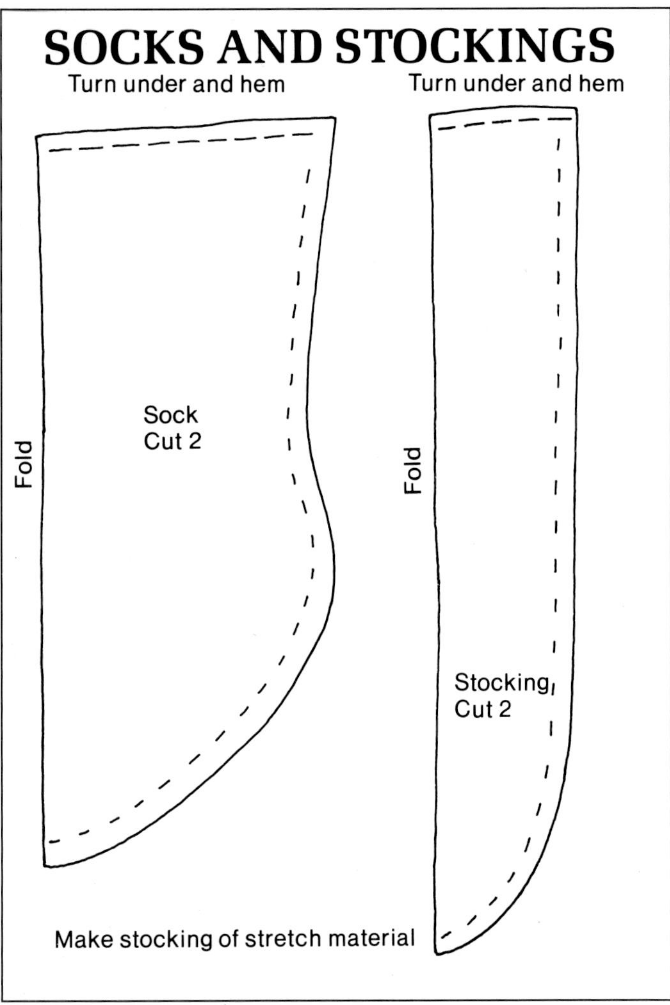

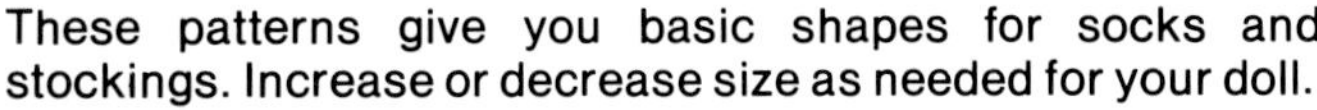
These patterns give you basic shapes for socks and stockings. Increase or decrease size as needed for your doll.

Underclothing from three 12-inch French dolls. Note different closings and decorations.

for doll stockings. Long, full-length gloves and mitts make excellent stockings. Many of these were silk and have held up well. Check antique stores or ask neighbors for old gloves and stockings.

Fancy or decorated stretch hose in shades of dark blue or burgundy are good for making stockings, and leotards make good stockings. They have so much stretch they usually fit, and they come in many colors and textures. Men's undershirts with ribs or mesh make fine white stockings. Baby's outgrown undershirts are useful. Tint or shade white to match an outfit.

Striped Stockings—For stripes fine enough for a doll's stocking, children's knit T-shirts are your best bet. The second best item is boy's socks. Pick up anything you find that you think you might be able to use. Decide which doll will get the socks or stockings later. To be authentic, stripes should be about 1/16 inch wide.

Often we have only one doll sock or stocking left on a doll. If it is a large doll, we may be able to make two stockings or socks for a small doll from it. An antique stocking is better because we can match the age of the doll. When a doll is marked *all original,* check stockings or socks.

Before making socks or stockings, try to find the approximate age of your doll. Make them as close as possible to what the doll was wearing when it was made.

UNDERCLOTHING

French dolls of the 1890s wore simple underclothing, such as drawers of white cotton, with a slit back. Drawers were held up with a drawstring at the waist that tied in the back. Over this was a short-sleeve chemise with a drawstring at the neck. A chemise fell halfway between hips and knees, and a petticoat tied in the back. Everything was tucked and trimmed with lace.

Underclothing of German dolls of the same period was similar. They wore full petticoats fastened with buttons and handmade buttonholes. A chemise fell below the hips and was low cut, without sleeves.

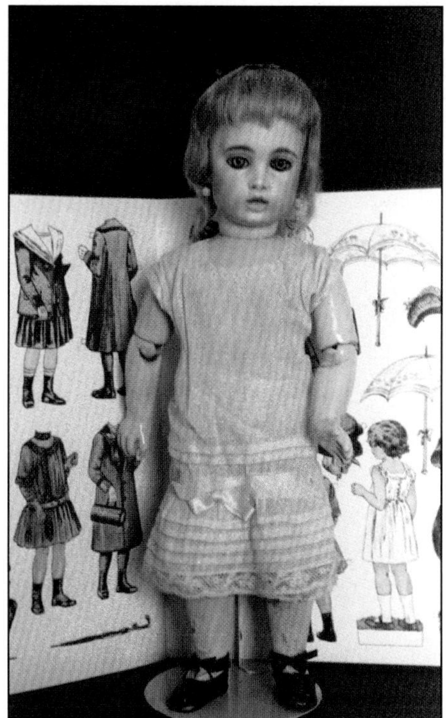
Paper dolls often show undergarments and outergarments worn at a particular time. Paper dolls behind this doll show variety of clothing. Doll wears A-line lawn slip with square neck. Armholes and neck are faced with inset lace. Band of inset lace goes around low waistline, with pink ribbon underneath inset. Bottom is edged in lace. There are four rows of tucks below and two above the insertion. Back closing has button and buttonhole. Matching lawn drawers are split-type, gathered on a waistband that buttons in back.

Our Simon and Halbig doll wears her cotton-lace, tuck-trimmed underclothing. Drawers are completely split, and drawers and petticoat are gathered on a tape to fasten.

Yellowed, three-piece cambric underclothing of this K(star)R 114 is original. Drawers and underskirt are finished with scalloped edging and tie with cotton drawstring. Slip top has blue ribbons at shoulder and lace trim. All are machine-sewn. This is an excellent example of underclothing from the 1910-to-1916 period.

Drawers were entirely split, which means legs were not sewn together except at the waistband, and buttoned in the back.

There were variations of these underclothes. Some dolls wore corsets, corset covers, flannel petticoats and a second petticoat. Sometimes drawers were split completely or split only in the back. Chemises could have a button at the shoulder for opening or a drawstring, but they usually slipped over the head. Sometimes drawers buttoned to a bodice.

Underclothing became simpler as doll making moved into the 1910-to-1920 period. A petticoat was attached to a top, and sometimes the chemise was eliminated. Drawers were buttoned at the side. Combination underwear, called *teddies,* with let-down seats were introduced. The petticoat was simplified into a button-shoulder slip. Drawers became panties and were shorter, with wider legs.

DECORATION OF UNDERCLOTHING

Many pieces of doll underclothing were embroidered, crocheted, tatted or trimmed with lace or tiny tucks. This fancy work, called *white work,* was sometimes done by a couturier, who originally designed and made the costume, or by the mother or grandmother who prepared the doll as a Christmas or birthday gift.

Embroidery was often done in the same color as fabric. As a variation, stitches were done in pastel colors, such as blue or pink. Usually only a few stitches were used—French knots, lazy-daisy-stitch, chain-stitch, outline-stitch and feather-stitch.

Lace is the most common decoration found on underclothing. Rows of insertion lace and tiny tucks were often used on petticoats. Necks and armholes were softened with lace at the edge.

Tatting seems to be a home product and was used on underclothing and dresses. Crocheting was used on the bottom of homemade petticoats and drawers.

Tiny tucks were the least expensive and most used of any decoration on underclothing. They were done by hand or machine. Besides being decorative, tiny tucks in the underskirt helped hold it out to make it more bouffant.

Simon and Halbig doll with leather body has three petticoats in addition to her chemise and drawers. Drawers are split in back and trimmed with lace. Bottom petticoat has inset lace.

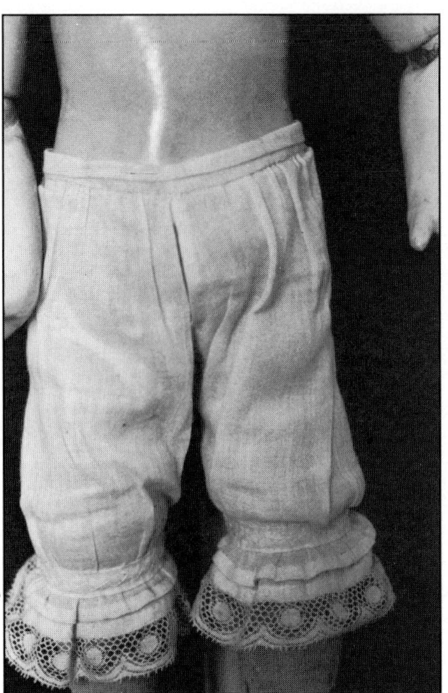

Jumeau drawers have pull string that draws extra fullness only in bustle area.

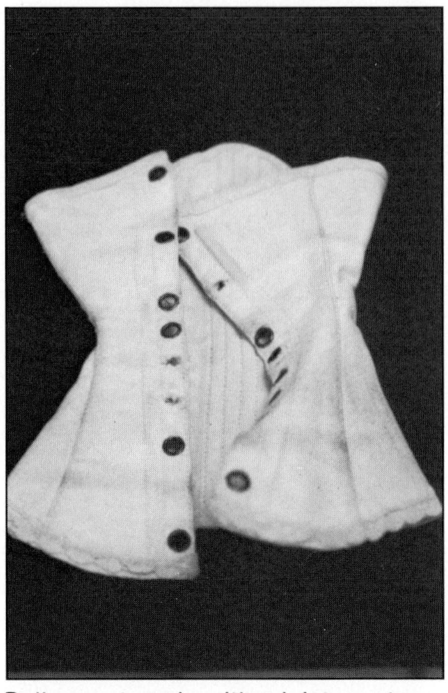

Doll corset made with miniature stays, similar to corsets for adults.

Handmade petticoat decorated with hand-sewn tucks and whipped-on lace. Underpants have crocheted edge.

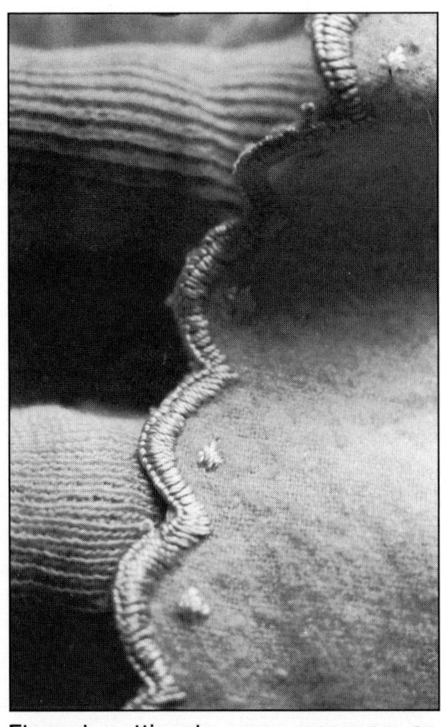

Flannel petticoats were common on dolls, but are often moth-eaten. Look at handwork on bottom of this petticoat.

Underclothing of SFBJ boy doll. This doll came in commercially made original clothing in its own box.

Jumeau wears one-piece, machine-sewn underclothing. Neck, arms and legs are lace trimmed. Top back opening is tied, and drawers have drawstring that draws extra fullness at bustle.

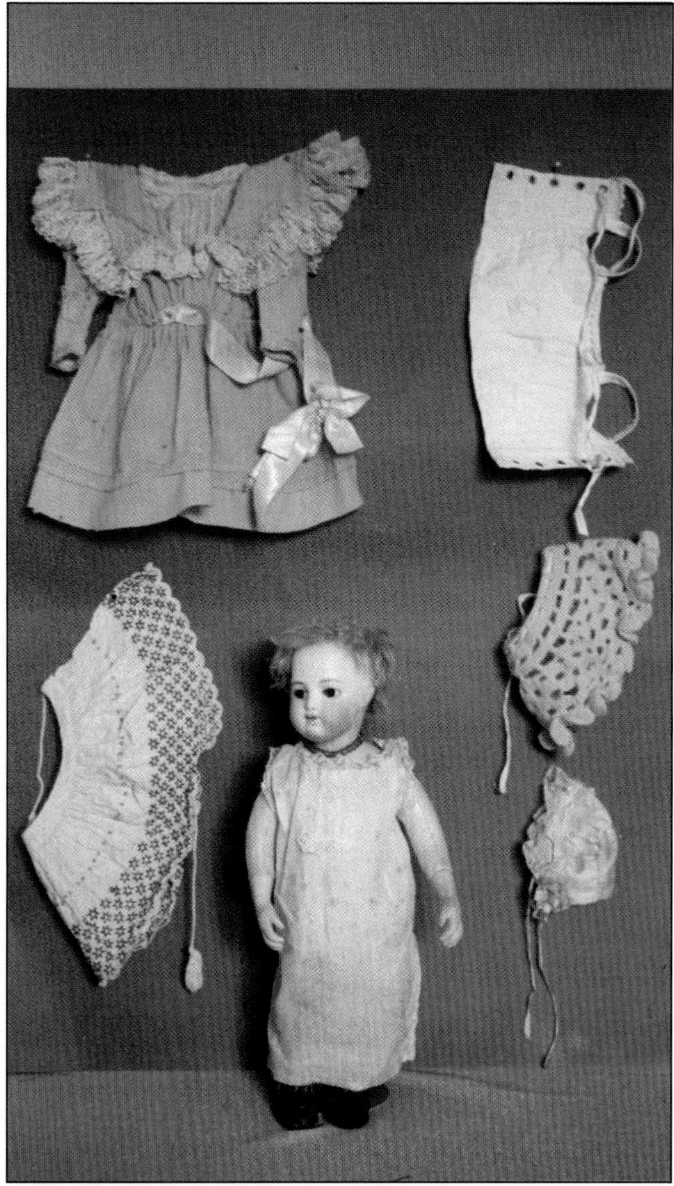

This Bru Breveté came from London in her trunk. She was dressed as a toddler in bright-pink, moth-eaten challis in Kate Greenaway style. Wide, notched collar has lace ruffle and braid. Guimpe is silk with many tiny tucks. Full skirt attaches to outside of bodice. Inside bodice is lined with loosely woven cotton, and back closure has tiny brass hooks. Doll wears lace-trimmed silk hood. As we undressed this child doll, she was full of surprises. First, she had a petticoat of cotton, then a hand-embroidered petticoat with red stars and tiny turquoise beads. Next, she wore a wool petticoat and a corset! Underneath was a commercial chemise. She had gray gloves, gray-cashmere cloak with cape collar, called a *pelisse,* two other dresses and a matching hat.

On this antique bonnet, bow loops are gathered and each loop brought to a point.

Completing the Costume

Ribbons

Ribbons are versatile decorations and have been used on doll clothes as insets, bows, ties and flowers. Ribbon comes in many colors, shades and tints, in many widths and in almost any material. Some new ribbon looks good on reproduction costumes because it is similar to the old. If you look carefully, you may be able to find old ribbon on doll clothes or in antique shops, attics or old chests. It can usually be found at doll shows.

RIBBON TREATMENT

Ribbon ends can be fringed, cut in a V or cut on an angle. Dip ribbon ends in white glue to keep them from raveling.

Ribbon can be stiffened using several different methods. Light stiffening can be done with spray starch and ironing. Equal amounts of white glue and water makes a stiff ribbon. Tied ribbons can be sprayed with Duncan's clear bisque stain or mat spray, available in ceramic shops.

Knots—Knots are often tied in ribbon as part of the decoration. They are tied on the ends of decoration ribbon and bonnet ties. Knots are tied in the middle of bow loops as part of a multibow rosette. See the decoration on the small crocheted bonnet, page 138.

Another knot or ball is sometimes used. See the antique bonnet with ribbon balls, page 138. They are made with hand-packed cotton. Ribbon is gathered around it and sewn into a ball. Balls of ribbon match the ribbon on the hat and hang by a thread as decoration.

Stitching Ribbon—Most costumers and bonnet makers are familiar with zigzag stitching across ribbon by hand to give a rounded, puckered effect. The angle makes a difference in the end design. This method was commonly used in French hand-sewing. See illustration on page 138.

Another method was to sew across the ribbon and pull it tight. Different widths make different-size puffs. This technique can be done on a curve for a different effect.

One popular decoration for doll clothing was *puffing*. A seamstress did this by running a line of fine stitches on both sides of plain-woven ribbon. Then she pulled a little on the threads to give a puffed effect in the middle. This decoration was tacked to the doll's garment and was an attractive addition. Many dress makers still use this method

Left: Black Steiner dressed in knobby silk. Bias pieces were used for shoulder straps and bow. It was swirled on underbrim of hat. Blouse is antique, pretucked cotton fabric. Cord is made with silk fabric.

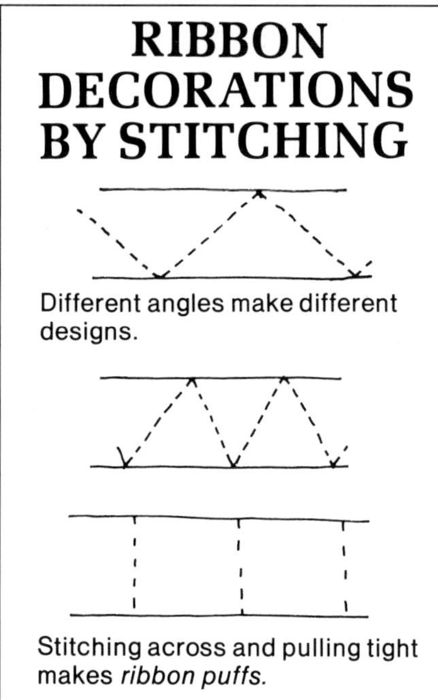

Create many different types of ribbon decoration by varying methods of stitching.

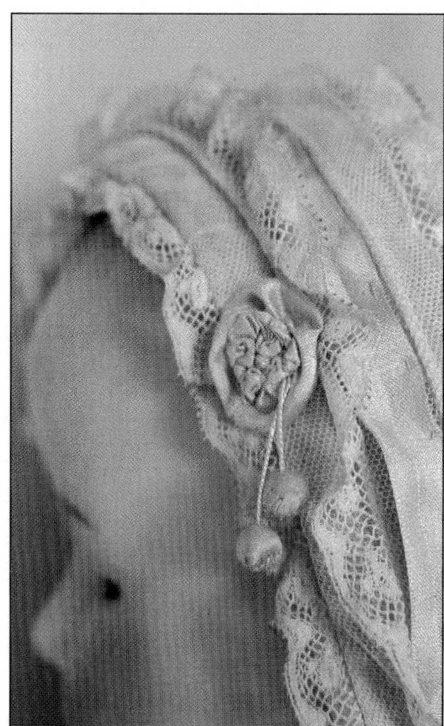

Ribbon flowers and tiny *ribbon balls*, ribbon with cotton sewn inside, hang on a thread.

Bonnet decorated with unusual bow of blue ribbon. Each loop has single knot tied in center.

today. Silk ribbon works best, but other plain-woven ribbon can be used.

Puffing can be done by pulling threads on each side of the plain-woven ribbon. Push the pucker along until you have enough ribbon to decorate the garment. It usually takes about twice as much ribbon as the measurement to get a good puffed effect. Tack this to the doll's garment.

Pleating Ribbon—Pleat ribbon around the face for bonnet decoration. It can be knife pleated or box pleated. Pleating ribbon can be done on any pleater used for doll clothing—follow directions on pleater.

Winding Ribbon—Make roses and other flowers by winding, twisting and making short loops with ribbon. Round flowers are made by gathering.

Thread Pulling—Thread pulling is easy. Unravel a few threads on each end of the ribbon. This lets you get at the two threads on each end to pull. Work gently so you do not break thread.

There are many variations of thread pulling. Each can be done with fine stitching, but it is faster to pull thread.

On a wide ribbon, pull three threads, one in the middle and one on each side. This gives double puffing. You can do more rows if ribbon is wide enough. This method is used to make Vs in French dresses.

Make a single row of ruffles by pulling two threads at one edge of the ribbon. Do not pull it too tight, or ribbon will wind up.

Another method is to pull two threads in the middle of the ribbon. This is often used on old bonnets and results in a double row of tiny ruffles.

On some old bonnets, we find a wide ribbon ruffled on the brim side, then shirred where it is mounted to the main part of the bonnet. This is done by pulling two threads in two or three different places on the ribbon. Threads are pulled on one side of the ribbon. The other side makes a nice ruffle for the brim of the bonnet. The pulled side is used as decoration.

There are many variations of thread pulling. They can all be done with rows of fine stitching or by pulling thread.

HAIR RIBBONS

Hair ribbons are found on almost every wig. They vary from tiny ribbons to giant bows on the top or back of the head.

Ribbon is the first material on a doll to deteriorate, and it was the first thing a child removed or changed. Rearranging a doll's hair seemed to be an inborn thing.

On many old German dolls, we have found ribbon on both sides of the head. On Bru dolls, we have found narrow ribbon on the top of the head where

Tiny silk roses, made from ribbon by doll costumer Shirley Jones, decorate this K(star)R 117 dress.

Dress made of ribbon, joined with insertion lace—a new dress from an old idea. This effect was used mainly on small dolls.

Material is sometimes cut in strips and used as ribbon, as shown on this Googly's bonnet.

hair was pulled back. On a Steiner with original hair, we found a double bow on each side connected by two bands of ribbon over the head. We have found hair pulled back and tied with ribbon.

Large hair ribbons worn by little girls and dolls became popular after 1900. We have not been able to find the origin of the bob haircut, but my mother cut my hair that way in 1919. This was about the only hairstyle that did not have ribbons. Ribbons were tied around the head in the 1920s.

Even though many dolls wore hats, they still had ribbons worked into their hairstyle.

TYPES OF RIBBON

Picot Edge—Ribbon of any width with looped thread along both edges. It was used to tie bonnets and edge dresses and sashes.

Seersucker—Puckered ribbon that does not lie flat because thread in some sections is drawn tighter. It was used most often as dress decoration and braid.

Plisse Edge—Ribbon with ruffling on one or both sides used on bonnets and dresses for decoration.

Moire—Water marked, as moire silk. Markings come out if pressed with a hot iron. Moire is often used with antique fabrics and was used on costumes for French fashion dolls.

Rococo and Variegated—Ribbons that change color, from light to dark. Rococo ribbon changes when moved from side to side. Variegated ribbon changes when moved from end to end. Color changes can be one color, from light to dark, or from one color to another. These ribbons were used on bonnets.

Satin—Ribbon with shiny, smooth surface on one or both sides. It is the most common ribbon used on dolls, and old ribbon of this type is often available. New ribbon comes in different qualities. The terms *single-faced* and *double-faced* are used with satin, meaning it is shiny on one or both sides.

Grosgrain—Heavy ribbon with a rib running across it, used as doll belts, bonnet ties and braid on costumes. Sometimes narrow grosgrain ribbon was braided as edging. This durable ribbon is often found with old materials.

Plain Woven—Ribbon woven the same as plain fabric. Silk ribbon is often plain woven. These ribbons are good for thread pulling.

Embroidered—Ribbon with designs embroidered on or woven in, used as decoration around skirts and as braid on sleeves. Designs must be in proportion to the size of the doll. Large designs are overpowering.

Iridescent—Ribbon woven of two colors of silk to give the color a changeable effect.

Woven Edge—Ribbon that has a tighter weave along edges to keep it from raveling. Most good ribbon has a woven edge.

Fused Edge—Fused edge is made by cutting ribbon

CUTTING AND MAKING BIAS STRIPS

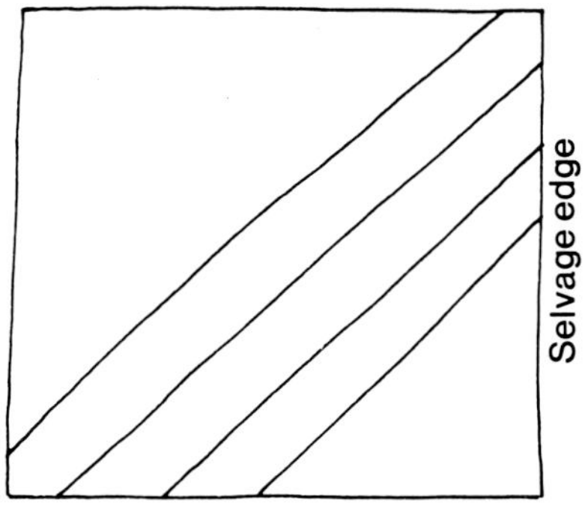

Selvage edge

To make bias strips, measure diagonally across fabric, cut strips, then sew ends together.

lengthwise, then using heat to melt the edge slightly. Only inexpensive ribbon has a fused edge.

Velvet—Ribbon with a cut pile, such as velvet fabric.

Ribbons made in France and available in the U.S. include plain silk ribbon, ribbon flowers, flowers on ribbon, rosebuds and variations. Some imported ribbon is old and some is being recreated that is suitable for doll clothes.

MATERIALS USED AS RIBBONS

Sometimes dress fabric can be used for bows, sashes and even part of a hat. On the black Steiner doll, page 136, our dressmaker used only the nobby silk of the dress for decoration.

We gave her about 7/8 of a yard of old striped silk. She used the stripes up and down for the skirt, but for the bodice and shawl collar she used fabric on the bias. She then made a bow of bias fabric to decorate the front.

Hat ties under the chin are round ties. These were made by rolling and sewing bias fabric with edges turned under.

The inside brim of the hat is covered with bias silk, then silk is slightly gathered where it comes to the crown. This gives lines in the pattern a little swirl. The back of the hat has a wide band and a bow of striped silk cut on the bias. Not all silk will behave this way and not all fabric patterns are as appropriate as this.

Another example of using fabric for ribbons and decoration was a Googly in an antique striped-aqua silk-taffeta dress. We gave the dressmaker 3/4 yard of antique silk taffeta that was striped with aqua, gray and white. Along with this, she used antique inset lace.

Stripes and bows of the striped fabric were cut with stripes *not* on the bias. For the collar, she cut two strips and made them meet in a V in the front, ending with a bow. Fabric was cut each time so the aqua stripe formed the center. There are three bows on the dress front, one at the neck and two below the waist at the end of the pointed collar.

The hat is a masterpiece. The dressmaker used the same silk cut in the direction of the stripes. She gathered this on the brim in tiny gathers, and stripes form a pattern.

The top of the hat was tied with three layers of overlapping ribbon made from silk. It was finished in the back with three-layer, graduating bows and two ties on each side of the bows. Ties or strings were made of the same fabric with the aqua stripe dominant.

On a large Bru dressed in shades of blue, antique silk brocade from the jacket was used to make a bow in the center back. The bow replaced a bustle. The same silk brocade was used for bows all around the bonnet. Ties for the bonnet were made from light-blue silk.

The 101 Pouty doll, page 92, shows how to get variation in braid. Her regional costume is decorated with braid in three sizes. Our doll costumer added bright red underneath the braid for the skirt. For the head piece, she trimmed the braid and added red underneath, along the top edge. Next she trimmed the shoulder with the narrow center part of the braid.

You can see by studying the photo that the braid was not colorful or wide enough for the skirt. It would have been too wide for the shoulder cross lap.

Making a Bias Strip—To cut a bias strip of material, first make a square by folding selvage edges of fabric together. The bias strip is cut from corner to corner. See illustration in previous column.

To make a ropelike string tie, fold a narrow bias strip. Turn under the raw edge, and overcast with tiny stitches. Do not press but leave round. To make a larger or thicker ropelike tie, use a piece of cord inside, and fold a bias strip of fabric over it.

Bias pieces of fabric have a slight give to them. You will find using bias strips and fabric cut on the bias helpful in fitting doll clothes and making decorations. On the black Steiner, the entire bodice is cut on the bias.

The use of bias is appropriate for lightweight fabric and heavyweight fabric, from silk to velveteen.

Roses are an old, charming idea. Follow instructions, then add your own ideas for making original silk roses. China silk is best, but soft satin can be used.

Antique fabric flowers decorate Steiner hat. These are simple to make to match or contrast with a bonnet.

SILK ROSES

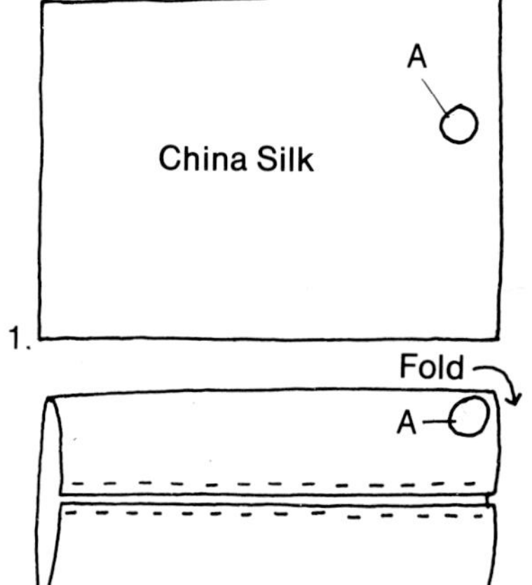

2. Baste across both edges. Do not press fold.

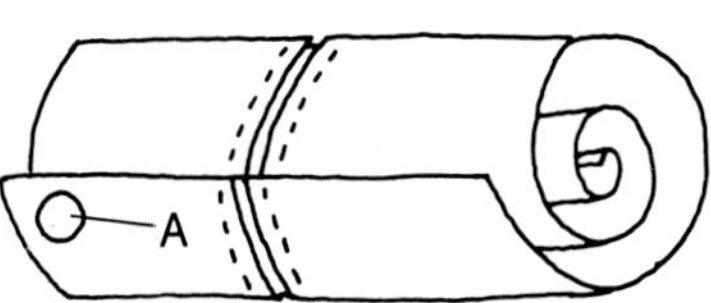

3. Roll silk tight at first, then more loosely.

4. Tie roll in middle.

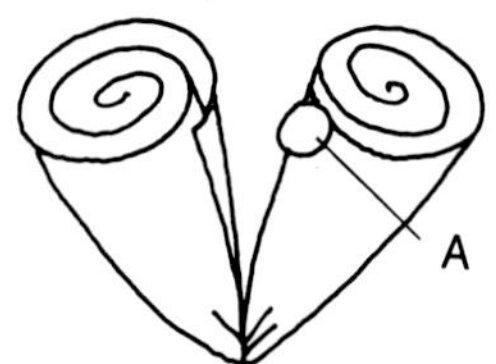

5. Bend in middle so heads are together.

6. Tack in a couple of places to hold heads together.

7. Make two more roses, and tack all backs together. Tack roses to back of bonnet or any place you desire.

Flowers

SILK ROSES

The antique bonnet of our Bru Cherish, shown above on left, has four white roses of China silk that almost cover the back crown. They are so attractive we took them apart to see how they were made. It was a surprisingly simple procedure and one that dressmakers and hat designers will use many times.

Make roses any size, but make them in proportion to the doll. See illustration to the right.

1. Take a strip of silk twice as wide as you want the depth of the flower. It should be half-again as long. Adjust the size of the rose to the size of the doll.
2. Fold both edges of the long side in, almost to the center, and baste in place.
3. *Do not press* the outer edge. Soft folds make a better petal.
4. Tightly roll silk, from point A. As you roll, roll more loosely.
5. Tie the roll tightly in the middle with thread.
6. Bend the roll in the middle so both roses face the same direction. Take a tiny stitch or two at point A to hold the heads together.
7. Make two more roses, and tack backs together.

On a 12-inch doll, we used a piece of silk 4x9". We have used this method to make pink, yellow, blue and white roses. They have all been beautiful.

We tried to make individual roses, but they did not turn out. We tried a darker piece of silk on the inside of the fold. We used bright pink under pale pink to achieve an interesting shading effect. We tried two roses of one color yellow and two of another color yellow. We liked it best with the roses in one color or all four a different tint of one color. This was done by cutting the original piece of silk in half lengthwise and sewing on half of a darker or lighter tint of the same color. Keep trying to make these roses until you get just what you like.

FABRIC FLOWERS

It used to be difficult to find flowers for hats and costumes. Today many are available on the market. But you may not always be able to find them in the right fabric, the right shade or the right size. It is fun to make them yourself.

The advantage of making flowers is you can use the same fabric as the dress. You can make flowers in proportion to the size of the doll. Use velvet, satin, silk or cotton fabric to make flowers. We use commercial stamens, No. 18 floral wire and floral tape from a craft store. You will need white glue, corn starch, a round measuring spoon and a stainless-steel table knife.

Whatever fabric you use, you need to size the back of the fabric to make the flower petals stand up and stay in shape. We cut the fabric in 8x8" pieces. Any size is acceptable if it can be easily handled. With a wide paint brush, paint the back of the fabric pieces with the mixture described below. When fabric is dry, press with an iron set on medium heat. Cut patterns for petals by tracing them on the wrong-side of the fabric with a pencil.

To make the glue-starch solution, mix 1/2 tablespoon of cornstarch with 1 tablespoon of cold water. Add 1/3 cup of boiling water, and cook over medium heat until thick. Remove from heat, add 1 tablespoon of white glue, mix and cool. Brush this mixture on the back of all fabric you use. When fabric is dry, press with an iron set on medium heat.

Wire leaves so they can be bent to fit in any arrangement without looking stiff. Cut pieces of wire a little longer than leaves to make a stem. Apply a thin line of glue down the back of the leaf, and put the wire in the glue. To make veins in the leaf, use a spray bottle of water and lightly spray each leaf. Place the leaf, face up, on a padded surface. Use the knife the same way you use an iron. Heat it in a candle flame, and press on each side of the wire. With the side of the knife, press creases for other veins.

Petals are shaped by placing them right-side up on a padded area, then pressing with a hot measuring spoon. This gives curve to the petals.

Cut the number of petals you wish. It is easier to make flowers if petals are cut from one piece and joined together. Mount stamens in the middle, and glue to the end of a wire. Push the other end of the wire through the center of the flower, and glue around stamens. Add more petals until you have the desired amount.

Make roses by rolling a single petal around the end of a wire. Add more petals one at a time around the first petal.

Many flowers can be made by cutting out small petals, putting in one stamen and a wire. Shade petals or darken tips with a felt pen. Make rolled-petal buds with a wire inside, and glue on green for sepals.

With flowers in bunches or halos, use them for hair and hats. Use your imagination in choosing colors, texture and shapes of flowers.

BREAD DOUGH

Bread-dough art is an ancient Equadorian folk art. Equadorian women make charming, elaborate Christmas tree decorations, animals, baskets and figures with bread dough.

Each year at the Tubac Art Festival, in Tubac, Arizona, Rosario Garza Cantu of Nogales, Mexico, demonstrates bread-dough art. She makes flowers from 1/4 inch to 4 or 5 inches. Her specialty is roses. She shades them the way flowers are shaded, and petals are as thin and perfect as real rose petals. Leaves are so delicate you can hardly tell a real leaf from a bread-dough one. Rosario uses the real leaf to press veins into the bread dough. Stems are flower wire wound with florist's tape.

Flowers are made from a small dab of dough, which is pinched until it is very thin. The first petal is rolled and pinched down for a stem. She pinches out more petals and places them around the rolled one.

She uses several colors of pink dough and pinches off bits of light and dark dough. They are mixed together to get the right shading for each petal, then wire is inserted into the wet rose. All pieces must dry for 24 hours before they are sprayed or pins mounted on them. They can be sprayed with gloss spray.

We have the formula for bread dough. It is so simple and versatile—every doll maker who does not know about it will be glad to have it! Use it for making flowers, earrings, ornaments for shoes, nosegays and other things you may need. It is good for repairing old dolls. You can replace broken fingers and toes, and fill in holes with this wonderful mixture. We have even used it to make a new joint.

Formula—Remove the crust from a piece of white bread, then knead the slice of bread on a piece of foil. Knead 1 tablespoon of white glue into it. Work glue with the back of a spoon first, then put hand

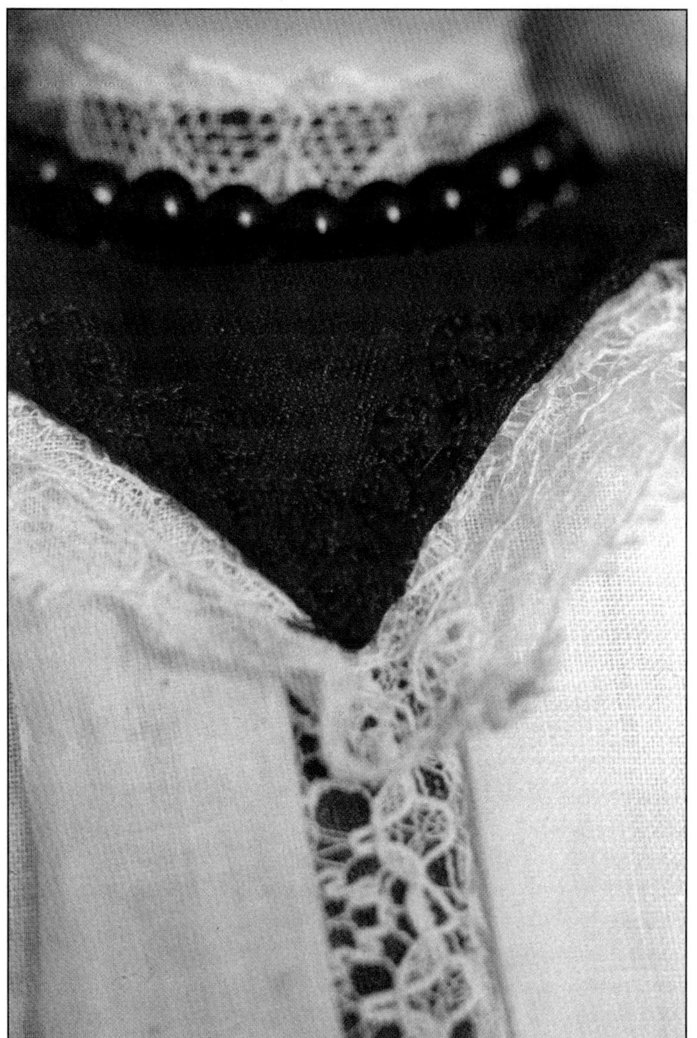

Ruby glass beads are original on this Jumeau.

Bonnet, made by modern-day costumer Hazel Ulseth, is decorated with matching feathers.

cream on your hands and work with the mixture. The more you work it, the finer it gets.

If you want to make small fruit or flowers, color dough with a water-soluble color. Use inks, water colors, Duncan bisque stains or other water-soluble paints. Separate dough into small balls, and add the color you need to each ball. Wrap balls in plastic wrap or foil to keep them from drying out.

If tightly wrapped, bread dough will keep for several days in the refrigerator. Use some hand lotion or cold cream on your hands before working with this mixture.

Other Decorations

DOLL JEWELRY

Doll jewelry is a part of a costume. Some old jewelry may remain with a doll, but often jewelry was changed from doll to doll, some from one generation of dolls to the next. Most original jewelry has been lost.

Many Brus and Jumeaus wore a choker of round red or white glass beads. We know these are original. Our Jumeau in her original box, shown in full-page photo on page 55, wears a short string of ruby-red

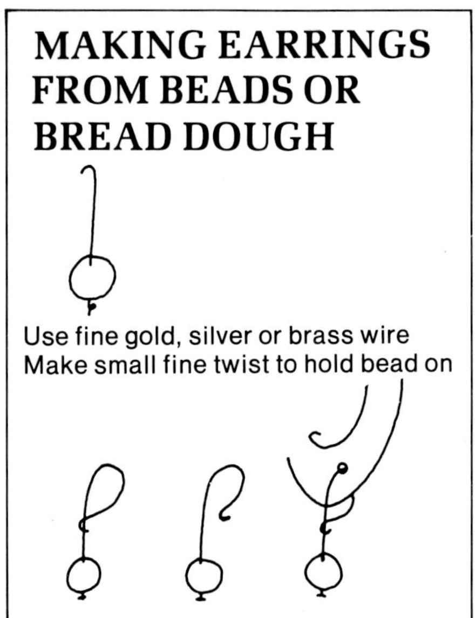

Use beads, bread-dough shapes or other decorations to make unique earrings.

Above: Smocking is used effectively on doll clothing. It has been used for dolls' and children's clothing since the 1880s.

Right: Five-inch all-bisque doll has dress made from silk handkerchief. Embroidery and edging are hand-sewn. Handkerchiefs for dressing small dolls are available at antique shows and shops.

glass beads that covered the crack of the swivel joint. See photo on page 143. One of our dolls has bronze-red beads with a pendant in the middle. Our large Crescent Bru, page 43, wears coral beads that we feel are original. Brus were often described as having coral necklaces. The small Bru Brevetê, page 155, has cut amber-color glass beads. Some lady dolls wore beads, long chains, pins or lorgnettes.

We have a Jumeau that has a child's play watch hanging around her neck and a boy Jumeau with a pocket watch on a chain. One of our lady dolls has a watch pinned to her dress and another has a watch she wears on a long chain around her neck.

One of our Long-Face Jumeau dolls has a gold chain with a heart locket. The locket has initials and appears to be a child's necklace. Other dolls wear inexpensive heart lockets around their necks. Lockets were a favorite piece of jewelry.

Some larger dolls wear bracelets. One gold bracelet on a Bru says *Bébé*. It could be the doll's, but most bracelets were probably added. We have two dolls with combs in their hair, a Jumeau Bébé and a French fashion doll. Except for an occasional string of inexpensive beads, we do not have any German dolls with jewelry that we believe was original with the doll.

One French fashion doll we purchased was described as wearing "original, handmade gold jewelry—earrings, necklace and hair combs." When we picked up the doll, it had no jewelry. The owner claimed she did not know what happened to it. We think she kept it for another doll.

EARRINGS

Earrings are part of the costume of French dolls. Be careful they are not lost when you costume a doll.

Most French dolls wore earrings. It is difficult to determine if they are original or if they are new.

Sometimes pins with color-glass heads or human earrings are used for dolls. Be careful with these—they may chip bisque.

Make Bead Earrings—If your doll has no earrings and you wish to make some, it is not difficult. Many people use small beads as earrings. Keep them in proportion to the size of the doll.

Make a bead into an earring by using fine gold, silver or brass wire. Put the wire through the bead. With needle-nose jewelry pliers, wind a little circle so wire does not slip through the bottom of the bead. Cut the other end of the wire so it is 1 inch long. Put the wire through the ear, and adjust it to the length you want. Bring the end of the wire down behind the ear. Trim it so it comes forward and makes a single hook around the piece containing the bead. Make two earrings alike. See illustration above.

Put a drop of white glue on the bottom end of the bead, and put some matching color over that. Earrings will appear to be old.

Other Shapes—Instead of glass beads, make interesting shapes, such as tear drops, squares and egg shapes with the bread-dough modeling mixture. See page 143 for more information on this procedure. Put these shapes on wire ends and allow them to dry. Spray them or dip them in nail polish. They can be any tint or shade of a color, or a mixture of colors. Make wires as described above.

We use the finest wire possible. There is less chance of damaging bisque, and finer wire shows less.

DYEING BUTTONS

Often you can find tiny white buttons to decorate

doll clothes, but it is harder to find colored ones. Tiny buttons are hard to find, but we have listed some places in the *Resource* section, page 158, that carry tiny buttons.

Small white pearl buttons come in heart and diamond shapes with off-center holes, ovals and other shapes. They are made for doll clothes.

You may want buttons to blend with the costume. If you do, tint them.

You cannot dye a button, but a button will take on an attractive tint. Use cold dye, watercolors, food coloring or almost any water-soluble color. Mix the dye or coloring with a little water in a small jar. Put buttons in the dye solution and leave them overnight. Buttons will absorb some of the color.

DYEING SHOES

Dye white-leather shoes with spray shoe dye that is available at shoe repair shops and some shoe stores. You can use bisque stain to paint shoes.

TINTING LACE

You may have lace that would look better with old fabric if it was a soft ecru or ivory color. If you are not using a lot of lace, it can easily be tinted.

Wind the lace snugly around a glass or jar, and anchor the end with a pin. Make some strong hot coffee or tea—instant tea or coffee works well. Pour it in a pot large enough to set the glass with lace down inside it. The liquid should almost be boiling. Tea makes a more-yellow color than coffee. We like both colors, so test two small pieces of lace. The color you choose depends on the color of the fabric you use with the lace.

Place the glass or jar in the hot coffee or tea. Make sure liquid covers the lace. Let the lace get darker than you want because some color rinses out. Leave it in the liquid for 3 or 4 minutes.

Rinse the jar and lace under cold running water. Do not remove lace from the glass. Watch the color, and when it is what you want, blot with paper towels. Let lace dry on the glass.

If you wish to tint lace other pastel colors, use liquid dye the same way. If you are dressing a large doll and have a lot of lace, wind the lace on a gallon jug. Another way is to dye lace loose in the solution, then wrap it around a jug to dry.

When you are finished, lace may be soft and fragile. If it is, spray with spray starch, then gently iron.

Ribbon can be tinted with coffee or tea, but it cannot be dyed wrapped around a glass. When ribbon overlaps, it does not tint evenly. Tint the ribbon loose in the solution, rinse it, then wind it on a glass to dry. Dye with colors the same way.

Stockings made of white stretch lace or shirt mesh are too bright on a doll dressed in old fabrics. Tint stockings in tea or coffee.

SMOCKING FOR DECORATION

Smocking was popular on children's clothes. It is a decorative device that has been used for over 100 years to adjust fullness of a garment or section of a garment. It is made of tiny pleats that are embroidered.

When costuming dolls, smocking can be used in many ways. It can be used for dress bodices, small sections of a bodice, shoulders and wrists of sleeves. It can be used to gather fullness around the waist.

Smocking can be done on a separate piece of material and added as decoration. Use it down the front of a dress or shirt. It makes an interesting collar or section of a bonnet. It is decorative on baby-doll clothes and was often used on fancy aprons. If smocking is kept in proportion, it can be used on any doll.

Pleating for smocking can be done by hand or with a pleater machine, available in quilting stores. Check in stores carrying sewing supplies for instructions and patterns for smocking.

THINGS TO SAVE FOR COMPLETING A COSTUME

The following items are good for saving and adding to your doll costumes. When you find them, keep them. You never know when you will need one to complete an outfit.

- Old buttons in small sizes
- Children's socks
- Glass beads
- Small, old jewelry
- Leather gloves
- Fine chains
- Silk
- Leather handbags
- Tiny buckles
- Handkerchiefs with lace trim
- Hats with usable parts
- Fancy handkerchiefs
- Silk thread
- Silk handkerchiefs
- Tatting
- Women's silk dresses or parts of dresses
- Pieces of lace
- Lightweight percale
- Hair ribbon
- Single doll shoe
- Good ribbon
- Single large-doll sock
- Clothes from other dolls
- Wigs from other dolls
- Silk flowers
- Men's T-shirts
- Fine wire
- Leotards
- Children's striped T-shirts

Tynie Babe, made by Horsman, wears crocheted costume. Fine, delicate design is appropriate for this small baby doll. Ruth Klein is the designer of this original outfit. Instructions can be varied for any small doll.

Crochet Baby Doll Pattern

Crochet clothes for dolls were shown in catalogs for all-bisque dolls. We have found crochet clothes only on German dolls. In 1910, the *Ladies' Home Journal* carried several crochet doll-dress patterns. Crocheted dresses were used earlier on tiny German dolls that came dressed. We have a set of these dolls in original crochet costumes.

ORIGINAL PATTERNS FOR TYNIE BABE

You can dress a doll from inside out with patterns for panties, booties, dress and bonnet. These patterns can be used for Tynie Babe and other all-bisque dolls. Directions for these patterns can be adapted for most dolls if you fit often and crochet by inches, instead of the number of stitches. The original pattern and crochet method were developed by Ruth Klein.

Materials Needed—The following materials are needed to make a dress:

- No. 13 steel crochet hook
- 2 spools of 300-yard Suisse all-purpose polyester sewing thread
- 1 spool trim color
- 1 yard 1/8-inch-wide silk ribbon

Gauge—40 chain stitches = 2 inches

PANTIES

Cloth diapers are optional, though on large dolls they seem more fitting. The waist measures 6-1/2 inches, so add about 1 inch for the necessary fullness.

Chain 7-1/2 inches

Row 1.

Single crochet in second chain from hook across. Keep chain straight. Chain 1 and turn.

Row 2.

Single crochet in turning chain. In each single crochet across. Chain 4 and turn.

Row 3.

Skip first single crochet, double crochet in next. Skip 1, double crochet in next, repeat across. Chain 1 and turn. Spaces made are for waistline ties of ribbon, cord or length of chain stitch.

Row 4.

Single crochet in first space, chain 3, 2 double crochet, chain 1, make 3 more double crochet. This makes shell. In next space, double crochet 3, chain 1, double crochet 3, and next shell is made. Continue across making a shell in each space. Chain 1, turn.

Row 5.

Slip stitch to center of shell, chain 1 space. Chain 3,

Left: Crown of this original Steiner hat is wired around head and has three wires sewn in pink-satin fabric across top. Triple flounce decorates brim of silk embroidered lace. Basic hat is made of buckram, lined with silk. Hat was decorated with flowers and leaves.

These 3- and 4-inch dolls wear outfits crocheted by Ruth Klein. She specializes in designing and making tiny costumes. Dolls are antiques.

work 2 double crochet, chain 1 and 3 double crochet. Double crochet in center of next shell 3 times, chain 1, 3 double crochet. Work across shell-on-shell, chain 1 and turn.
Row 6.
Repeat row 5. At end of row, slip stitch to top stitch of chain 3 to join waist. Be sure work is free of twists.
Row 7.
Slip stitch to center of shell, then work shell-on-shell around end by slipping stitch to top of first chain 3.
Row 8.
Repeat row 7.
Try on doll for length. It should fit from waist to top of leg. Add another round if needed.
Row 9.
Crotch and leg area—make shell-on-shell as in row 7 over 4 shells. Chain 1 and turn.
Row 10.
Slip stitch to center space. Work shell-on-shell as before.
Rows 11-18.
Repeat row 10 eight times to make 10 rows of 4 shells.
Row 19.
Divide work in half, and match last row of 4 shells to 4 shells in back. Slip stitch evenly to corresponding back shells.
Row 20.
Leg area—decrease row. Make shell-on-shell around leg and 5 over crotch area using a smaller shell of 2 double crochet, chain 1 and 2 double crochet. Join with slip stitch to first shell.
Row 21.
Single crochet in chain 1 space, single crochet in space between shells. Continue around leg.
Row 22.
Pick up loop in 1 single crochet. In next single crochet, work all loops off as 1 single crochet.
Row 23.
Repeat row 22 from front to back. Test on doll leg for snug fit. Decrease if necessary.
Row 24.
Chain 3, double crochet closely around leg for cuff. Cut thread and knot several times. Attach thread to opposite leg. Repeat leg-shaping rows. Lace cord or ribbon through waistline spaces.

BOOTIES

Chain 6 stitches
Single crochet in second chain from hook and in next 5 stitches. Work 3 single crochet in end stitch and back opposite side of chain. Continue working in single crochet for sole of bootie. Increase at each end—2 single crochet in 1—on each side of toe and heel. Work until piece fits sole of foot on doll.
Row 1.
For upper section, single crochet in back loop only. Single crochet around with no increase.
Row 2.
Repeat row 2 until boot fits foot. Pull in toe section with decrease on each side once or twice as necessary for close fit over toes.

Right: Woven, soft-straw bonnet with antique flowers. Ribbon is woven into straw. Doll is marked only with a 14.

Row 3.
Chain 3, skip 1, double crochet in next from one side to other to make spaces for ties.
Row 4.
Make shell in each space using 2 double crochet, chain 1 and 2 double crochet per shell. Trim with roses on toe or use bows, rosettes or French knots. Lace ribbon through spaces and tie on.

BONNET

Chain 4, join with slip stitch to form ring
Row 1.
Chain 1, single crochet in center of ring 10 times, join and chain 1.
Row 2.
Single crochet in each single crochet around, increase every fourth stitch, chain 1 and turn.
Row 3.
Work single crochet from wrong-side in each single crochet, with increase in every fourth stitch. Join, chain 1 and turn.
Row 4.
Repeat rows 2 and 3 until circle measures 1/2 inch in diameter. Change to half double crochet and continue to work rows 2 and 3. Increase about every sixth stitch.
Row 5.
After 4 rounds of half double crochet, change to double crochet with increase every eighth stitch. When circle measures 2-1/4 inches across, double crochet to last 20 stitches. Do not increase again.
Row 6.
Chain 3, turn and double crochet to opposite side. These 20 stitches are back-neck area.
Row 7.
Repeat rows 5 and 6 until cap fits head of doll from mid-ear to mid-ear over top.
Row 8.
Chain 4, skip 1, double crochet in next. Repeat across, making spaces for ribbon.
Rows 9, 10, 11.
Make shells in each space. Three rows of shell-on-shell are made for ruffle. Cut thread, attach trim color and make picot edge. Cut thread, and fasten securely.
Rows 12, 13, 14.
Attach thread to edge of back 20 stitches. Make spaces across and make 2 rows of shells with picot trim on edge. Fasten ribbon on each side after threading through spaces. Attach small bow. Thread ribbon through front spaces, and tie under chin. Tack at each ear, and add rosette or trim as desired.

DRESS

BODY OF DRESS

Chain 4-1/2 inches to fit loosely around neck
Row 1.
Single crochet in second chain from hook and each chain across. Chain 1 and turn.
Row 2.
Single crochet in turning chain and in next 4 stitches. In next single crochet, make increase, work 2 single crochet in 1 single crochet. Repeat increase across every sixth stitch, then chain 1 and turn.
Row 3.
Single crochet in turning chain and in each single crochet across. Chain 1 and turn.
Row 4.
Repeat row 2.
Row 5.
Repeat row 3.
Row 6.
Repeat row 2.
Row 7.
Repeat row 3. Repeat row 3 over next several rows. Fit on doll. Yokes should lay flat around neckline and back edges should be straight. If necessary, increase or decrease.

Yoke will be about 1/4 inch deep and lie smooth. Single crochet in turning chain and in next few stitches to arm area back of shoulder. Chain 17, skip 13 stitches and single crochet in each single crochet across front. This creates the sleeve opening. Measure yoke. Fold in half to determine opposite sleeve area, and mark with thread or safety pin. Single crochet to first mark, chain 17, then single crochet from second marker across back. Chain 1 and turn.

Single crochet in each single crochet across, with 1 single crochet in each stitch of underarm chain. Chain 1 and turn. Check garment on doll to be sure arm and hand go through opening. Garment should lie flat on body with straight back edges.

Single crochet in turning chain and in each single crochet across, chain 1 and turn. Repeat to below bustline. Pull up loop on last stitch, and cut thread. Leave length of thread to tie together. This is a good place to do sleeves and collar.

Right: Monday, our K(star)R Googly, is dressed in peacock-blue and bronze satin. It is a strange color combination, but dolls were often dressed in what was left from something else. Lace around sleeves has turned bronze. Lace sewn under edge of skirt has turned blue. Maybe dress was washed in water that was too warm or maybe doll was left in rain. Skirt is sewn on the outside of the yoke, which was common on dolls of this date.

SLEEVES

Row 1.

Attach thread to sleeve opening at front or back of dress. Make 13 shells around opening—chain 3, double crochet 2, chain 1, 3 double crochet. The first shell is made. Skip 1 stitch, make shell in next, 3 double crochet, chain 1, 3 double crochet. Join with slip stitch and repeat shell-on-shell procedure, as in panties, page 147.

Row 2.

Make 4 rounds of shell-on-shell.

Row 3.

Decrease 1 single crochet in each shell, 1 in space between.

Row 4.

Decrease to fit arm and hand of doll, then make double crochet band as with pantie leg. Cut thread and attach trim color.

Row 5.

Single crochet in each double crochet around arm.

Row 6.

Slip stitch to join last round. Chain 3, single crochet in same space as chain 3. Pull tight to make picot. Single crochet in next 3 stitches, make another picot. Continue around. This makes 1 picot on top of each shell. Cut thread and knot several times. Make other sleeve using same method.

COLLAR

Make collar with one or two rows of shells around neck. Trim with picot edge in trim color. The dress on page 147 has two rows of shells with pink picot edge.

FINISHING

To finish dress, tie together threads on row 12. Make knots small and tight, then cut close.

Row 1.

At end of last row of dress, chain 4 and turn. Skip first single crochet, double crochet in next. Skip 1, double crochet in next. Continue across, chain 1 and turn. Spaces are for ribbon trim.

Row 2.

Single crochet in space, then chain 3, double crochet, chain 1, 2 double crochet. The first shell is made. Make shell in each space across—double crochet 2, chain 1, double crochet 2. Chain 1 and turn.

Row 3.

Repeat shell-on-shell row, then slip stitch into top chain of first shell to join skirt.

Row 4.

Slip stitch to center of shell, and work in rounds for balance of skirt.

Row 5.

Work shell-on-shell until length is correct.

On last row, make picot, and single crochet around bottom edge. Cut thread, and secure ends. Attach thread to back of neck, chain 5, skip 2, single crochet in next. Make 3 loops down back for buttons. Sew beads or buttons on opposite side.

Thread ribbon sash through spaces from back to front. Fasten ends of ribbon on each side at back. Tie small bow in front. Button loops are spaced at neck, across ribbon space and in between. Front of dress has four lengths of ribbon threaded from top to bottom between shell rows. Four rosebuds are placed below collar. Tack ribbon in place at top and bottom.

Right: Gowned in her rust-red, cotton-cambric frock, this Simon and Halbig doll sits in a chair. Dress is old and faded, and may be the only one she has ever worn. Dress lacks design, yet sleeves are two piece, which indicates some style. It is lined and has self-fabric ruffle at bottom. Dress goes well with doll's gray eyes and well-blushed cheeks.

Glossary

Alencon Lace—Needlepoint lace outlined with cord.
All-Bisque—Term used when entire doll is made of bisque.
Antique Costume—Costume over 75 years old.
Antique Doll—Doll over 75 years old.
Arm's Eye—Armhole.
Auto Bonnet—Hat with tight, turned-back brim and slightly puffed crown.
Balayeuse—Dust ruffle on the underside of skirt that shows below the skirt.
Ball-Jointed—Type of doll joint using wood ball in the socket for flexibility in movement.
Balmoral Boots—Low boots that lace up front.
Baschlik—Scarf wrapped around head and over a hat.
Basque—Extension of bodice below the waistline.
Batiste—Semisheer, lightweight cotton fabric.
Bavolet—Curtain across the back of bonnet to shade neck.
Bébé—French childlike doll.
Bedfordcord—Heavy fabric with cords running with warp.
Beefeater—Hat with soft, round crown and flat brim made by shirring fabric over wire.
Bellows Pocket—Pocket made with bellowlike pleats.
Beret—Flat circle or pancake-shape hat, with a band to hold it on the head. It was shown in 1911 and may have been used before that. Large beret is called a *tam-o'-shanter.*
Bertha—Lace or ornamental collar around shoulders.
Biggin—Large mob cap.
Bishop Sleeves—Full sleeves gathered in wristband.
Bisque—Fired form of porcelain clay that was fired until it has chemically changed or melted. It is like material of fine dishes, only without glaze or shine.
Blouse—Bodice that usually blouses at waistline.
Blouse Waist—Bodice that blouses over waistline.
Bodice—Upper part of dress or underwear.
Bolero—Hat with conical crown and small brim.
Bretelles—Over-the-shoulder decoration or decorated suspenders.
Breveté—French word for *patented.*
Brocade—Heavy silk with a textured pattern.
Broderie Anglaise—White embroidery, often with eyelets.
Buckram—Stiff, coarse, inexpensive cotton, heavily sized.
Cambric—Slightly lustered cotton fabric.
Capote—Bonnet with soft crown and stiff brim; also cape or overcape.
Cartridge Pleats—Tight gathers.
Cascades of Lace—Many rows of gathered lace.
Cashmere—Soft, lightweight, smooth material of twill weave, usually wool.
Challis—Soft, light, silk-and-wool-blend or wool-and-cotton blend fabric.
Chapeau—Any fancy French hat or bonnet.
Character Dolls—Lifelike representations of real people, especially babies and children. Dolls with realistic expressions.
Chemise—Shirt worn next to the body, sometimes called a *skirt;* plain dress dolls were sold in.
China Silk—Thin, plain silk with slight luster.
Cloak—Loose-fitting outer garment.
Clocks—Stocking decorations running up from the ankle.
Coat Sleeves—Sleeves with two seams. Used on dresses and coats.
Collectables—Dolls between 25 and 75 years old.
Color Rubs—Places where cheek color is rubbed through to expose white bisque.
Combination—Underbodice with attached drawers.
Contemporary Costume—Clothing made about the same time as the doll, but not necessarily for the doll.
Couturier—Designer of fashions for women.
Crinoline—Petticoat made of horsehair or hoop petticoat.
Damasse Silk—Brocade silk fabric.
Demitrain—Small train resulting from fullness at back of skirt.
Déposé—French word for *registered.* French doll makers used this term on heads and shoes.
Dolly Face Dolls—German dolls with plump cheeks, open mouths and teeth. They were not modeled after a child, but were an idealized portrait of a child of no particular age.
Dorset Thread Button—Button made of flat metal disk covered with threads radiating from center hole.
Drawn Work—Decoration made by pulling thread out of fabric and hand-stitching remaining thread to make design.
Embroidered Ribbon—Ribbon with designs embroidered on or woven in, used as decoration around skirts and as braid on sleeves.
En Coeur—Heart-shape neckline.
English Net—Fine-mesh fabric made of cotton; background fabric of many types of lace.
En Tablier—Skirt trim imitating an apron.
Faille—Ribbed silk fabric recognized by its cord surface.
Farmer Satin—Lustrous cotton fabric used for lining.
Fichu—Scarf worn at shoulders or neckline.
Flirty Eyes—Eyes that move from side to side.
Fly-Fringe—Cord fringe with knots used as trim.
Foulard—Lightweight silk with plain twill or satin weave.
Frill—Narrow, gathered ruffle.
Frock—Dress with back closure.
Fused-Edge Ribbon—Made by cutting ribbon lengthwise, then using heat to melt edge slightly. Only inexpensive ribbon has fused edge.
Gaiters—Covering for lower leg and top of foot.
Gibson Pleats—Shoulder pleats stitched to yoke depth.
Gigot Sleeves—Long sleeves, full in the upper part and tight over forearm.
Gown—Dress, usually with front closure.
Gretchen Dress—Dress hanging freely from yoke; bodice with high waistline.
Grosgrain—Ribbed fabric. Cords are heavier than poplin, rounder than faille.
Grosgrain Ribbon—Heavy ribbon with rib running across it used for doll belts, bonnet ties and braid on costumes.
Guimpe—Bodice worn under a jumper or low-necked dress.

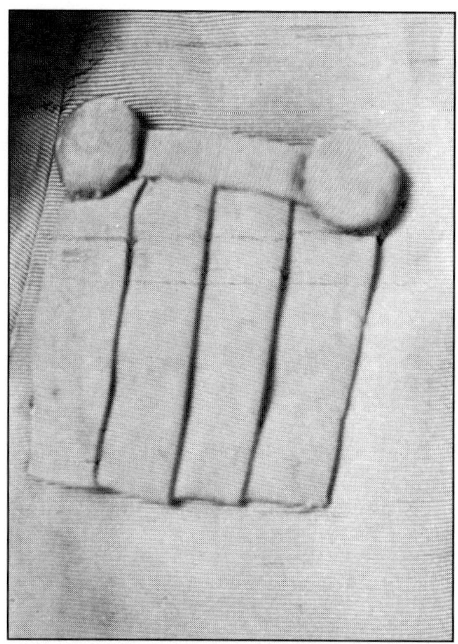

Pockets with large pleats that expand when filled are called *bellows pockets.* They were used on original dress of marked Schmitt doll.

Bru Breveté in original chemise. Her wig is lambskin and boots are marked *B.*

Dorset thread buttons have metal-disk base with center hole. Thread is wound through hole until no disk shows. Often elaborate designs were worked out with more than one color of thread. Buttons were used on clothing and shoes.

Gypsy Hat—Wide-brim hat with ties extending over the top of the crown and brim, often worn by Gibson-Girl dolls.
Hairpin Work—Lace made on hairpins.
Hood—Tight-fitting bonnet with no brim.
Hoop Petticoat—Underpetticoat with hoops of cane, wire or bone.
Insertion Lace—Lace inserted in fabric.
Iridescent Ribbon—Woven of two colors of silk to give it a changeable effect.
Jne—Mark found on Bru dolls, meaning *Junior.*
Knickerbockers—Full breeches, usually gathered in a band below the knee.
Lady Dolls—Dolls with adult-female figures.
Lawn—Cotton fabric similar to linen.
Leglets—Pantalets without body section, only legs.
Lustering—Cotton lining fabric with lustrous surface.
Mantilla—Small or short mantle, usually deeper in back.
Mob Cap—Gathered circle, usually trimmed with lace. *Biggin* is an extra-large mob cap.
Mode—Thin, lustrous silk fabric.
Modern Dolls—Dolls less than 25 years old.
Moire—Corded silk or silk-and-cotton fabric with water-marked effect.
Moire Ribbon—Water-marked ribbon similar to moire silk. Markings come out if pressed with hot iron.
Molded Hair—Dolls with hair formed in the mold. Hair was not added.
Mother Hubbard—Free-hanging dress, cloak or night-gown gathered on yoke.
Mousseline Desoie—Sheer silk fabric similar to chiffon.
Muslin—Plain-woven cotton fabric.
Nainsook—Thin, lightweight cotton.
Normandie Bonnet—Hat with high, half-moon-shape puffed crown with many variations of brims.
Nun's Veiling—Lightweight wool fabric made with plain weave in plain colors, similar to wool batiste.
Old Costume—Costume of undetermined age, but not modern. Older than 35 years.
Organdy—Sheer, stiff, lightweight cotton.
Original Costume—Clothing made for a doll at the time the doll was produced or made at home as the doll's first dress.
Pantalets—Long pants worn by females, usually as undergarment.
Paperweight Eyes—Eyes with glass bulge on the outside, giving depth to eyes. Used only on French dolls.
Pate—Covering for open head, usually cardboard in German dolls and cork in French dolls.
Peau de Soie—Heavy silk with fine, grainy surface produced by tiny cords. Long-wearing and serviceable.
Percale—Cotton fabric with plain weave, usually recognized by firm construction, smooth, dull finish and printed pattern. Also available in plain colors.
Petticoat—Underskirt with waistband.
Picot-Edge Ribbon—Ribbon with looped thread along both edges, used to tie bonnets, edge dresses and sashes.
Picture Hat—Hat or bonnet with wide, off-the-face brim.
Pilisse—Cloak with cape.

Mob cap made by gathering edge of circle of fabric. Usually frill of lace was added.

Bretelles are over-the-shoulder straps or ruffles. On front of this SFBJ dress, bretelles go down to waistline.

Capes with overcapes are called *capotes.*

Pinning Blanket—Long petticoat slit down front. Made to wrap around and over infant's legs.
Plain-Woven Ribbon—Weave similar to plain fabric. Silk ribbon is often plain woven. These ribbons are good for thread pulling.
Plastron—Panel of contrasting-color fabric down the front of dress or bodice.
Plisse-Edge Ribbon—Ribbon with bit of ruffling on one or both sides, used on bonnets and dresses for decoration.
Poke Bonnet—Hat with projecting front brim, high, rising small crown and ties under chin.
Polonaise—Dress with overskirt draped in back.
Pongee—Mediumweight silk fabric in plain weave distinguished by irregular threads and natural beige color.
Poplin—Fine-ribbed silk, wool or cotton fabric.
Princess Style—Gored, flowing style without waistline.
Queen Anne Collar—Square-cut collar.
Ribbon Necklace—Band of ribbon or other fabric worn tightly around the neck.
Robe—Open-front gown.
Rococo and Variegated Ribbon—Ribbons that change color. *Rococo* changes when moved from side to side. *Variegated* changes when moved from end to end.
Rompers—Child's garment with bloomers instead of skirt at bottom.
Sarsnet—Cotton fabric with luster.
Sateen—Cotton fabric with luster on right-side. Used for dressing French dolls.
Satin—Lustrous silk material in satin weave.
Satin Ribbon—Ribbon with shiny, smooth surface, which can be on one or both sides of the ribbon. It is the most-common ribbon used on dolls. Terms *single-faced* and *double-faced* are used with satin, meaning it is shiny on one or both sides.
Seersucker Ribbon—Puckered ribbon that does not lie flat because thread in some sections are drawn tighter. It is used most often as dress decoration and braid.
Set Eyes—Eyes that do not move.
Shift—Chemise or underskirt.
Sleep Eyes—Eyes that open and close.
Stomacher—Ornamental, stiffened panel work used as front of bodice.
Taffeta—Plain, closely woven, stiff silk fabric with dull luster.
Tam-o'-Shanter—Large beret.
Tarlatan—Inexpensive gauzelike fabric used to dress German dolls.
Teddy—Combination undergarment.
Tête—Jumeau mark. *Tête Jumeau.*
Toque—Small, round, close-fitting French hat with or without brim.
Velvet—Pile fabric. Pile is usually cut close.
Velveteen—Cotton, with cotton backing and cotton pile.
Wescott—Very short, sleeveless jacket.
Woven-Edge Ribbon—Ribbon with tighter weave along edges to keep it from raveling. Most good ribbon has woven edges.

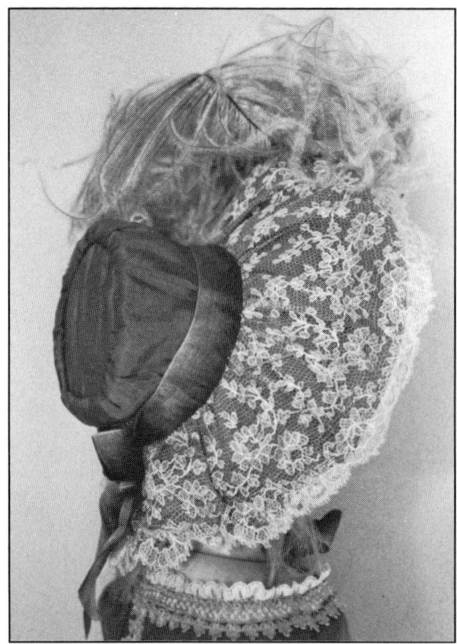

A *picture hat* is an off-the-face hat with a large brim used on many commercially dressed dolls. It calls attention to doll's face.

Plastron fills in low V-neck of French dress and is usually shirred or gathered as shown on this antique Bru dress.

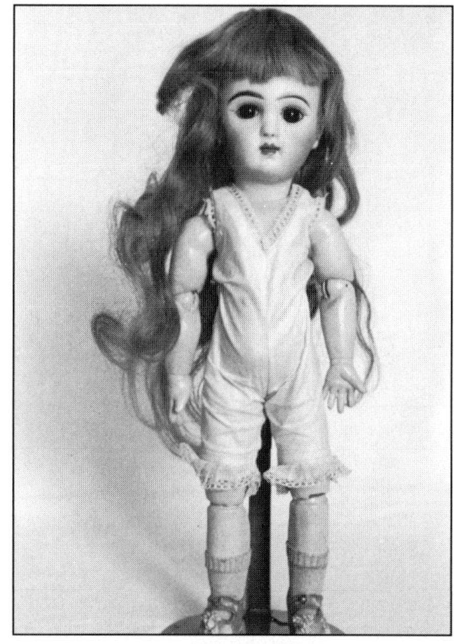

Combination underpants and top is called a *teddy.* They were first used in the 1890s. This is an original Jumeau combination—V-neck is almost a trademark of Jumeau underclothing.

BOOKS AND PAMPHLETS

The books, pamphlets and articles listed below may be difficult to find. A few can be found in bookstores or libraries. Those that can be ordered from Doll and Craft World and Hobby House Press are noted, and addresses can be found on page 158.

Alexander, Lyn. *The Doll Dressmaker's Guide to Pattern Making.* Available from Doll and Craft World or Hobby House Press.

Alexander, Lyn. *The Doll's Shoemaker.* Available from Doll and Craft World or Hobby House Press.

Back, Pieter. *Textile, Costume and Doll Collections in the U.S. and Canada.* Available from Doll and Craft World or Hobby House Press.

Bailey, Albina. *How to Make 19th Century Shoes for Dolls.* Available from Doll and Craft World or Hobby House Press.

Bailey, Albina. *19th Century Bonnets and Hats for Dolls.* Available from Doll and Craft World or Hobby House Press.

Bailey, Albina. *19th Century Hairstyles—Hair Accessories.* Available from Doll and Craft World or Hobby House Press.

Basic Principles for the Care and Preservation of Period Costumes. National Museum of American History, Washington, D.C. Available at museums.

Doll Patterns. Reprints from 1881. Available from Doll and Craft World or Hobby House Press.

Durand, Diane. *The Art of English Smocking.* Available from Doll and Craft World or Hobby House Press.

Ein, Claudia. *How to Design Your Own Clothes and Make Your Own Patterns.* Available from Doll and Craft World or Hobby House Press.

Fikioris, Margaret A. "Textile Cleaning and Storage." *Museum News,* Vol. 55, No. 1, Sept-Oct., 1976. Available from museums.

Foulke, Jan. *Dolls and Values, Blue Books, 5th edition.* Cumberland, MD, Hobby House Press, 1983.

Foulke, Jan. *Kestner—King of Dollmakers.* Cumberland, MD, Hobby House Press, 1980.

French Fashion Plates from the *Gazette, Du Bonton, LePape* 1912 to 1925. Available from Doll and Craft World or Hobby House Press.

Guldbeck, L. *The Care of Historical Collections.* Associates for State and Local History. Available at museums.

Hat Making for Dolls 1855-1916. Reprints available from Doll and Craft World or Hobby House Press.

"How to Wet-Clean Undyed Cotton and Linen." Information Leaflet No. 478, Smithsonian Institution Museum of History and Technology, 1967. Available from museums.

Jendrick, Barbara. *Doll's Dressmaker.* 1896 reprints available from Doll and Craft World or Hobby House Press.

Kämmer and Reinhardt Catalog of Dolls, reprinted by Doll Research Projects. Available from Doll and Craft World or Hobby House Press.

Klein, N. *Repairing and Restoring China and Glass: The Klein Method.* Order direct: P.O. Box 245, Harleyville, PA 19438

Long, Ida and Ernest, *A Catalog of Dolls, 1877-1961.* Order direct: P.O.Box 272, Mokelumne Hill, CA 95245.

Magazines, such as *Peterson's, Delineator, The Doll Dressmaker,* and *Mme. Demorest,* Available from Doll and Craft World or Hobby House Press.

Mini-Wigmaking. Available from Doll and Craft World.

Morgan, Mary. *How to Dress an Old Fashioned Doll.* Available from Doll and Craft World or Hobby House Press.

Noble, John. *Treasury of Beautiful Dolls.* New York, Hawthorn Books, 1971.

"Procedures for Cleaning Cotton Textiles." Eleanor Touceda Workshop, No. 4, Sept. 1951. The Textile Museum, Washington, D.C. Available from museums.

Putnam, K.G. *Caring for Textiles.* New York, Watson-Guptill, 1977.

Rennelt, Francis. *Collector's Book of Fashion.* New York, Crown Publishers, 1982.

Sears, Roebuck Catalog reprints available from Doll and Craft World or Hobby House Press.

BOOKS & PAMPHLETS CONT.

Seeley, Mildred and Colleen. *Doll Collecting for Fun & Profit.* Tucson, HPBooks, 1983.

Serkis, Susan. *The Wish Booklets.* West Point, 1965.

The Young Ladies' Journal. Reprints available from Doll and Craft World or Hobby House Press.

Ulseth, H. and Shannon, H. *Antique Children's Fashions.* Cumberland, MD, Hobby House Press, 1982.

Victorian Costumes. Reprint from *Harper's Bazaar,* 1867 to 1898. Available from Doll and Craft World or Hobby House Press.

Westfall, Marty. *The Handbook of Doll Repair and Restoration.* New York, Crown, 1979.

1914 Marshall Field's & Co. Catalog, reprinted by Hobby House Press.

RESOURCES

All The Trimmings
P.O. Box 24222
Louisville, KY 40224
Organdy, dotted Swiss, batiste, nainsook, voile and other fabrics and trims

Barglebaugh, Helen
118 Old Sutter Ave.
Jamaica, NY 11420
Shoe buckles and eyelet kits for shoes

Betty's Fabrics
821 State St.
Santa Barbara, CA 98101
Fine dress fabric and silks

Britex Fabrics
146 Geary St.
San Francisco, CA 94108
Fine cottons, nainsook, dimity and other fabrics

Brookstone Co.
127 Vose Farm Road
Peterborough, NH 03458
Tools, hemostats, magnifiers, pantographs

California Millinery Supply Co.
718 S. Hill
Los Angeles, CA
Hat supplies

Carriage House Antiques
2 Lincoln West
New Oxford, PA 17350
Lace, edgings, lawn, nainsook, voile, organdy

Conair Corp.
Miniature curling iron, 3/8-inch curl, called Conair Mini Curls, Model CD14. Good for human hair and mohair

Conservation Resources International Inc.
111 North Royal St.
Alexandria, VA 22314
Museum supplies for preserving dolls

Creative Silk
820 Oakdale Road
Atlanta, GA 30307
Silk

DeMeo Brothers Importers and Distributors
39 West 28
New York, NY 10003
Hair supplies

Doll & Craft World Inc.
125 Eighth St.
Brooklyn, NY 11215
Doll books, wigs, doll supplies

Doll Chapeaux
435114 E. 6th Ave.
Portland, OR 97281
Bonnet patterns

The Doll Dresser
P.O. Box 10787
Glendale, CA 91209
Authentic patterns for doll dresses

Doll Repair Parts, Inc.
9918 Lorain Ave.
Cleveland, OH 44102
Doll shoes, elastic and other doll supplies

Doll-Tiques
7836 Gratio
Richmond, MI 48062
Smocking machine

Dolls by Dottie
2910 Centerville
Dallas, TX 75228
Wigs, shoes, shoe buttons, bodies and other supplies

Dollspart Supply Co.
5-15 49th Ave.
Long Island City, NY 11101
Wigs, eyes, cloth bodies, equipment

Elizabeth Zimmerman Ltd.
Babcock, WI 54413
Fine knitting needles, lace needles—1-1/4mm, 1-1/2mm, 1-3/4mm

Elsie's Exquisiques
205 Elizabeth Drive
Berrien Springs, MI 49102
Fabric, buttons, lace, ribbon

Exotic Silks
252 State
Los Altos, CA 94022
Silk

Frank's Silhouette Parisian
P.O. Box S
Laverne, CA 91750
Doll-dress patterns

Heirloom Patterns
Paule Fox
38936 Chicago Ave.
Wadsworth, IL 60083
Doll-dress patterns

Helmon Label Co.
5143 W. Diversey Ave.
Chicago, IL 60639
Makes labels of your design

Hobby House Press
900 Frederich St.
Cumberland, MD 21502
Antique pattern reprints, doll books

Home Silk Shop
2002 E. McDowell
Phoenix, AZ 85006
Silk

Home Silk Shop
330 S. Cienega Blvd.
Los Angeles, CA
Silk

Home-Sew Inc.
Bethlehem, PA 18018
Tiny buttons and lace

Lady K Fashions
Box 845
New Port, OR 97365
Doll-dress patterns

Lyn's Doll House
Box 8341 DA
Denver, CO 80201
Doll-dress patterns, shoe patterns

MacDowell Doll Museum
Route 1
Box 15A
Aldie, VA 22001
Repairs bisque dolls

Manny's Millinery Supply
63 West 38th St.
New York, NY 10018
Hat supplies

Meyer Jacoby & Sons Inc.
32 W. 20th St.
New York, NY 10011
Wigmaker

Mini-Magic Carpet
3675 Reed Road
Columbus, OH 43220
Patterned silk, straw hats, French lace

Naibert, Janice
16590 Emory Lane
Rockville, MD 20850
Fancy French trim, ribbon, buttons, some fabric

National Art Craft Co.
23456 Mercantile Road
Commerce Park
Beachwood, OH 44122
Lace, doll globes, craft supplies

O'Brien, Anne
11208 Tiara Street
North Hollywood, CA 91601
Millinery supplies, covered wire, feathers, silk flowers, straw hats

Reinhold Lesch
D8633 Rodental Coburger Strasse 47
Pasyach 17 West Germany
New glass eyes for dolls

Schoepher
138 W. 31st St.
New York, NY 10001
Old glass eyes

Seeley Ceramics
9 River Street
Oneonta, NY 13820
Reproduction molds, slips, etc. for reproduction-doll making.

Smith, D.
2125 W. 19th Pl.
Eugene, OR 97405
Hats for dolls

Standard Doll Co.
23-83 31st St.
Long Island City, NY 11105
Tiny buttons of all sizes, doll supplies, doll stands

Standard Leather Co.
3415 S. Brand
St. Louis, MO 63118
Leather for shoes

Stevens, Mary K.
121 E. Main St.
Roselle, IL 60172
Patterns and doll supplies

Tandy Leather Co.
Check local telephone directory
Leather for shoes, markers to stamp shoes

Thimble House
R.D. 1, Box 406
Center Valley, PA 18034
Makes bonnets for French and German dolls

Thousand Fabrics
611 S. Fairfax Ave.
Los Angeles, CA
Silk

Treadleart
25834 Narbonne Ave.
Lomita, CA 90717
Thread, disappearing markers, sewing supplies

Ulseth, Hazel
4483 Grellick Road
Traverse City, MI 49684
Doll-dress patterns

Wemzel, May
38 Middlesex Drive
St. Louis, MO 63144
Publishes Costume Quarterly

White, Lucy
P.O. Box 982
Westbrook, CT 06498
Lambskin and mohair for making wigs

Yesterday's Patterns
P.O. Box 2053
Falls Church, VA 22042
French dress patterns

Index

A
A.T. doll 42, 43
All-bisque dolls 147
Antique costume 6, 10
Antique fabric 41
Antique paper dolls 16
Antiques 39
Armand Marseille 70, 71
  Googly 72
  Oriental doll 72
Artist's doll 15
Auctions 15, 103

B
Baby Millie 15, 108
Baby dresses 15
Beads 142
Bébé 48, 144
Belton 8, 9, 24, 25
Bergmann 66
Betty Bonnet paper dolls 16
Bias strips 140
Bisque stain 82, 88
Black Bru 48
Body
  leather 95
  twill-covered composition 94
Bonnet
  cotton 113
  pattern 150
Bonnets, also see Hats
Books and Pamphlets 157
Booties pattern 148
Boots, see Shoes
Bow loops 137
Bread dough 87, 142
Breveté 18, 135, 144
Brim shapes 119
Brim variations 119
Bru 12, 19, 38, 43, 46, 140, 143
  baby doll 43
  Bébé 48, 144
  black 48
  Breveté 18, 135, 144
  Circle and Dot 18, 46, 47, 48, 123
  Crescent 43, 144
  Jne 101, 117
  Jne 9 48
  open-mouth 43
  shoes 48
  singing 46
Buckles 28
Buttons 26
  dyeing 144
Bye Lo Baby 68

C
Catalog 5, 20, 30, 56, 66, 70, 103, 104
Character doll 63, 72
Child's antique dress 15
Children-dressed dolls 20
Circle and Dot Bru 18, 46, 47, 48, 123
Cleaning
  bisque heads 81
  leather body 88
Clothes moth 26
Clothing
  decoration 20
  wool 18
Color 8, 12, 38, 98
Color wheel 100
Contemporary costume 10
Costumes
  antique 6, 10
  contemporary 10
  costs 40
  mail-order 34
  new 25, 94
  old 10, 25, 94
  original 10, 13, 43
  preserving 8, 28
  reproduction 6, 8, 13, 27, 34, 35, 36, 41
Costuming Suppliers 157
Couturier costumes, Jumeau 49
Couturier, doll 15, 30, 32, 40, 41
Crescent Bru 43, 144
Crochet clothing 147
Crown variations 118

D
Decorations 26
Designing hats 116
Doll body shapes 93
Doll couturier 15, 30, 32, 40, 41
Doll dresser 30
Doll dressmaker 8, 30
Doll, size 40
Dollhouse dolls 16, 17, 18
Dolly Dingle paper dolls 16
Dolly face dolls 66
Dress patterns 150
Dressel 66
Dresser, doll 30
Dressmaker, doll 8, 30
Dry-cleaning 25
Duncan bisque stain 82, 143
Dyeing
  buttons 144
  wigs 106

E
Earrings 143, 144
Eden Bébé 114
Eye repairs 88

F
F.G. doll 40, 44
Fabric
  antique 41
  old 38, 39
  weights 39
Fashion dolls 5
Flocked hair 107, 109
Flowers, fabric 142
Flowers for hats 111
French Bébé 130
French doll bodies 93
French hats 113

G
German doll bodies 93
German dolls 130, 131, 144, 147
German hats 113
Gibson Girl 63, 68, 70
Glossary 154
Googly 72, 95, 104, 136, 139, 140

H
H-doll 29, 43, 44, 45
Hambuger and Co. 66
Hand-sewing 8, 13, 20, 22, 34
Handwerck 66
Hats and bonnets 111
  brim shapes 119
  brim variations 119
  crown variations 118
  designing 116
  flowers 111
  making 117
  making pattern 116
  material 114
  measuring 116
  mob cap 114, 117
  picture 116
  Red Riding Hood 116
  soft straw 116
  straw 111, 113, 114, 118, 149
  wool 111
Heubach 12, 72, 74, 109, 112
Hilda 68
Hilda bonnet 119

I
Insect
clothes moth 26
museum beetle 26

J
JDK 13
Jewelry 142
earrings 144
Jullien doll 10
Jumeau 12, 15, 36, 37, 43, 48, 49, 51, 52, 54, 55, 111, 123, 134, 135, 143
Bébé 121
Long-Face 49, 50, 51, 144
commercial costumes 49
couturier costumes 49
dress 26
reproduction 15
shoes 49

K
K(star)R101 74, 78, 92, 99, 140
K(star)R109 78, 79
K(star)R114 74, 75, 133
Pouty One 74, 75
K(star)R115 74, 78
K(star)R117 74, 75, 139
K(star)R character doll 74
K(star)R Googly 78, 150
Kämmer and Reinhardt 18, 66, 74, 77, 102, 104, 105
Kate Greenaway paper dolls 16
Kley and Hahn 64, 112
Kestner 68, 70, 120
Bye Lo Baby 68
Gibson Girl 68, 70
Hilda 68
Kewpie 68
shoes 70
Kewpie 68

L
Labels 12, 40
Lace 39
tinting 145
Large dolls 13
Leather doll bodies 93
Lettie Lane paper dolls 16, 20
Long-Face Jumeau 49, 50, 51, 144

M
Machine-sewing 8, 13, 34
Mail-order costumes 34
Making hats 117
Making pattern for hats 116
Marque 12
Material for hats 114
Measuring hats 116
Milliners 116
Moving dolls 28
Museum 20, 26, 28, 30, 50, 51, 103
Museum beetle 26

N
New costumes 25, 94

O
Old costumes 10, 25, 94
Old fabric 38, 39
Open-mouth Bru 43
Oriental doll 68, 72
Original costumes 10, 13, 43
Outdoor clothing 18

P
Panties pattern 147
Pantograph 95
Paper dolls 16, 133
Betty Bonnet 16
Dolly Dingle 16
Kate Greenaway 16
Lettie Lane 16
antique 16
Paris Bébé 7, 8
Patching holes 87
Pates 107
cardboard 107
cork 107
plaster 107
Patterns 6, 8, 15, 16, 20 78, 93
decreasing 95
enlarging 95
fit 94
making 94
size 95
use of 96
Petticoats 15
Preserving costumes 8, 28

R
Remounting swivel head 82, 84
Repairing
bisque heads 82
composition body 87
leather body 88
papier-mâché body 87
Reproduction costumes 6, 8, 13, 27, 34, 35, 36, 41
Reproduction doll 18, 36, 93, 88
Reproduction-doll artist 6, 40
Reproduction Jumeau 15
Resources 157
Restringing
French body 84, 85
German doll 86
Schmitt body 84
composition body 81, 87
Restringing dolls 81, 85
Ribbon
balls 138
pleating 138
puffs 138
pulling 138
winding 138
Ribbons 26, 28, 137
hair 138
knots 137
material 140
puffing 137
stitching 137
types 139
washing 111
Roses 141
making 141
silk 139

S
SFBJ 1, 18, 49, 58, 58, 60, 91, 109, 134
original costumes 58
Satin 26
Schmitt 4, 5, 13, 60, 61
Set eyes 90
Setting eyes 90
Shoes 10, 12, 13, 26, 38, 121
Bru boot 124
French ankle-strap 126
French boots 122
French slipper 125
German ankle-strap 128
Jumeau ankle-strap 127
Jumeau slipper 126
bluette 130
commercial 122
copying 124
decorations 128
designing 124
dyeing 145
flowers 130
hints for making 130
leather slippers 122
making pattern 124
markings 48, 49
materials 126
pattern 122
putting together 128, 129
rose 130
sandal 125
size guide 122, 123
slipper 126
storing 28
taking apart 122
Shoes, Jumeau 49
Shoes, Kestner 70
Simon and Halbig 32, 63, 66, 69, 97, 123, 133, 134, 152
119 doll 73
Oriental doll 63
Singing Bru 46
Sleep eyes 90
Smocking 144, 145
Snow Angel 2, 18, 30, 31, 32
Socks 10, 26, 28, 130
Socks and stockings 132
Soft straw hat 116
Steiner 54, 59, 83, 89, 106, 141, 146
A-series 56
Black 136, 137, 140
commercial chemises 58
Petite 57
reproduction dress 56
wire-eye 54
Stockings 26, 121, 130
commercial 131
making 131
striped 132
Storing dolls 28

T
Thread, old 38
Thuillier dolls 42, 43
Tinting 145
Trim 26, 39
Trunks 12, 19
Tynie Babe 147
Types of eyes 90

U
UFDC 43, 74
Underclothing 121, 132
chemise 132, 133
corset 133, 134
corset covers 133
decoration 133
drawers 132, 133
petticoat 133
teddies 133

W
Washing 16, 25, 30
Weights of fabric 39
Wigs
all-bisque dolls 108
Bru 103
caring for 106
combing 106
dyeing 106
F.G. 104
German styles 105
human hair 103, 104, 106,107
Jumeau 104
lambskin 103
making 108, 109
Marque 104
mohair 103, 106, 107, 108
preserving 106
repairing 107
Schmitt 104
Steiner 104
styles 103
styling 106, 107
Thuillier 104
washing 106
wool 103
Wool 20

X
XII doll 67